The Literary Essay
From Character to Compare/Contrast

Lucy Calkins, Kate Roberts, and
Kathleen Tolan

Photography by Peter Cunningham

HEINEMANN ◆ PORTSMOUTH, NH

This unit within the argument writing progression

GRADE 5

In *The Research-Based Argument Essay*, students build powerful arguments using carefully-weighed evidence, analysis, and rebuttal of counterclaims.

In *Shaping Texts*, students write memoirs that combine essay and narrative structures to convey significant insights and personal themes.

THIS UNIT

GRADE 6

In *The Literary Essay*, students craft essays that make arguments about characters and themes, learning strategies essayists use to gather, analyze, and explain evidence from the text to support their claims.

GRADE 7

In *The Art of Argument*, students learn to write essays that build convincing, nuanced arguments, balancing evidence and analysis to persuade readers to shift their beliefs or take action.

This unit within the grade 6 progression

UNIT 1

In *Personal Narrative*, students write true stories, learning strategies to generate meaningful story ideas, manage pace, elaborate on important scenes, and deepen insights.

THIS UNIT

UNIT 2

In *The Literary Essay*, students craft essays that make arguments about characters and themes, learning strategies essayists use to gather, analyze, and explain evidence from the text to support their claims.

UNIT 3

In *Research-Based Information Writing*, students learn ways to research and write informational essays, books, and digital presentations or websites to teach their readers about a topic, using increasingly sophisticated ways to draw on and structure information to explain a position or make a call to action.

This book is dedicated to the magnificent, awkward, blooming brilliance of the eleven-year-old.
—Kate

Heinemann
361 Hanover Street
Portsmouth, NH 03801–3912
www.heinemann.com

Offices and agents throughout the world

The authors and publisher wish to thank those who have generously given permission to reprint borrowed material:

Excerpts from "Raymond's Run," copyright © 1971 by Toni Cade Bambara; from *Gorilla, My Love* by Toni Cade Bambara. Used by permission of Random House, an imprint and division of Random House LLC. All rights reserved. Any third party use of this material, outside of this publication, is prohibited. Interested parties must apply directly to Random House LLC for permission.

Cataloging-in-Publication data is on file with the Library of Congress.

ISBN-13: 978-0-325-05944-0

Production: Elizabeth Valway, David Stirling, and Abigail Heim
Cover and interior designs: Jenny Jensen Greenleaf
Series photographs by Peter Cunningham and Nadine Baldasare
Composition: Publishers' Design and Production Services, Inc.
Manufacturing: Steve Bernier
Printed in the United States of America on acid-free paper

18 17 16 15   VP 2 3 4 5

Acknowledgments

THE WORK THAT LED to this book has been a long time coming. For decades upon decades sixth-grade teachers have been straddling the gap between the solid teaching of elementary school and the middle school years ahead. Sixth-grade teachers have always worked to bring their students together, to hold them to high standards, and to move them forward all in the same moment. And of course it is not new to teach sixth-grade students how to write powerful essays about texts. We are so grateful to and in awe of the teachers of the past and the present who have blazed a trail in this work with middle schoolers, who have stayed committed to workshop teaching and to the belief that our students are more important than our assignments.

As is the case with any curriculum that is not written by a particular teacher for his or her particular students, our sixth-grade teachers have worked with materials that they tweaked, adjusted, and adapted for many years now. We would like to thank all of the middle school teachers who have been waiting for this series and who have done all of the foundational work of teaching, trying, and revising that makes up the lessons in these pages. This book, this series, stands on the shoulders of your work.

Many teachers piloted the lessons found in these pages, and students from across the country did the work we outline here, providing invaluable feedback for our revisions. In particular, we would like to thank Cathy Alberico, Damian Jones, and Sarah Reedy from the Carroll Gardens School for Innovation; Rachel Lane, Jesse Lumsden, and Candice Simon from the Brooklyn School for Collaborative Studies; and Steve Petrella from the Central School in Simsbury, Connecticut. These teachers went above and beyond to be sure that the lessons you find here are both rigorous and realistic for a wide range of students. They embraced (and put up with) long conversations over email and phone, repeated visits, last minute changes, deadlines, and an experimental process that pushed us all to get better and to reflect on our practice.

This project was truly a collaborative effort. So many people stepped up to the plate repeatedly to be sure that we got the work right—both for our own high standards of practice as well as for the realities of a middle-school classroom. Julia Mooney, Karen Kawaguchi, Tracy Wells, and Felicia O'Brien spent hours upon hours refining the lessons and writing within these pages—they were stalwart in their commitment to understanding the nuts and bolts of this work and to being sure that it would be clear to all who read this book. We want to thank them for their work editing as well as for their daylong conversations about the true meaning of "boxes and bullets." This book would not be the same without you. Others pitched in as well, often just when we needed it most—thank you to Jenny Bender, Lisa Cazzola, Sara Johnson, and Audra Kirschbaum Robb for your expertise, effort, and talents.

We are especially lucky to work with the team at Heinemann, a publishing company who stands for all that is right for students, whose high standards are a light in the field, and who are always looking out for what is best for teachers and students. In particular, Kate Montgomery has led the work of this series with grace and foresight. We cannot imagine this series without her. Shannon Thorner, Elizabeth Valway, and Abby Heim have blazed the trail to production and publication, making sure that all of our i's are dotted and t's crossed, designing, reminding, and making sure that the book you hold in your hands is as perfect as possible. We are indebted to your work, your organizational skills, and your patience. Heinemann has a way of making you feel like you are family, and we are so grateful to be a part of theirs.

The class described in this unit is a composite class, with children and partnerships of children gleaned from classrooms in very different contexts, then put together here. We wrote the units this way to bring you both a wide array of wonderful, quirky, various children and also to illustrate for you the predictable (and unpredictable) situations and responses this unit has created in classrooms around the nation and world.

—Lucy, Kate, and Kathleen

Contents

BEND III Writing Compare-and-Contrast Essays

Welcome to the Unit

THIS UNIT MAY SEEM DAUNTING AT FIRST, but it needn't be. It is no wonder that many of us balk at the concept of spending weeks teaching students to become more powerful literary essay writers; the stakes feel high and the outcome at times can seem less inspiring than the beauty of a well-crafted narrative. However, there is great power in this unit—and great beauty as well. How you teach students to write literary essays in middle school has great ramifications for their school life, because they will be writing about their reading in greater frequency as they grow older and move on to high school and college. The skills they develop in the next few weeks can help build a foundation for this critical work. At the same time, the ability to step back from a text they have read or heard—be it a short story, a novel, or a popular television show—and articulate an interpretation of that text clearly and emphatically can be every bit as powerful as a writing a story from their own lives. Think about it: we are as a people surrounded by more text now than at any other time in human history. The power to be thoughtful about those texts and to write those thoughts down with skill and precision is every bit as important and essential to the life of a modern citizen as the ability to write a Small Moment story or an argumentative essay.

Many times the literary essay has been relegated to the land of assignment, but in this unit you will take your students through three incarnations of essays—character-based, theme-based, and compare-contrast—each one building on the last. This repeated practice is essential to the work of helping your students to become more independent and confident in their literary-essay-writing abilities. That being said, each incarnation of essay will dig deep into the rich skills of literary essay writing. You will spend time modeling thinking and writing, and coaching students to develop strong claims about the texts they are reading, you will confer and pull small groups in response to your students' needs, and your classroom will be overflowing with well-crafted

mentor essays and useful charts—all in an effort to teach your students that writing literary essays is a skill that they can improve upon no matter at what level they begin, no matter what teaching they have had in the past.

This unit begins by teaching students to read texts more closely and with a greater focus on the details. In addition, across a series of lessons you will teach your students to think big about the texts they are reading—forming their own theories about the character in the first bend of the unit, then the theme of the text in the second. In this process you will uncover another great source of power of the literary essay: the fact that by learning to write essays about the texts they read, students will not only become more powerful writers, but they will become more powerful readers. In this way, a literary essay is like a Trojan horse of literacy teaching: inside its relatively simple structure lies so much of the breadth and depth of what we strive to teach our students about both reading and responding to texts powerfully.

The skills learned in this unit will take your students far. First and foremost, students will learn to express their thoughts while reading—to name their ideas succinctly and to back up those ideas and observations with strong evidence. They will learn to evaluate the strength of the evidence they choose, to write it with voice and clarity, to incorporate quotes with context and precision. This unit will help your students above all to learn that not only can writing be a way to hold onto one's thinking about a particular subject or, more specifically, about a particular text, but that writing can also help them clarify and elaborate on that thinking.

Here, in this unit, you will be teaching many of the foundational moves of essay writing—that essays have a structure that is common to them, that there are claims, with supports, and evidence. But literary essays live a bit in both worlds—the world of argument writing as well as the world of informational writing. While on the one hand, it is undoubtedly an essay in structure and skill, it is a little bit less of an argument than its cousin, the research-based information essay (the next unit in this series). That is to say, when your writers posit that a character embodies a certain trait in a story, it is unlikely that someone who has read that same story could say, "No they certainly do *not* embody that trait." In this, literary essays are not exactly arguments. In many ways they inform you of the ideas found in a text. But this genre does not exactly fit with what we have come to know about informational writing either. And so here we treat the literary essay as an essay in form and skill but with less pressure on the writer to argue his point as much as support it—a perfect unit for your students at this time of the year.

OVERVIEW OF THE UNIT

Most likely you do not know exactly what your students have learned about literary essays in the past. Your students may be coming from many different elementary schools, and even if they are coming from one school, you will have new students or you may not be close enough to know exactly what was taught in earlier grades. You will begin this first unit of middle school essay writing with "the boot camp," so named because it attempts both to assess to some degree what your students know and do not know about essay writing as well as to introduce in broad strokes some of the root moves of essay writing that you will develop later on.

You will then move onto a series of lessons that will both develop a foundation for writers' claims as well as improve upon their reading skills—first by teaching them to read a text closely to find the details that illuminate great things about a character, then by examining those characters more deeply by considering their motivations and desires. Then you will teach students the rudimentary moves of an essayist: how to develop a claim and articulate it, how to plan for an essay, the art of writing about evidence. Before you move on to your next essay you will push your students to explain how their evidence supports their thinking, a skill essential to sixth-grade essay writing and one of the more exciting and challenging sessions in this bend.

After drafting and revising a simple essay about character in the first bend, you will ask students to repeat this cycle in the second bend, this time angling their essays to consider the theme of the text they are analyzing. They will be learning new essay-writing skills—from crafting powerful introductions and conclusions to incorporating quotes deftly and accurately, but at the same time they will be asked to write their second essays with greater independence.

They will reflect on their writing throughout, using both the checklists for opinion and argument writing as well as mentor essays written by you and former students. All along the way you will be beside them, whispering, "You know how to do this, remember, take a look here . . ."

Finally, you will teach your class to compare two texts through the lens of a common theme, teaching them to consider the similarities and differences in the ways two texts deal with an issue or problem. This bend, being the final one, will lean even more heavily on your students' prior learning. In many ways, they will be writing this essay by themselves, with only the resources you have given them throughout the unit for support. In this bend you will be teaching your students how to juggle these resources, how to set goals and revise using what they know.

ASSESSMENT

There are multiple ways to assess what your students know about essay writing before you start teaching them. Of course, this is of the utmost importance, because otherwise you run the risk of reteaching much that has already been learned or jumping so far ahead that you leave your class in the dust behind you. Some teachers take a few days at the start of the year to assess the big three in writing: narrative, argument, and informational writing. Others choose to preassess a few weeks before the unit begins, giving themselves ample time to sort through the work and mine the data. Of course, in this unit the first session also acts as a sort of assessment. You will be able pretty quickly to see what many of your kids know and are comfortable with in literary essay writing. This issue here is simply that you are scaffolding so much that it is not a true assessment of your students' independent abilities.

We have provided you with instruments—learning progressions, rubrics, checklists, and leveled exemplar texts—that will help you to see where, in the trajectory of writing development, each of your students lies. These tools will help you to see clearly what some steps are to improvement. With your assessment and these instruments in hand, you will be able to track each student's progress—and to help your students to see themselves improving.

For this assessment to truly track what your students know coming in and what they have learned from you and your teaching, you will need to be careful not to scaffold the work of this assessment. You can remind your students of the basic qualities you'd expect in an essay, but then you'll have to step back and leave them to their own devices. Be sure that your students know that this assessment is just that—a way for them to show off what they know and a way for you to tailor your teaching to fit their needs. We suggest you begin with the following prompt, repeating it on the day of the assignment:

"Think of a topic or issue you care about, an issue about which you have a very strong opinion. Tomorrow, you will have forty-five minutes to write an essay in which you will write your opinion or claim and argue why it is right, telling reasons why you feel that way. When you do this, draw on everything you know about essays. If you want to find and use information from a book or another outside source, you may bring that with you tomorrow. Please keep in mind that you'll have forty-five minutes to complete this, so you will need to plan, draft, revise, and edit in one sitting. In your writing, make sure you:

- Write an introduction
- State your claim
- Give reasons and evidence
- Organize your writing
- Acknowledge counterclaims
- Use transition words
- Write a conclusion."

Afterward, you will want to assess where each writer falls in the Learning Progression for Argument Writing. While a literary essay is not a perfect example of an argument, and shares many qualities with informational writing, it's structure and skills most closely align with this progression and these Common Core standards, so we suggest that you assess students across these lines.

GETTING READY

As in the first unit, *Personal Narrative*, the writer's notebook continues to be an essential professional writing tool for your budding essayists. You and your students will use the notebook to write-to-think about characters and possible themes, jot down ideas for claims, collect evidence to support claims, flash-draft whole essays, and capture key writing strategies. Encourage your students to use their notebooks as living, breathing instruments—something they use not only in the classroom or for writing assignments, but to write down ideas and thoughts when they are still fresh or to delve more deeply into an idea they had in class.

We suggest that you also collect examples of literary essays written by sixth-graders, perhaps from earlier years, to help your students see real-life examples of the kind of writing they will be doing in this unit. We provide examples on the CD-ROM, but the most engaging examples will come from your own students or students of fellow teachers.

For a mentor text, we invite you to use "Raymond's Run," by Toni Cade Bambara, throughout the sessions (on CD-ROM), so that students can become familiar with reading and working with this text. Students will also need to read additional short texts to analyze and write their essays, and we make suggestions in the unit. Of course, you can choose any authors or stories that you and your students love or know well.

Essay Boot Camp

IN THIS SESSION, you'll teach students that when writing an essay, writers start with a clear sense of the structure in which they'll be writing and then try shaping the content to fit into that structure, changing the structure around if the content requires them to do so.

GETTING READY

✔ Be sure that you approach this minilesson with the simplest version of "The Three Little Pigs" fresh in your mind or an alternative bare-bones story if you so choose (see Teaching and Active Engagement).

✔ Chart paper and markers (see Teaching and Active Engagement)

✔ "Boxes-and-Bullets Essay Structure" anchor chart (see Teaching and Active Engagement and Share) ⊙

✔ Students will need their writer's notebooks during and after the minilesson.

✔ For homework, each student will need to read at least one of the short texts suggested for the next session. We recommend the following:

  ✔ "Thank You, Ma'am," by Langston Hughes
  ✔ "The Gift of the Magi," by O'Henry
  ✔ "Everything Will Be Okay," by James Howe (the mentor text for the *Personal Narrative* unit)
  ✔ "Freak the Geek," by John Green
  ✔ "Your Move," by Eve Bunting
  ✔ "Stray" by Cynthia Rylant

  Alternatively, you may decide to choose your own favorite stories (see Share).

COMMON CORE STATE STANDARDS: W.6.1a,b,c,d,e; W.6.4, W.6.5, RL.6.1, RL.6.2, RL.6.3, RL.6.5, RL.6.10, SL.6.1, SL.6.2, SL.6.6, L.6.1, L.6.2, L.6.3

I N MANY WAYS, your sixth-graders are educational immigrants. They have arrived on the shores of middle school, carrying with them the wealth of their experience in elementary school, ready for new opportunities and new lives. And while they are excited to meet the challenge, a challenge it is: there are bells going off every forty-some-odd minutes and different teachers for each subject, each with different demands and personalities; there is a new building, new kids, new rules.

And there is often a great divide between what you think students can do and what they actually know how to do. This divide works in both directions: at times you may assume a lack of knowledge where there is great depth of it; other times you might assume that kids know things and are stunned to find that they do not.

By the end of this bend, your students will have drafted a literary essay about a character. But you will spend this first day pushing your class to write an entirely different flash-draft of an essay about a character in a very accessible story that your whole class knows well. You'll see that we have chosen to channel the class into writing an essay about the third pig in the fairy tale "The Three Little Pigs." We've also done this boot camp using the iconic superhero Superman, and that works if your class knows that story well enough (from movies—including sequels or remakes, comics, video games) to be able to produce the evidence they need to support a claim. Either way, the point is to spend just one day in a whole-class, intensive writing experience and to do so in a way that is clearly not serious essay writing but is instead a fun sort of exercise. Hence the choice of well-known texts and, as you will see, a very obvious thesis.

We have found that this "essay boot camp" allows you to induct all your students into using a simple structure for essay writing. This structure will be old hat for some of them, but it is bound to be new (or an important reminder) for others. Teaching this very simple version of essay structure right at the start of your unit means that you are front-loading what can otherwise be time-consuming work of teaching essay structure. Often essay units become so mired with lessons on body paragraphs and topic sentences that they never get to the heart of literary essay writing, which is thinking—deeply—about reading and articulating those thoughts—powerfully—in writing. This intensive boot camp on essay structure allows you to bring kids up to speed and also to determine just how much time you will need to spend teaching into the frames of an essay.

The work here is no-frills. It is the airline dinner of meals. It begins with an assigned claim about a statement, several body paragraphs, and a closing—all within ten minutes. You may extend that window of time (quietly) just a bit if you need to do so, but this is what you need to know: your students can do this.

"'You can do this,' you will convey to your writers through every word and action. And they can."

Okay, it may take them twelve minutes, not ten. Some may not complete the concluding paragraph. Some may forget to indent their paragraphs. The work won't be perfect. But in classrooms across even the high-need schools of New York City, every kid has written a part of an essay within this little window of time.

"You can do this," you will convey to your writers through every word and action. And they can.

Although every writer will not completely finish the draft today, every writer will have experienced essay structure. Toward the end of this unit, you will invite students to do some large-scale revision on these early pieces. By then, their abilities to plan and structure an essay (as well as their stamina) should have developed to the point where they will each be able to write a full flash-draft essay, all on their own, within fifteen minutes. As students become adept at writing within the familiar structure of the five-paragraph essay, you will be amazed at how easily they can produce quick little flash-draft essays—and that skill will be incredibly useful across all the content areas.

You may skip this boot camp, of course. It is especially self-contained and for that reason, easily dropped. But we encourage you to start here, with the simplest of ideas, helping students coming from all sorts of places to begin their middle school essay work by saying, "All together now . . ."

One final note: before teaching today, you will want to scan the upcoming minilessons and make some decisions. For today's homework, students will need to reread the text they will be working with throughout the bend, a text they have already read and interacted with. Meanwhile, it is equally important that the text you study together as a class both engages kids and holds big ideas about character and theme that students will be able to discover and discuss and write about, with your guidance. We think that "Raymond's Run," the story we selected for the upcoming minilessons, will engage students and inspire deep thinking and insightful writing, and we welcome you to use it if you don't have another text already in mind.

Essay Boot Camp

CONNECTION

Rally your students to work on writing essays by talking up the usefulness of the genre.

"Writers, our new unit is on writing about reading, but you'll still do this writing in your writer's notebooks, so get them out, and fold a page over or use some other strategy to make a divider, setting off this new unit," I said and then waited for the students' attention to be back with me.

"When people want to compliment a musician, sometimes they will say, 'That girl has some serious chops.' *Chops* kind of refers to talent, but more than that, *chops* is about someone's grit and guts—the fact that they are trying something bold and working hard at it.

"Writers, you are starting to have some serious writing chops. I think you are ready to graduate to another really important kind of writing. Today you are going to start your first middle school essay unit on literary essays. I know some of you have written essays before and others of you haven't, but that's okay, because what we are going to do today will get everyone on the same page. And the chops you'll get from this unit? Well, what you do during this unit is definitely going to make you more skilled at expressing your ideas."

"Here is the thing about essay writing: if you can write essays well, that skill will take you places. You'll use this skill to ace any high school writing you need to do, or to get into colleges (with scholarships). And people write essays all the time in life, even though grown-ups might not call them that. People embed essays into emails trying to persuade their bosses to do something, into reviews of great video or computer games or shows. One eighth-grader wrote an essay attacking a passage in a standardized test called 'The Pineapple and the Hare,' and his essay went viral and made the test-maker take that passage off the test, nationwide!"

Point out that today's boot camp minilesson will be different than usual and explain that the class will work together on a quick essay just for practice.

"Writers, today we are not going to have a typical minilesson where I teach you something, you try it, and then you go off to work independently. Because I want to give you a feeling for what it's like to write an essay, we will work together to do a writing-in-the-air of an essay, which you'll then each flash-draft into your notebooks, as practice. As we do this, it will help you get a feel for how writers structure, or organize, essays."

◆ COACHING

As you become accustomed to these writing units, you'll see that there are lots of ways we suggest you talk up the power of hard work, perseverance, and, to use a word from Paul Tough's How Children Succeed *(Mariner Books), grit. This discussion of writing chops is one way to convey this message.*

I like beginning a unit by conveying a sense that we're entering a new chapter in students' writing lives. And I do believe that essays are fundamentally different from stories.

You are using a lot of lingo that kids will know if they have grown up within writing workshops (and specifically within this series) but otherwise will not know. Writing-in-the-air is a phrase that means that the writer dictates aloud what she would say if there was time to actually write it. A flash-draft is a draft that is written, fast and furiously, in one sitting. It isn't really different than a draft, but the words are meant to rally kids into writing especially quickly, with an experimental feel, knowing the draft may or may not work.

✿ **Name the teaching point.**

"Today I want to teach you that when writing an essay, it can help to start with a clear sense of the structure in which you'll be writing, and then you almost pour your content into that structure, changing the structure around if the content requires you do so."

TEACHING AND ACTIVE ENGAGEMENT

Tell kids they are going to write an essay about a fairy tale, then give them time to talk together and to join you in recalling that fairy tale, highlighting the aspects that you'll mine in the essay.

"Today we're going to write a flash-draft essay, all in one day, which is a lot (I know), but this will get you warmed up for writing a real literary essay. I've been thinking about a story that everyone in this room knows, so we can all write about it, and I've settled on a real classic: 'The Three Little Pigs.' You know it, right?"

Some of the kids laughed and others gave me skeptical looks.

"I know, I know. This is a silly fairy tale for kids—but actually, people often come up with big ideas about the simplest stories. Here's another reason I chose this story. Today's work will move quickly and it's not easy. You'll be happy it's the three pigs we're thinking about and not more complex characters—trust me! Later, you'll have a chance to read and write about harder stories.

"Before we go any farther, get the story into the front of your mind by quickly retelling it to each other. Work in clusters, pairs, whatever. Go!"

The room erupted into conversation. As students talked, I listened in and then voiced over, "Think especially about the *third* little pig, because I think he's going to be our focus. Keep talking."

Recalling the class's attention, I said, "So writers, you've got the story in mind. You remember that the three pigs each built themselves their own home: one out of straw, one out of sticks, and the third pig, one out of bricks (that must have been a lot of work!). Then the wolf came, and he called . . . what?"

Some kids laughed awkwardly. I started them off and let a few students join me as I said, "Little pig, little pig, let me in."

Resuming my retell of the story, I said, with a smile, "And one after another, each of the pigs answered . . ."

This time, more kids chimed in, now embracing the drama, "Not by the hair on my chinny chin chin!"

You can make the teaching point memorable by adding gestures. Keep in mind that speech writing courses suggest that large-scale gestures—those in which there is air between your arm and your body—convey "an air of confidence." So with your arms, make a structure—spread out on the imaginary table before you—and then pour in the content.

By providing students with a rationale for this choice of text, you accomplish two things. First, you prevent your sixth-graders from disengaging from the lesson simply because it spotlights a story they read as little kids. Second, you convey that they are in on the plan, which is sure to catch their attention. By poking fun at "The Three Little Pigs," you introduce the light tone that is essential to essay boot camp.

Enjoy this. You are being a bit silly to suggest the kids write an essay on "The Three Little Pigs." So play around a bit—without elongating things, because the pace needs to be extremely fast. This whole minilesson needs to last all of ten minutes, and that is entirely possible, but not if you are ponderous, not if you wait until everyone is silent before talking, not if you elaborate on and extend everything that is said.

"Imagine calling that out when you are the third and only remaining pig, after you've watched your brothers get eaten! That third pig is no wimp, is he? Do you recall what the third pig does at the end?"

The kids and I agreed that the third pig, in the end, outwitted the wolf by suggesting he come down the chimney and join him for dinner—which ended up being a dinner of wolf, because the pig had a pot boiling under the chimney.

Set the kids up to coauthor a thesis statement. Give them the starting claim—an obvious one—and get them to talk in pairs to generate reasons that fit into the template you give them. Coach into their work.

After recapping the story, I said, "So, writers, to write an essay, you need an idea that is important to you. You could take a week coming up with an idea, but remember, you're writing this whole essay in one day, so I'm going to shorten that part of the process by suggesting you write an essay using the claim or thesis, 'The third little pig is an admirable character.' Now, whenever you write anything, it helps to think about the structure you will use. When writing a story, you took on the structure of a timeline or a story mountain, but to write an essay, you start with a structure that is not a timeline but an outline. One of the simplest ways to outline, to organize an essay, is to write about your reasons.

"Let's do that. So for now, take the thesis and come up with your reasons: 'The third little pig is an admirable character because A, because B, and most of all, because C.' Will you talk together to come up with what your first reason could be, your A, what your second reason could be, your B, and so on? Go!"

I quickly jotted the thesis statement along the top of a sheet of chart paper, boxing it out and putting two bullet points below.

> The third little pig is an admirable character because A, because B, and most of all, because C.

√ One reason …
√ A second reason …

Eventually, of course, you will want students to move toward writing their own more complex thesis statements, but for now, the goal is to get everyone going writing fairly simple, straightforward essays. Note that our use of the word because is actually a place holder. Eventually students will learn to use more precise words: "one sees this when . . . ," "evidence for this can be found at the start of the story when . . . ," "one example of this is . . . ," "one way in which this is true is . . . ," "one reason for this is . . ." The word because can be stretched to accomplish a lot of different jobs; for now, just know that it works not only in this essay but in many essays, and later you'll teach students more precise ways to set readers up for what they'll learn in the essay.

Then as the students talked, I listened in and voiced over tips and corrections. "Try actually borrowing the line, 'The third pig is admirable because A! Because B! And most of all, because C!' and just fill in the holes," I said. "Make sure your categories don't overlap. You can't say he's admirable because he's brave and then say because he stands up to evil—those are the same." I added, "As you do this, think about whether you are going to be able to find support from the story to defend your point. If you don't have any examples, your claim won't stand."

Convene the class, collect suggestions for the next portion of the shared essay, and synthesize them into the frame for a shared essay.

"What is your first reason he's admirable?" I asked, calling on Cindy (whom I'd already identified as having a solid answer).

Cindy pitched in, "Because he works hard, like making the brick house and all?"

Nodding, I said, "Some of that will be in your evidence. For now, we just need the reason." I dictated the new draft we now had for the class essay:

> The Third Little Pig is admirable because he works hard, because he . . .

I touched the next bullet, and gestured to another student to pitch in his ideas, and then to a third. Soon we had this thesis:

> The Third Little Pig is admirable because he works hard, because he is brave, and because he outwits his enemy.

Set members of the class up to use what will now be a shared box-and-bullets plan to write-in-the-air their own version of the essay's first paragraph.

"Okay, we have a claim and ways it's supported, box and bullets. That's our structure, our plan. Now you pour your content into that structure. To do this, imagine what you would write if you had time to do so by writing-in-the-air your first body paragraph. Think of scenes or details from 'The Three Little Pigs' that you can use to support, to illustrate, or to give an example of the fact that the third little pig works hard."

As you listen in, you are also deciding which students you will call upon and in which order. You probably will want your reasons to match the sequence of the story, so you won't want the first reason to be that the little pig outwits the wolf. What he does first is to build the house out of bricks (not straw, not sticks). So listen in to find a student whose first reason matches that portion of the story.

Notice that I tailored what a student offered to fit the lesson. I did not try to work with the student in the moment, as often this kind of back-and-forth uses a great deal of time without much true instructional purpose.

You can make this more clear to your students by pointing back to your claim box and bullets you wrote on chart paper.

After a moment of silence, I said, "You are going to need to write this as a paragraph, not just a sentence, so imagine the detailed story of what the character did, or must have done if it isn't spelled out, that shows he works hard." Again I left a bit of silence. "This is actually a bit tricky, so help each other, and remember, as you do this, write-in-the-air how the essay will go. Start with the thesis, then the topic sentence, then your evidence. Get started, and I'll come around."

As I listened in, I voiced over. "Love it! I love hearing you dictate the topic sentence for your first body paragraph: 'One reason why the third little pig is admirable is that . . . For example . . .'" I revealed chart paper on which I'd written out this template for a body paragraph:

One reason why [character] is [trait] is that . . .
- For example, A
- For example, B

I also voiced over saying, "Here is a tip. See if you can retell the part of the story that goes with your point by using what you already learned about writing narratives."

Recall the class, and drawing on what you heard, dictate a draft of how the thesis and first body paragraph might go, absent any discussion of the evidence because that will be "written" next.

After a bit, I recalled the class and said, "I'm hearing some great ideas. Let me see if I've captured what many of you are saying," Then I dictated this first bit of an essay:

The Third Little Pig, in the fairy tale "The Three Little Pigs," is an especially admirable character because he works hard, he is brave, and especially because he outwits his enemy.

The first reason that the Third Little Pig is admirable is that he works very hard. He builds his own home, which must take a lot of work. He builds it out of bricks, which must have taken an extra amount of work. He carried all those bricks to one place, laid them one by one on top of each other, added in the cement. He made one wall, another, another, another. He even built a roof and a chimney. This shows that the Third Little Pig works hard and I admire him for that.

"Essayists, there are two other jobs I want to help you to do. The first is this: after citing an example, you need to 'unpack' it, or analyze how it fits with your point. So you need to add something like 'This shows . . .' or 'This illustrates . . .' and then explain how the example fits the claim about the third little pig. *And* repeat your claim. Then you will need to write a transition that gets you started on the next body paragraph, using terms like 'Another reason . . .' or 'Although one reason is . . . another reason is . . .' Again, write-in-the-air with each other, and do these two things."

A chart showing a sample thesis and evidence illustrates the boxes-and-bullets plan.

As the students talked, I revealed a chart that scaffolded the work they were doing.

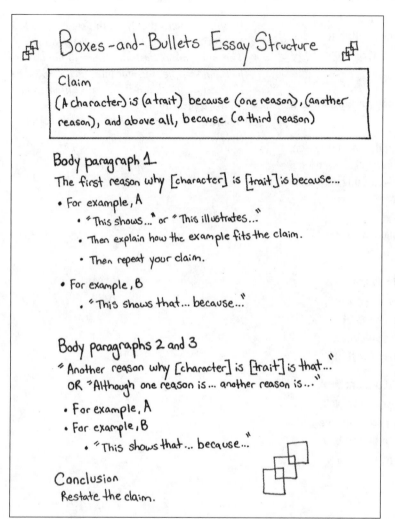

Boxes-and-Bullets Essay Structure

Claim
(A character) is (a trait) because (one reason), (another reason), and above all, because (a third reason)

Body paragraph 1
The first reason why [character] is [trait] is because...

- For example, A
  - "This shows..." or "This illustrates..."
  - Then explain how the example fits the claim.
  - Then repeat your claim.

- For example, B
  - "This shows that... because..."

Body paragraphs 2 and 3
"Another reason why [character] is [trait] is that..."
OR "Although one reason is... another reason is..."

- For example, A
- For example, B
  - "This shows that... because..."

Conclusion
Restate the claim.

I also listened in. "It is so wise that you are using words like *also* to help readers follow your thinking," I said to one student. To the class, I voiced over, "Some of you aren't writing-in-the-air but are instead talking *about* what you'd write. Go back to the start and dictate what you'd write, word for word, then keep going into the part that unpacks the example and the part that transitions to the next part of the essay."

Your students will remember from previous units that writing-in-the-air occurs when a writer says the exact words he might write to a partner. Even though students have been asked to do this often, it's worth taking the time to ensure that they are actually dictating the words they intend to write rather than merely discussing their ideas.

Debrief. Consolidate what you hope students have learned by naming what they just did.

"Writers, did you see the way we started by naming our claim and several supports for it? Then, in your first body paragraph, you repeated the claim and the first way it is supported. Then you told the story of an incident in the story that supports that claim and closed the paragraph by saying a bit about *how* the example supports the claim and also by restating what you were aiming to prove. Wow! That is a lot of work for one little paragraph!"

Set students up to practice by writing-in-the-air the entire essay, including the second body paragraph, as a prelude to flash-drafting the entire essay. Coach into their work.

"Right now, with your partner, write-in-the-air your second body paragraph, this time supporting the second reason, which is that the third little pig is brave. Do your best to quote the text exactly." The room erupted into talk. Before long, after hearing some more and some less successful efforts, I called out, "You've got it!" and I restated what I heard some of them saying aloud, once again starting at the beginning of the essay.

> The Third Little Pig, in the fairy tale "The Three Little Pigs," is an especially admirable character because he works hard, he is brave, and especially because he outwits his enemy.
>
> The first reason that the Third Little Pig is admirable is that he works very hard. He builds his own home, which must take a lot of work. He builds it out of bricks, which must have taken an extra amount of work. He carried all those bricks to one place, laid them one by one on top of each other, added in the cement. He made one wall, another, another, another. He even built a roof and a chimney. This shows that the Third Little Pig works hard, and I admire him for that.
>
> Another reason that the Third Little Pig is admirable is that he is brave. He watched a giant angry wolf with big teeth blow down his brothers' houses and eat them up but still, when the wolf came to the Third Little Pig's house this pig was brave. He didn't run and hide. Instead when the wolf called, "Little Pig, Little Pig, let me come in," the Third Little Pig called out, "Not by the hair on my chinny chin chin." That shows that he is brave because he is not intimidated by the scary wolf, even though he has good reason to be.

LINK

Remind students that writers often brush up on the structure of the genre before diving into writing in it. Ask them to use the thinking of the past few moments to help them do that now.

"Fabulous! I don't want to say another word. Just start writing. You are going to flash-draft an entire essay in your writer's notebooks on the admirable character, the Third Little Pig (although if any of you are game for a challenge and want to argue that the Big Bad Wolf is admirable, or evil, you can do so). Feel free to borrow the reasons and evidence we've shared in class or to make up your own, but here is the thing—you only have thirteen and a half minutes to write the whole essay, so get started!"

Remind students that flash-drafting means fast and furious writing to get ideas down on paper. The end result of flash-drafting will not be perfect and sets the stage for later revisions. Clarify for students that a flash-draft differs from a draft—a piece of writing that is the product of significant time and effort and probably multiple revisions.

The truth is that the kids may not completely finish this essay, but if you act confident that they will, there is at least a good chance that your confidence will carry the day. Note that you are not doing a final debrief about ways this work is transferable. Generally you would do so, but for now, it seems more important to channel them immediately toward the page while the oral draft is still in their minds.

Ratcheting Up the Level of Student Work

B ECAUSE THE MINILESSON WAS AN UNUSUAL ONE, involving extended guided practice, your kids will have less writing time than usual, and therefore you'll have less time for conferring as well. Although you won't want to pull a chair alongside one writer and engage in a long talk, you absolutely *will* want to be involved in the work that students are doing. The best way to do this will be to observe their work and to either interject small comments, almost whispering in as an individual writer works, or to call out voiceovers that relate to the whole class. Either way, your coaching will aim to ratchet up the level of students' writing by reminding them of moves that are integral to writing in an essay structure and by nudging them to write quickly and powerfully.

At the start of the very brief writing time, you will probably want to nudge writers to get themselves started writing without delay. In this world of high-stakes testing, it is important for students to grow up understanding that there are times when writers need to write with great dispatch. After all, on SAT and ACT tests, students are given less than half an hour to read the prompt and plan and write an essay. A study conducted by an MIT professor and cited in the *New York Times* found that students' scores on the essay portion of those tests are directly correlated with the length of their essays. Those students who produced an essay that spanned two sides of a page—writing the entire essay in that amount of time—almost always scored far better than students who wrote just a page. For today's work, there is no reason for delay. The content and wording of the essay are already established. So this is a perfect occasion to nudge students to get themselves off the starting block right away.

Compliment and push writers with strong, decisive gestures that carry heft. A bold thumbs-up sign, a marginal exclamation point: these can mean more than you dare to believe. So, too, can short comments mean the world. "Fabulous, you've gotten half a page written," you might say to one writer. "You're on a roll. That whole page will be filled in three minutes." These prompts are meant for individuals, but if you raise your voice just a bit, others will overhear you, and that will help your cause. "Keep your hand moving," you will tell another writer. "Don't stop, mid-sentence. Just keep going. Keep your hand moving down that page."

Once students have gotten themselves started, you'll want to shift your prompts so that now you are reminding them to incorporate transitional phrases. Chances are good that you will need to remind them to indent when they come to new body paragraphs. Paragraphing is a very big deal when writing an essay, so make a fuss about this. Of course, once students are within their body paragraphs, you can coach them to write more than one example, to "unpack" or discuss the example in relation to the opinion statement, and to recap what they have said at the end of each paragraph. Don't worry that any of this is done perfectly—this is not a piece of writing that writers will publish. It is, instead, what we sometimes refer to as "an exercise text."

MID-WORKSHOP TEACHING   **Essay Body Paragraphs Have Beginnings, Middles, and Ends**

"Writers, I know you know that stories have beginnings, middles, and ends. When writing an essay, each body paragraph also has a beginning, a middle, and an end. The beginning of the paragraph will usually contain a transition that hooks the new reason to the others and to the claim. The middle will need to reference the story with details, and the end will need to unpack the references, the evidence, perhaps by saying, 'This shows . . .' or 'This illustrates . . . ,' and certainly by restating the idea you are writing about. Reread and make sure you are writing in paragraphs (you might have more than one paragraph in a part) and that each paragraph has a beginning, a middle, and an end. Back to work."

Reflecting on Being an Essayist

Channel writers to reread their own and each other's essays and to annotate them with notes about how they can make these better.

"Writers, can I stop you? Last night I read something about how people get good at things—at anything. You know I am always studying that! Anyhow, it turns out that world-famous chess players spend as much time reviewing their game and critiquing what they did as they spend playing chess. I know that might sound totally irrelevant, but for you to become world-famous essayists, I figure you need to spend time reviewing your essay and critiquing what you did, just like the chess players do, and studying essays that others write, as well. So for share today, will you and your partner look at one person's essay or the other's and annotate it, almost as if you are the teacher making comments? Note the things the essayist has done well, and jot suggestions, because after you annotate your essay, you'll rewrite it. I know we don't have time in school, but you can do that at home. Get started."

As students worked, I listened in. A few talked a bit about the fact that they'd had a hard time figuring out what to say in the final paragraph. One said that talking it out first helped, which is true for a lot of writers! I pointed out to them that among other things, they could look to see ways in which writers had followed the template on chart paper at the front of the room.

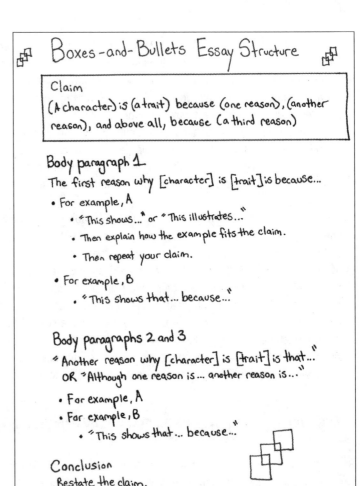

REFLECTING ON ESSAYS AND THEN WRITING A NEW DRAFT

"Tonight, finish annotating your essay, noting in the margins and with stars and underlines and arrows and happy and sad faces—any marks you want—what you think about the essay. Then write a new draft, a fabulous draft, of the essay.

"Tomorrow we will all work as a class with 'Raymond's Run' (you'll remember that story well because I read it to you just a few days ago), and each of you will work with another familiar story of your choice from these options: 'Thank You, Ma'am,' by Langston Hughes, 'The Gift of the Magi,' by O'Henry, "Everything Will Be Okay," by James Howe, 'Freak the Geek,' by John Green, 'Your Move,' by Eve Bunting or stories recommended by your teacher. Take home one or two that you especially like to reread, so that you are ready to write about it when you come in tomorrow. You will work on that one story not just tomorrow but also for the next two weeks."

We asked each student to select one of several familiar short stories—all ones the class has read. One choice is presumably Howe's "Everything Will Be Okay," which, of course, students know from the previous writing unit. We've also often used a combination of some of these: "Thank You, Ma'am," by Langston Hughes, "The Gift of the Magi," by O'Henry, "Freak the Geek," by John Green, "Stray," by Cynthia Rylant, and "Your Move," by Eve Bunting. You could choose these same texts or others that reflect your students' particular interests. You'll notice that some of these are more complex than others. You'll of course want to choose texts your students are able to read. If your plan for Session 2 is for students to work with novels they've read earlier rather than with short stories, remind them to bring in novels for the next class. Tell them the novel they select should be one they've reread and know very well and that they will be using the same text for writing essays in upcoming classes.

Growing Big Ideas from Details about Characters

IN THIS SESSION, you'll teach students that to generate ideas for an essay about literature, writers reread a text very closely, paying attention to important details about the characters and thinking about the author's intentions.

GETTING READY

✔ Before starting the session, each student will need to have read at least one of the short texts suggested for this session. We recommend the following:

  ✔ "Thank You, Ma'am," by Langston Hughes

  ✔ "The Gift of the Magi," by O'Henry

  ✔ "Everything Will Be Okay," by James Howe (the mentor text for the *Personal Narrative* unit)

  ✔ "Freak the Geek," by John Green

  ✔ "Your Move," by Eve Bunting

  ✔ "Stray" by Cynthia Rylant

  Alternatively, you may decide to choose your own favorite stories.

✔ "How to Write a Literary Essay about Character" anchor chart (see Connection, Active Engagement, and Link)

✔ Copies of the shared class text, "Raymond's Run," by Toni Cade Bambara, one per student (provided on CD-ROM). You should also have an enlarged copy of the excerpted passage, written on chart paper or displayed for the class (see Teaching and Active Engagement).

✔ "Thought Prompts that Help an Essayist Think and Write" chart (see Teaching and Active Engagement)

✔ Chart paper and markers (see Teaching)

✔ Students' writer's notebooks and pens (see Active Engagement)

✔ The short texts students will study across the unit (see Link)

COMMON CORE STATE STANDARDS: W.6.1.a,b; RL.6.1, RL.6.2, RL.6.3, RL.6.10, SL.6.1, SL.6.6, L.6.1, L.6.2, L.6.3

T O WRITE DEEPLY ABOUT TEXTS, students will need to have read those texts deeply to begin with. As my grandmother used to say (to my unending horror), "You can't make chicken soup out of chicken poop." This is true for essays as well—you cannot write great essays out of weak thinking. This session teaches students that by reading a text closely, their writing about those texts improves.

While the previous session was a one-day stand-alone, today's session launches students into a stretch of work that will span the first bend of this unit. Today your students will get started working closely with a familiar short story, growing an idea about that story that is worth developing into a character-based literary essay. It is important that students mine a text they have already read so that writing time is reserved for writing or for the special kind of close rereading one does when writing about reading.

You could conceivably alter this bend by asking students to write about a whole-class novel if you and your students have been studying one together and they are close to finishing that work. We prefer to teach into more independence, recognizing that choice is especially critical to young adolescents' engagement. If students are writing essays about novels, remember that they need to have already completed their reading, because today they will be rereading a text. This means that you'll need to figure out a way for them to have read the texts in advance of writing workshop.

Either way, you will teach students that to read a text closely, one must reread. You will model how to focus attention on the details of a text and highlight the fact that even the smallest detail in a text can spark rich thinking. You will teach students that to write effective literary essays, it is important to read analytically, thinking about the author behind the words, aware—and wary—of the choices that have been made.

There is one other reason to spend time teaching your students to attend to the details of a text; by looking at a text closely, even students who have not yet fallen in love with reading will find something to latch on to—some small detail or moment that resonates with them and hooks them in to the world of the story.

Growing Big Ideas from Details about Characters

CONNECTION

Remind the class of the work they did in the previous session, and help them to anticipate that today they'll launch similar work, only on a larger and more ambitious scale.

"Right now, will you open your notebooks to the page on which, last night, you wrote your revised essay about the 'Three Little Pigs,' and will you glance over it, asking one very important question: 'What did I learn from doing that essay that I can use again, when writing a more intellectually ambitious essay?'" I left a pool of silence, and then after a bit said, "Star places in your draft that represent lessons you learned. And the lessons might be reminders of things you knew already but have forgotten.

"You're not going to talk about those lessons right now, but carry them with you, because starting today, you are going to work on a much more ambitious character essay. Your essay will take four or five days to write, and it will be lots better than the essays you whipped out yesterday. But the process of writing these essays will be largely the same, and again, it helps to start by thinking about the big claim that you want to make about the text—and in this case, about the character.

I revealed a chart in which I'd recorded the following steps:

> ### How to Write a Literary Essay about Character
>
> - Reread selected bits.
> - Notice details, think, talk, write to explore: "Why this detail?"

❧ **Name the teaching point.**

"Today I want to teach you that to get big ideas about texts—and eventually grow those ideas into a literary essay—it pays to notice important details the author has included about the character, and then to reflect on the author's purpose for including a detail, and to jot down those thoughts."

Notice that this minilesson begins with asking students to be active and reflective. Their engagement in your whole-class teaching is the sun, the moon, and the stars. The challenge, of course, is to get them engaged but to keep your minilessons tight and efficient to save time for the engagement that matters most—that is, for students' engagement in their own writing.

TEACHING

Demonstrate the way essayists mine texts to notice details that reveal something important.

"The writer Stephen King wrote, 'Good books don't give up their secrets all at once.' I love this quote. I love it because it tells us that there is great reward in paying attention to the details in stories, that if you do, you will uncover the big ideas that make the story important. In this bend of the unit, you'll be writing essays about characters, and of course, paying attention to the details of a character is an especially important thing to do because characters are people. Just like you can't know everything about a person the first time you glance at them, you can't know everything about a character the first time you meet the character in the pages of a story.

"To learn how to write essays about character really well, we're not going to mine 'The Three Little Pigs.' Instead, we're going to return to a really well-written story that we read earlier, 'Raymond's Run.' There is a copy for each of you on your table. You remember this story about the tough girl with a brother who has some special needs and her discovery that even though he has problems, he's a great runner, just like she is.

"To grow a claim about Squeaky, the protagonist in this story, you and I need to do some work that you'll also end up doing with whatever story you choose to work with later today." I gestured to the chart I'd begun.

> * Reread selected bits.
> * Notice details, think, talk, write to explore: "Why this detail?"

"We first need to reread a part of the story that shows what the protagonist is like, and we need to reread closely, with pen in hand. After that, we'll need to take some of what we notice and think *hard* about why the author might have put in this particular detail.

"So let's get started by doing some rereading. Remember, we need to go right to a part of the story that shows the character we're writing about. Point to the first part of 'Raymond's Run' that you think shows Squeaky." They did, and I scanned the room. "Almost all of you pointed out that we could even read just the start of the story, so let's do that. Will you reread your copy while I read aloud? And as we read, let's underline details about Squeaky that show what she is like as a person. After each part that shows a lot, let's stop and think, 'Why might the author have chosen this particular detail?'"

I read, and underlined as I did, pausing a bit after the second underline.

> *But now, if anyone has anything to say to Raymond, anything to say about his big head, <u>they have to come by me.</u> And I don't play the dozens or believe in standing around with somebody in my face doing a lot of talking. <u>I much rather just knock you down</u> and take my chances even if I am a little girl with skinny arms and a squeaky voice, which is how I got the name Squeaky.*

Tell students that it's their responsibility to hang onto the copies of their selected stories, for their work today and in future classes, as well as for homework. If they have a writing folder they use for their ongoing work or a special pocket in their writer's notebooks, the stories could reside there for the next several weeks. They should also keep a copy of the shared text, "Raymond's Run," in their writing folders or notebooks. Remind students that they will be referring to this story throughout the unit.

I am asking students to join me in reading for important details because I want them to be active in the lesson, right from the start. Although I begin with a demonstration, very quickly I'll ask them to do this work themselves, and it's essential that they are with me.

You could, of course, have just gone to the start of the story and started to read there, but remember that you are trying to leave a trail that kids can follow. Say they are writing about a novel—they can't just reread starting at the beginning and proceeding through the text. So you add in the step of selecting the passage to leave a trail that kids can follow, with success, when they do this work on their own.

"I bet by now you have underlined some parts, haven't you? Did some of you underline the phrase, 'I much rather just knock you down' like I did?" Many kids agreed that they'd thought that line was significant too. "I thought it said a lot when she said, 'If anybody has anything to say about Raymond they have to come by me,' but this next line is even stronger." I reread it, acting it out. "This is a pretty intense thing to say, right?" The class nodded: a consensus had been reached.

Demonstrate that instead of just noting an important detail, essayists ask, "Why might the author have included this?" Show that you can do this thinking by writing, though you will actually write-in-the-air.

"Writers, when essayists find a detail that seems important, they don't just gloss by it. Instead, they think about it more, talk about it more, and often write about it, even. Only the writing isn't something for other people to read. It's just writing-to-think. Do you remember that I said earlier, essayists ask, 'Why did the author include that detail?' Let's think about this detail in the story, trying to grow big ideas about it by asking that question, but here is one more tip. Because we aren't going to know for sure why the author did anything and we are just speculating, it helps to use thought prompts like these":

Thought Prompts that Help an Essayist Think and Write

✓ Maybe the author included this because...
✓ On the other hand, perhaps...
✓ Or it could be that...
✓ I wonder if...

"I'm not going to *actually* write-to-think, I'm going to say what I would write aloud, but will you pay attention to how I am doing this sort of writing and thinking? In a minute, you are going to take another detail in the story and do the same work I try to do, thinking big ideas about small details."

I shifted my posture, becoming a writer/reader in front of the class. "Hmm, . . ." I scratched my head, then picked up my marker. "Remember, our question is Why does the author have Squeaky say that she'd knock people down if they have something bad to say about her brother? One thing we know for sure is that this wording, in the story, it isn't an accident. Toni Cade Bambara chose Squeaky's way of responding (and these exact words) for a reason. There's a purpose behind it. So we need to ask, '*Why* does Bambara include this detail about Squeaky? Hmm . . .'"

Voicing my thoughts out loud, I touched the relevant thought prompts as I wrote-in-the-air:

Notice that before you get going, thinking aloud in front of the class, you definitely need to set kids up so they understand their role. And you need to do just one kind of thinking at a time. When kids are more proficient at this, they'll be able to think like you do—shifting from one kind of thinking to another with finesse. For now, they are novices. That's why you are explicitly teaching these steps.

The most important word that I've said might be hmm. *It's crucial for us to show students that ideas don't come to any of us right away. So often, students expect ideas to be right there, fully articulated, in their minds, and they don't understand the experience of waiting for an idea to come.*

I notice that when people say mean things about Raymond, Squeaky reacts by saying, "I much rather just knock you down . . ." I wonder why Bambara included this detail about Squeaky—that she wants to knock people down. **Maybe the author** wants to show us that Squeaky is really really angry over how people treat her brother. **On the other hand, perhaps Bambara is showing us** that Squeaky really loves Raymond—she loves him so much that she's willing to fight for him. **Or could it be that Bambara is trying to show that** Squeaky thinks it works better to fight than to talk through stuff?

Debrief, naming the strategies you just modeled so students can try them in their own work.

"Writers, what I did just now is the work literary essayists do. They reread a passage from the text, pausing when they find a detail about the character that merits thinking. You watched me thinking about that little detail by asking, 'Why *might* the author have included this?' And because I was speculating, wondering, I used phrases like 'Maybe . . .' and 'On the other hand, perhaps . . .' When I kept using words like *maybe*, that helped me keep writing more stuff. Literary essayists do that, and you could try that today if you like.

"Here's the thing. If I hadn't been planning to write an essay about this story, I would have zoomed right past the detail that Squeaky can't tolerate people talking to her about Raymond—that she 'knocks them down.' But writing helps a person see more—in life, and in texts. After this, bear in mind that it always helps to wonder *why* the author of a text may have chosen a specific detail, a word, an action. Authors write on purpose—they make deliberate choices. It's your job as readers and as essayists to take notice."

ACTIVE ENGAGEMENT

Ask students to reread aloud to each other another passage from the shared text, paying attention to another detail that might reveal the character, and then to write off from what they notice.

"So give this a try yourselves. The section we were looking at continues," I said, displaying the next portion of the story on a document camera. "In your own copies of the story, reread the next few lines, paying attention to details that reveal Squeaky. Decide which partner is going to read aloud—and which partner is going to have responsibility for listening and following along, underlining the details that seem significant. Stop at 'I'm the swiftest thing in the neighborhood.'"

I listened as around the room, one student read to another. As I saw what students underlined, I did the same on the enlarged text.

And if things get too rough, I run. And as anybody can tell you, I'm the fastest thing on two feet.

There is no track meet that I don't win the first place medal. I used to win the twenty-yard dash when I was a little kid in kindergarten. Nowadays, it's the fifty-yard dash. And tomorrow, I'm subject to run the quarter-meter relay all by myself and come in first, second, and third. The big kids call me Mercury cause I'm the swiftest thing in the neighborhood.

Notice that in this active engagement section, we give students a second experience working with the class's shared text. This allows us to tuck more instruction into the lesson; you will note a few tips that we incorporate into this work. If your students resist writing and have a hard time generating things to say, we recommend you alter this active engagement so that students talk with someone else who will be writing about the same story as they have selected. Together, they choose a detail that is worth mining and begin to discuss how that detail reveals the character. That talking can then scaffold the writing work you will be asking them to do today. Always be aware that you can adjust your teaching so that it is more supportive or more challenging. In this session, our choice is the more challenging option because we leave students to fare on their own when writing about the stories they selected.

After a minute, I said, "If you didn't yet find a detail worth discussing, reread and find one now," and I pointed to the second bullet on the chart.

> • Notice details, think, talk, write to explore: "Why this detail?"

"Start writing." As students did this work, I read the passage aloud, highlighting some significant parts. "As you try to figure out why the author included the detail—what she says about Squeaky—remember to use those phrases."

Thought Prompts that Help an Essayist Think and Write

- Maybe the author included this because . . .
- On the other hand, perhaps . . .
- Or it could be that . . .
- I wonder if . . .

As students worked, I coached, "You picked out a detail. Now push yourself to think, 'Why *might* the author have included that detail? What is she trying to say about Squeaky?'" And, after another moment, "If you feel 'done' with one detail, pick another!"

Recruit the class to listen to and build upon what one student has done.

"Writers, listen to what Jamhil wrote. Before Jamhil shares what he wrote, listen to the passage he found significant and think about this bit of the story yourself."

> *And tomorrow I'm subject to run the quarter-meter relay all by myself and come in first, second, and third.*

"You found the passage? Squeaky vows to run this race all by herself, and therefore she is going to come in first, second, and third place? (My hunch is that when you think about being in a running race, you don't think of racing yourself, and therefore coming in every place.) Jamhil, good job realizing this shows a lot about Squeaky." I said to the class. Then I began sharing his work. I said, "Jamhil first wrote this":

> I think Bambara wants to show that Squeaky is a good runner.

"Here's the cool thing. After he wrote that, he said to himself, 'Wait, I can use *maybe* and come up with some other ideas.' Listen to how he uses a few *maybes* in what he writes next."

Jamhil read:

> Or <u>maybe</u> she wants to show that Squeaky is really egotistical, like she is a rapper saying, "I'm the best!" But it is sad she is running by herself. <u>Maybe</u> the author is trying to show that

If time is running out, cut this part of the mini-lesson. This gives you another chance to bring home your point, but it is expendable. Be sure your entire minilesson can fit into ten minutes so that students have time to work.

If you do decide to highlight the way one student has written a thoughtful entry by using maybe *to get himself speculating, be sure to nudge a student to do this.*

You could report on Jamhil's thinking, as if he were a past student of yours, but it is far better if you can talk about what a student in your own class says. As you do, be sure to emphasize the strategy the student is using instead of whether or not his ideas are "good." In this instance, it helped to show what the writer did first, then what the writer said to himself, and what he did next. Of course, I really didn't know the thoughts that Jamhil said to himself—so some of this needs to be improvised.

Squeaky doesn't have any friends because she is running all by herself and winning all the spots. I bet <u>maybe</u> she doesn't have friends because she is always attacking other kids.

Debrief in a way that highlights what the one student has done and how you hope others will do this as well.

"Writers, do you see that when Jamhil asked why the author included a detail about Squeaky, he started off thinking the detail showed a sort of obvious external trait—her talent for running? But then he thinks more about what the detail really shows, and goes deeper. He next talks about how that detail shows Squeaky's *internal* state. Is she egotistical? Lonely? That's the kind of thinking work that will lead to a powerful essay."

LINK

Channel students to start using the strategy you taught with the short story they chose to study. As soon as an individual begins writing about details in the text, send that person off, so those needing help remain and get that help.

"Today you learned that to get big ideas about texts—and to eventually grow those ideas into a literary essay—it pays to notice important details the author has included about the character, and then to surmise the author's reasons for including those details, recording your thoughts." I again gestured to the chart showing the beginning of the process for literary essay writing.

> How to Write a Literary Essay
> About Character
>
> • Reread selected bits.
>
> • Notice details, think, talk, write to explore: "Why this detail?"

"Right now, get out the short story that you have chosen to work with and go right to a part of it that you think really reveals the main character. Put your finger on that part." I waited for them to do this. "Now, reread that part really carefully, underlining key words, key details. You should be rereading about four lines, not ten."

I gave them a minute to do this. "Open up your notebook, and begin writing about what you are thinking. Start as I did: 'I notice that the author says . . .' Go!"

I watched as students got started, and as soon as I saw one of them seem engaged, I tapped that student on the shoulder and whispered, "Go back to your seat and keep writing." After most students had been dispersed, I suggested the remaining students pair up with someone who was writing about the same story and read a passage aloud to each other and talk together about it.

Generating Meaningful Ideas, Right from the Start

WHEN YOUR STUDENTS WERE WRITING PERSONAL NARRATIVES, getting a lot of writing done was easier for them than it will be today. They could select an event, recall what transpired, and essentially creep through their memories of the event, recording all that they remembered. Now you are asking for them not just to recall and record, but to generate ideas and content. You will find that many of your students write a bit and then feel finished. A good deal of your teaching will center around helping them to see more in the text, to write more. And a good deal will revolve around helping them to not stop working. If you haven't yet gotten to students

to coach them into elaboration, they can at least write about a succession of details, though this may take some encouragement.

Your first goal, then, will be to support productivity. You will probably want to circulate quickly among your students, making sure they are engaged in this work. As you do this, note first the good things that your students are doing. Nothing will recruit their energy more than you functioning as a talent scout. Notice, for example, if a student has marked up the text she is reading—underlining, adding arrows, circling. Close

(continues)

MID-WORKSHOP TEACHING   Link Ideas in the Story

"Writers, let me interrupt you to push you a bit farther. When I did this, the entries I wrote first contained some great ideas, but each idea and each entry felt a bit like an island. The ideas I had at the beginning of the story are just sitting there, unconnected to the rest of the story, to what happens after, and to the ideas I developed about later sections of the story. One way to make your entries and your ideas feel less like islands is this: after you have read on and written more, you can return to an entry you wrote early on to reread the entry in light of all the reading and thinking and writing you have done. Then add a blurb at the bottom of your writing that starts off, 'What I am thinking now is . . .' or 'While this idea made sense at first, now I am thinking differently because . . .'

"Who would like to try this with me now?" Stephen raised his hand. "Great, Stephen. Go ahead and share an idea you had at the beginning of 'Thank You, Ma'am.' That's what you're reading, right?"

Stephen nodded and cleared his throat, "So, at the beginning of the story I wrote, 'The woman is kind of scary. You shouldn't mess with her.'"

"That's a terrific start-of-the-story idea. But I bet you are thinking something more complicated about her now that you are rereading the later parts of the story. Just dictate your thinking, writing-in-the-air, starting by saying, 'What I am thinking *now* is . . .'"

Stephen said, "Umm . . . What I am thinking now is . . . that she doesn't play around, because she has been through a lot, and she wants to help Roger through, like, tough love." Then he added, "But it's still love. She has a lot of love too, I guess."

I nodded. "So, Stephen, do you see that you could put your ideas together, saying something like, 'At first So-and-So seemed . . . but then I realized that really . . .' How many of the rest of you are game to try what Stephen has done—returning to an early entry, rereading it in the light of all you now know, and writing, 'At first . . . but now . . .'"

Most of the students indicated that they'd give this a try, and I sent them back to work.

> "Remember the school picnic when I climbed that cliff." This quote makes me think James is trying to be brave for Isaac and for himself. I think the author included this detail because she/he wanted to show that James was trying to be brave so his little brother wouldn't worry about him.

FIG. 2–1 Isis writes off a quote in her notebook.

attention to the text will pay off. Make a bit of a fuss about this if you see it. Notice if a student seems to have written one burst of thinking and then returned to reread the short story yet again, to think at a deeper level. Again, as you comment to her that the sort of rereading and rewriting she is doing will definitely pay off, make sure that those sitting nearby know, too. Notice, too, if a student has tried to reach for precise words, saying things in ways that aren't clichéd. Often this can lead to confusing prose, but the intent to capture an idea that isn't easily pinned down is worth celebrating.

You will also want to notice and address predictable problems. Some writers will focus on the plotline of the story rather than on developing ideas that emerge from it. They will retell a key scene or summarize the plot. This can be a way for a reader to prime the pump, so support the practice, but suggest that the student then push himself to grow an idea. Sometimes using little sentence starters, such as these, can help: "The thought I have about this is . . ." "This makes me realize that . . ." "I think this is important because . . ."

Sometimes you will find that students get stuck thinking about a character's emotions. While feelings are a great place to begin when thinking about characters, simply saying, "The woman in 'Thank You, Ma'am' is angry" is not going to uncover the depth of meaning of the text that you expect sixth-graders to generate. While naming a character's emotions is a grand way to begin an analysis, if the thinking work stops there, you will want to help your writers identify the next steps. Teach your students to step back from the emotion and the event of the text and to ask themselves, "What kind of person would feel and act this way?" or to begin with another prompt: "This is the kind of person who . . ." Or they could ask, "*Why* might this person be this way?"

One of the best scenarios you may encounter will be that some of your students do this work especially easily. When writers are ready for next steps, you might challenge them to notice that with every choice the author makes, he or she is trying to show you something, teach you something not just about the character but about life. Teach your students that when people read stories, they are immediately on the lookout for what this story is *really* about. (Meanwhile, note that you will teach this to the whole class later in the unit, so this is a preview of that teaching, and you can often populate later teaching with examples of work from your class.)

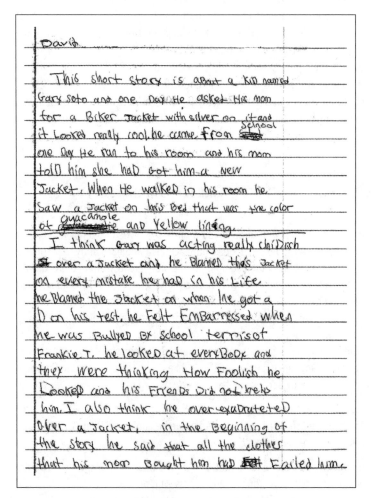

FIG. 2–2 David pushes himself beyond retelling the text in this notebook entry.

Thinking Gets Better through Talk

Talk up the value of talking about ideas, and then ask one member of each partnership to share her thinking and the other to talk back to it in ways that develop ideas.

"One of the most helpful lessons I have ever learned is that my thinking gets better when I talk to other people. This is true in my life, and this is true also in my work as a writer. It helps to run ideas by other people so they can remind me of things I haven't considered, or disagree with me, which then leads me to strengthen, clarify, or revise my thinking.

"Give it a go. Find someone who has read the same story as you (don't leave anyone out, you can be in triads). Talk out your ideas. But here's the thing. The goal is not just for one person to say, 'I wrote this,' and the other person to nod and say, 'Well, I wrote this.' Instead, the idea is to think about one person's ideas only and for as long as you can, have a long conversation about just those ideas.

"The hard job for you, as the listener, is to find places in what the other person has said that you can add onto. You might say, 'Yeah, *but* what about . . . ?' Or '*But* could it maybe be that . . . ?' Or 'I see what you are saying, *but* is there another place where that happens?' The goal is to grow ideas by talking about them and especially by using the word *but*. That is, try to think a little differently than the first person. You may find yourself adding on to the ideas or disagreeing with part of them, questioning if that's the best evidence."

HAVE A DIALOGUE ABOUT YOUR IDEAS ON THE PAGE

"While it is very helpful to have a partner coaching you in these moves, the real work is to be able to do this work on your own. Tonight, reread what you have written about the story you have selected, and conduct a written conversation on the page. Maybe you'll write, 'Yeah, but what about,' and then shift back to writing. Keep throwing the conversational ball between yourself and your imaginary partner to let those questions, those challenges, push you to develop your own ideas.

"Then, write another entry about the story and the character that interests you in that story. When you enter our classroom tomorrow, you will to need to have your story read and marked up pretty thoroughly, and you will need to have at least three entries."

Writing to Discover What a Character Really Wants

IN THIS SESSION, you'll teach students that literary essayists think and write about what motivates characters and what characters really want, and then they use this writing as the basis for their essays.

GETTING READY

✔ An enlarged copy of the excerpted passages from the shared class text, "Raymond's Run" (From Session 2; it is assumed that students have their own copy of the shared text for this and future sessions.) (see Teaching and Active Engagement)

✔ Chart paper and markers (see Teaching and Mid-Workshop Teaching)

✔ Your own writer's notebook (see Teaching)

✔ The texts students worked with in the previous session (see Link)

✔ "How to Write a Literary Essay about Character" anchor chart (see Link and Share)

✔ "Thought Prompts that Help an Essayist Think and Write" chart (see Mid-Workshop Teaching)

✔ Copies of Figure 3–2 for each student (see Share)

COMMON CORE STATE STANDARDS: W.6.1.a,b; W.6.2, W.6.3.b, W.6.10, RL.6.1, RL.6.3, SL.6.1, L.6.1, L.6.2, L.6.3

W HEN YOU CONSIDER THE PEOPLE YOU KNOW WELL, it is likely that your full relationship with them feels more like a novel than a note, more like an epic poem than an advertising slogan. There is so much to say about the people closest to us. The same could be said of the characters in the texts that move us. There is so much to say about Katniss, about Auggie, about Scout and Tom. And yet often when students write about and discuss the characters in their texts, their thoughts come out in three-word sentences with a period set so finally that you can practically hear the implicit "The End!"

In this session, you can help change that. First, you will teach your students that one way to find more powerful ideas about a character—ideas worth really writing about—is to investigate what makes them tick, what motivates them to do the things they do—and to investigate, too, what a character really wants out of life or from other people in the story. By spotlighting these queries, you position students to come up with more interesting ideas about their characters, ones that are not obvious, and you also position them to write with greater volume and independence. Later on in the session, you will teach students to elaborate on their thinking by using a few simple prompts that nudge the thoughts that may lie unarticulated in their heads to the surface of the page.

How easily this lesson goes will depend on what kind of reading work your kids bring to the table. To have powerful thoughts about a character, it helps to know the angles and aspects of characters that will reward attention. This session assumes that students have already learned that it pays off to think about a character's traits, choices, and relationships. You'll come to this session with the tone of "obviously this is what you would think about when you think about characters," and then you'll move on to a more complex way of thinking—in this case, to think about characters through the lens of motivation—what causes them to act the way they do.

If your class has not had this rich work in thinking about texts—if they have not, for example, had a lesson or series of lessons on how to consider the ways that a character's choices affect both the character and the secondary characters—then you may want to take a bit of time here to do some of that teaching. While you cannot fit an entire reading unit into this slot of time, you can outfit your students with some powerful reading and thinking strategies that will help them as they begin to collect ideas for essays.

"There is so much to say about the people closest to us. The same could be said of the characters in the texts that move us."

In this session, then, you will continue to show students the power of looking closely at people, at characters. More specifically, you will teach them that when readers know what to look for, their thinking multiplies, for they can see nuances and meanings they would have missed had they just skimmed the surface of the story.

Writing to Discover What a Character Really Wants

CONNECTION

Using an example from school life, point out that when we think about people, we often think about what they want and that it's useful for essay writing to think of characters the same way.

"Yesterday, coming back from lunch, I couldn't help but notice there had been some sort of drama in the cafeteria. As I was eavesdropping, I noticed how intuitive you all were about what was going on, how insightful you were about people and what motivates them. It struck me that the work you did yesterday in analyzing your classmates is also the work essayists do when they analyze texts! When you were talking, I heard a few of you say things like, 'The thing about her is that she just wants people to understand her, and if she feels misunderstood, she flips.' The way you were thinking is *exactly* the way essayists think. They analyze what motivates a character to understand what the character *really* wants. Today I'd like to push you to try that 'cafeteria-thinking' out on the characters in your stories."

❖ **Name the teaching point.**

"Today I want to teach you that when literary essayists are writing about characters, one way they make their ideas more powerful, more intriguing, is by looking beyond the obvious details about the characters to think about what motivates them—to figure out what the character really wants from other people and from life."

TEACHING

Stress the value of thinking about a character's motivations, emphasizing that what a character seems to want on the outside may not be the deeper motivation.

"Okay, so one way we can get started is to just think to ourselves for a moment, what does our character—Squeaky—want? What motivates her to act all tough and prickly and defensive? As we try to answer this question, it's important that we go beyond the obvious, the external—just like Jamhil did when he went beyond noticing Squeaky's talent for running to consider her loneliness. I mean, the first thing that comes to my mind is that Squeaky wants people to stop being jerks, but let's go deeper than that.

"You know, my dad never had a ton of money, but he always wanted this British sports car, a weird car if you ask me. But even though he said that he wanted that car, I think really what he wanted was to feel successful. It's this kind of

◆ COACHING

For all of their shrugging shoulders and sucking of teeth, adolescents want nothing more than to be seen and valued. By noting the drama of the day before, without knee-jerk disapproval, you are valuing their lives and their problems, equating their everyday lives to their academic work.

thinking work we want to do—so that we point out not that Squeaky 'wants people to stop picking on her brother,' although that's true, but something about how she wants to feel, or what she wants her life to be like, or how she wishes her relationships were."

Channel students to ponder the protagonist's real motivation and to be ready to share their thinking.

"We are going to go pretty deep with Squeaky here, and one thing I notice is that sometimes it takes me a second to have a good thought, you know? So let's pause for just a bit so you each have a chance to think about the question 'What does Squeaky *really* want, from other people and from life?' Use the whole story to help you answer this."

In the silence, I looked up to the ceiling, as if pondering deeply myself. After an interval, I said quietly, not wanting to stop their thinking, "After you have time to think, I'm going to ask for people to offer up ideas, to just speak out, and I'll write down what you say. I'm not going to call on you, so you'll have to remember that if it is quiet, it is your turn to talk. Okay, let's think in silence together, What does Squeaky *really* want?"

Invite students to share their thinking.

I waited twenty seconds and then gently asked students to begin voicing their ideas. There was silence at first, and then Stephen said, "She wants people to stop making fun of her brother." I nodded, smiled, and gestured for others to chime in.

Slowly voices started to add ideas to the mix. Diamond said, "She wants to win everything. She keeps saying she's the fastest and no one can beat her. And she practices her running all the time."

Crystal offered, "She acts really tough toward people. I don't know why. But even though she is tough, she really loves Raymond."

Frankie jumped on this and added, "I think she acts tough, but she is really lonely. At the end, I think she wants to be friends with that girl, what's her name?"

Natori's hand shot up. "I know, I know. She acts all tough, but she also has a soft side, because she really loves Raymond. She is tough because she is so protective of him. She would do anything for him."

I jotted notes capturing these ideas, writing fast and furiously so as not to stem the tide, and then stopped the class.

Debrief by naming what students have just done that you hope they do often when they write about literature. Then set students up to do the next step—to take one of their ideas and think/write long about it.

"Wow. You really get people! You get that what people want on the surface—a new car, for people to stop picking on them—isn't usually what they want most of all, what they want deep inside. What they *really* want is usually a feeling,

You will not find anything quite so magical as the silence of a group of sixth-graders sitting in a room together, thinking. You may need to remind a couple of your writers with a finger to your lips, and it may not always be perfect, but giving your students time to consider a question you have asked is integral to them being able to answer it. It may help if you repeat the question a few times, whispering, "What does Squeaky really want?"

Stephen's idea is totally obvious and not exactly the deep thinking I was hoping to yield—and he knew that. He contributed with a tone of voice that signaled he knew he was making my question seem silly. Here I make the choice to let this go or to talk to him after class rather than in front of others. I also chose to silently communicate that I got the joke—and even appreciated his wit. It seems important to let kids have their small victories.

You are going to want to decide now whether you'll be writing your own literary essay or borrowing the literary essay that weaves in and out of this chapter. This entry contains seeds of the literary essay that becomes important to the next six sessions, so borrow or adapt the following entry if you are going to want to lean on the essay within this book.

a way of living, a new kind of relationship; it's human nature to want these things. And in Squeaky's case, even though she tells us she wants to win that race—and I agree with all of you that she does want this, desperately—it seems like maybe she wants some deeper things, too.

"I bet you know what essayists do next, after listing possible motivations a character seems to have," I said, pointing to my writer's notebook to signal my intended meaning. When students began to say, 'They write?' I nodded, picked up my notebook, and started to scrawl in it. Students could not see what I was writing, which allowed me to write extra quickly, scrawling across the page. I deliberately took one of the ideas they'd offered.

> Squeaky seems tough and angry, wanting to knock down people, but even though she seems tough, what shines through is how much she loves Raymond. He is disabled in some way, I am not sure how exactly, and having him tag along could make some people crazy. But she wants to stay near him to look out for him. They go everywhere together. If people tease her brother or treat him badly, Squeaky gets mad. She knows he is different and that he can't protect himself.
>
> PROTECT.
>
> That is a good word for what Squeaky does. Squeaky wants to protect her brother from the world. She watches that he walks on the safe side of the sidewalk and knocks anyone down who so much as looks at him. It is like she sees the whole world as enemies to her and to Raymond. **Maybe** she's gotten tough because people have made fun of her and she uses that toughness to protect Raymond. But while she thinks she is just protecting Raymond, she is also pushing people away and I sort of wonder if she is lonely, deep down.

ACTIVE ENGAGEMENT

Set your class up to try the work you've demonstrated. In this instance, ask students to try to talk long about the character's motivation. Coach in as needed, suggesting they trace the idea through the beginning, middle, and end of the story.

"Your turn. I know you'll be thinking and writing about a whole different short story later today. But just to get your muscles for doing this work as strong as possible *before* you tackle a story all on your own, will you and your partner take another idea about what motivates Squeaky and talk about it together? The important thing is not just to say the idea to each other, but to grow some thinking about it. You can push your thinking by saying, 'Maybe . . .' You can also do what I did and think about examples from the start of the story, the middle, and the end."

As I listened in, I heard Jaz say to Sarah, "Um, okay. Let's take the idea that she wants to win everything, Because she does. All the races, for example."

Sarah checked in with me, and then followed with a sheepish, "Maybe she wants that because . . . ?"

Because I was writing in my notebook, tilted up toward me, I also tucked a crib sheet containing the prewritten entry. The truth is that when writing in your own notebook in front of the class, you can pretend *to write, scrawling wiggly lines across your page (quickly!), and meanwhile you can actually read aloud what you have already written (crib sheets) as you pretend to write that.*

Notice that when writing this entry, I've written about how the idea I have relates to the beginning, the middle, and the end of the text. It helps to have a strategy in mind for what you are doing when you write publicly. Later in this minilesson I will tell students the plan I had up my sleeve that led to this piece of writing.

Jaz glowered, and I coached into the conversation, "Sarah, Jaz isn't the only one who could follow up on your prompt. You could answer your own question."

Jaz looked triumphant and Sarah said, "Okay. Uhh . . . Or maybe . . . maybe the author has her wanting to win the races because . . . umm . . . she wants to feel good about herself?"

I gave them a thumbs up, added in another prompt ("This is significant because . . .") and moved on to listen in for half a minute to Natori and Kayla, who were in a heated conversation about whether Squeaky *had* to be mean. Was she protecting her brother or her image (or both)? I tried to listen to another partnership but found that Sam and Eli were just staring at each other, clearly feeling like they were done talking. I nudged them to reread the story, looking for examples of their point, and to say, "For example . . ."

Share a strategy that one partnership used that will help students if they get stuck doing this work.

"Writers, I want to share a strategy that Sam and Eli tried just now. They said their idea and then sat there—done." I imitated how they'd just sat for a bit, scanning the room, waiting for others to be done as well. "But then they got the idea to reread the story and see if they could find evidence for their idea! Instead of just sitting there, they reread—and you know what? I'm pretty sure they are not just going to find evidence for their original idea, but they are also going to find that their original idea evolves, that it becomes more complicated.

"So if you ever find yourself feeling stuck in today's workshop or future times when you are writing about reading, try Sam and Eli's strategy of going back to the text to reread and rethink."

LINK

Remind students that expert readers know which features of a story are worth studying and that it pays off to study a character's wants and motivations.

"You've spent today reading texts closely, noticing the kinds of details that get you growing ideas about characters." I gestured to the chart I created the day before. "Let's record this work. You'll be doing this again and again as you write literary essays, so this chart can be a way to keep yourselves on track." I turned back to the chart and added a third bullet point:

How to Write a Literary Essay about Character

- Reread selected bits.
- Notice the details, think, talk, write to explore: "Why this detail?"
- **Think, "What does the character really want?" and write long.**

Notice that here I attribute my own suggestion to these two somewhat recalcitrant students. This is intentional. They may not have come up with the idea themselves, but they used it, and my goal here is not to spotlight my own role in this, but rather to help them feel ownership of the work they did. Also, I want kids in the class to know that they can be their own problem solvers.

"So today you'll continue working to grow ideas about the story you have selected. You might return to thinking about the details in a text, writing long about them. Or you might think about character motivations. I imagine you will fill at least two pages of your notebook with entries today.

"But just one tip before you start. You'll recall that yesterday I suggested you reread passages that seemed important to you, looking for details in them. Instead of thinking all about character motivations in general, you might again first select important scenes and, only then, try to pinpoint, in those scenes, what the character wants, deep down inside, or what is motivating the character. Your writing and your thinking will be best if it is lodged in very particular parts of the story."

Notice that minilessons are cumulative, so that at the end of today's minilesson, I send students off to do the work they learned about today, and also to use what they learned yesterday. If yesterday's teaching doesn't even last until today, the chances aren't great that it will become a lifelong strategy!

Helping Students Write with Engagement and Precision

REMEMBER THAT YOUR STUDENTS will be working with stories other than "Raymond's Run." The first thing you'll need to do is to get your students to go to selected scenes, reread them, and then use those scenes to help them find and jot possible character motivations. That process of jotting character motivations should be as brief as the process of listing possible personal narrative ideas was in the earlier unit. That work just primes the pump and gets students ready to write. The real work of this session involves taking one of those motivations and writing a half-page entry about it, and then taking another. Of course, ideally, the entries will be longer than that, with lots of text citations, but it is early in the unit, so you should expect that some students will find it hard to elaborate extensively.

Early on in any unit, one of your responsibilities is to find ways to recruit students' engagement in the work. If some of your students seem to resist, it will be important

(continues)

MID-WORKSHOP TEACHING   **Using Thought Prompts for Elaborating**

"Class, I'd like to share some work that Sarah found helpful. She's writing about the story 'Popularity.' She was having a tough time keeping her thinking going down the page. It seemed like she ran out of things to say, so then she was just doing busy work. We talked about this and she remembered some prompts that she learned in previous years and that are helping her keep her thinking going." I looked at Sarah, giving her a cue that her part was coming up. "Sarah will let you in on the prompts that helped her. I'll add these to a chart we started yesterday, only I think we better rename the chart."

Sarah stood nervously, inspiring one of her friends to yell out "Go, Sarah!" which got the rest of the class laughing for a second. I motioned for Sarah to begin. She did. "Um, so, so the best prompt that I have is 'This is important because . . .' It really helps to, um, I guess it gets me to think about why my idea matters to the story."

Listening, I recorded, "This is important because" on the chart. I asked, "Does anyone else remember some thought prompts from our earlier lesson that helped you to elaborate? Let's think of a few more points to add to our chart." After a brief discussion, my chart looked like this:

> **Thought Prompts that Help an Essayist Think and Write**
>
> ✓ Maybe the author included this because...
> ✓ On the other hand, perhaps...
> ✓ Or it could be that...
> ✓ I wonder if...
> ✓ This is important because...
> ✓ For example...
> ✓ The reason for this is...
> ✓ On the other hand...
> ✓ So what I am really trying to say is...

"Class, Sarah is going to let you study her entry later to see if you get some tips from it. Meanwhile, see if this list can help you think and write more."

---

to try to turn that around now. That's why, in the minilesson, we made two students who were resisting the work famous for inventing a strategy. In your conferring, too, you'll want to reach those who are reluctant and turn them around. Chances are good that students who aren't engaged will feel as if the work of writing a literary essay doesn't connect to them and their lives. You'll want to help these students know that just because they are writing about someone else's story does not mean they cannot write about personally important topics and ideas. Teach them that it actually helps to think about questions such as these: Which characters do they most relate to? Which scenes resonated for them? Which problems, issues, and ideas are important in their lives as well?

They won't be writing about "Raymond's Run" but about one of the short stories from their packet. However, you can use "Raymond's Run" to make your point, perhaps explaining that if you want to think about, say, the role of running in the story, you can think, "How does this connect to my life?" You don't run, but you play basketball. So you can think, "What does basketball do for me in my life? How is that the same, and how is it different from the role that running plays in Squeaky and Raymond's lives?" You can then coach the students to think in similar ways about whatever story they are reading. By spending some time thinking about aspects of that story that resonate for a particular student, you can give those students strategies that allow them to be more insightful about the stories they are analyzing and writing about.

As you look over your writers' shoulders, you may see some essayists relying on generic words to describe complicated characters or ideas. The character is *nice*, the changes are *hard*, the lesson is to be a *good* person. Students who have written literary essays in previous years have the vocabulary to be more precise, more descriptive, but they may not be using it, so by all means simply ask them to revise some of their jottings to reflect the language they have at their fingertips. If you have some students who do not seem to you to have been taught to generate precise words to describe a character, introduce them to some powerful language that they will use over and over again as they begin their careers as literary essayists. Set these students up to collect and record synonyms for easier, more generic words they know.

You could start by drawing four boxes, with simple trait or feeling words at the top of each one:

Nice	Mean
Brave	Afraid

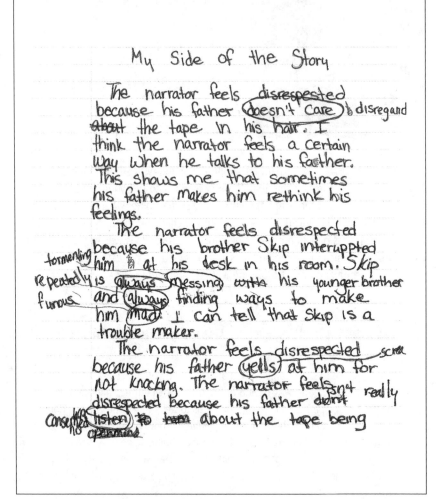

FIG. 3–1 Natori lifts the level of her vocabulary as she writes.

Then, in a small group, have students begin to brainstorm words that mean sort of the same thing as one of the generic terms they've been using—say, *nice*. Point out that many words that *seem* similar in fact represent slightly different shades of the word, for example, *content*, *happy*, *ecstatic* (or *want*, *yearn*, *crave*), and get students thinking along spectrums of similar words. As students work, they can rank the words they collect, from most nice to least. Over time, charts or personal word walls such as these can help develop students' academic vocabulary.

Setting Goals for Future Work

Coach students to study a mentor entry to name what that writer has done that they, too, could try.

"Writers, I know you are accustomed to studying the published work of famous authors and thinking about what that writer has done that you could try. But to write an essay well, there is behind the scenes writing-to-think that makes a world of difference, and people don't usually get a chance to

In the story <u>Popularity</u> ^it says that the character wants to be popular. I think this because in the story there are many details that show this. One detail I found was that the main character, Allen S, and Allen G. spend their recess at the oak tree and circle it while trying to find 4 leaf clovers. And if they ever found one they would wish for that they would be so popular that they never would have to spend another recess together again. This shows that the main character is maybe lonely, not popular, outcasts, and maybe a little shy. I think the author put this detail in because he wants you to know that they are outcasts and don't fit in. That is one detail to show that the main character in <s>Popularity</s> is <s>not popular,</s> yet.

FIG. 3–2 Sarah uses a thought prompt to keep her thinking going down the page.

James

James wanted to be in the K-Bones because he wanted to be cool, he wanted respect, and he wants to show he's brave. However, throughout the story James realizes its stupid and turns down Kris' offer.

I think James wants to be apart of the K-Bones to be cool. He acts sneaky when he waits until his mom leaves the bus stop, and thumps on the wall so Mrs. Lopez thinks him and Isaac are there. Maybe James doesn't want to get in trouble, but the struggle of being cool tempts him to do stupid things. Or maybe, James just doesn't want to seem punk in front of Kris. I think what James really wants is to be accepted by the K-Bones. So what I am really trying to say is, James is a good kid but will do whatever it takes to be cool, and be accepted.

FIG. 3–3 Crystal revises an entry after studying a mentor entry.

study that kind of writing. The great thing about working alongside each other is that in this class, you *can* study what writers do in their notebooks, what writers do to grow ideas—because that's what you all are doing.

"So I'm going to ask you to start and study part of Sarah's entry (the one we talked about in the mid-workshop), and specifically, I'm going to ask you to notice one really terrific thing that Sarah has done that you could try (see Figure 3–2 on page 33). Now, here is the hard part. Then you'll turn to your writing and try your hand at whatever you notice Sarah doing that you thought was so admirable. You can study Sarah's writing with a partner, but of course, you'll be revising your writing on your own".

STUDY A MENTOR ENTRY TO EXPLORE NEW WAYS OF THINKING ABOUT A SHORT STORY

"For homework tonight and across the next few days, I'm going to ask you to do a similar kind of writing as you did today. Remember to look at Sarah's writing and be willing to think, 'I haven't tried that yet,' and then give that new way of thinking and writing a go. Look at the writing I've done in class, too, and see if any of that can nudge you to try new stuff in your entries about your short story. I've tried to put the tips you have learned so far onto our anchor chart. I imagine you will write at least one to two more pages tonight for homework, so be sure you make a good plan now for what tips you can use."

How to Write a Literary Essay About Character

- Reread selected bits.

- Notice details, think, talk, write to explore: "Why this detail?"

- Think, "What does the character really want?" and write long.

- It can help to use thought prompts (Maybe... Perhaps...)

- Think about the deep down, internal motivations.

- Once you have an idea and some evidence, reread again, reread more of the text, reread more closely, and expect your original idea will change.

Crafting Claims

T HE TIME HAS COME for your class to develop and choose a claim. Students— and teachers, you too!—may be used to calling this a *thesis statement*, which is an appropriate term. We've opted for *claim* here, in part to align closely to the Common Core's terminology and in part to allow for the possibility of introducing counterclaims. *Claim* and *thesis* are synonyms, so you'll see both terms throughout this book.

This is a big moment. And like any big moment, this one has the potential to set students up beautifully or to derail them a bit. There are two common ways for writers to become derailed at this point. The first is that the push to get a claim can lead writers to grab onto whatever looks like the easiest, most obvious idea to write about, which can then lead them to steer clear of the richer, more interesting and more challenging ideas. That may not be the worst thing for those of your students who are new to writing essays. For some, it may be fruitful to write about fairly obvious ideas at this point, saving the more challenging work for later. But mostly, you want this unit to lead students to think more deeply because they are writing. The second risk is that writers might grab onto an idea that pertains to the most powerful part of the story but that doesn't (like a big idea hug) encompass and embrace much of the story.

To us, choosing a claim is much like choosing a prom date. It's not as life altering as choosing a partner to marry, but it sure is something that will stick with you for a while. You don't want to grab the first person—or the first claim—that comes your way. Instead, you want to reflect for a moment, imagining the whole night from beginning to end—the dinner out with friends, the prom itself, the photos and the after-party. Does this person fit into the whole night, or is he just a good fit for the after-party?

So in today's session, you'll teach your students to search their notebooks and their thoughts for any claims that might be contenders and then to step back and ask themselves whether these claims feel precisely right and whether they apply to the whole story or just to one part of it. Claims should encompass most of the text; writers should be able to find evidence for a claim across the course of the story, not just in the beginning, or at the end.

IN THIS SESSION, you'll teach students that essayists mull over their ideas about the character and then choose one they can craft into a claim that feels worth thinking and writing about and that may eventually drive an essay.

GETTING READY

✔ "How to Write a Literary Essay about Character" anchor chart (see Connection, Teaching and Active Engagement, and Share) 💿

✔ Students' writer's notebooks and pens (see Teaching and Active Engagement)

✔ Your own notebook that captures the class's thinking about "Raymond's Run" or this same thinking on chart paper, enlarged to share with the class (see Teaching and Active Engagement)

✔ A few white boards and markers, for several students to capture the claims that are generated (see Teaching and Active Engagement)

✔ Chart paper and markers (see Teaching and Active Engagement)

✔ The texts students worked with in the previous session (see Connection and Link)

✔ A copy of the class essay on the *third little pig*, generated in Session 1, enlarged for the class to see (see Share) 💿

COMMON CORE STATE STANDARDS: W.6.1.a,b,c; RL.6.1, RL.6.2, RL.6.3, RL.6.4, SL.6.1, SL.6.3, SL.6.4, SL.6.6, L.6.1, L.6.2, L.6.3

Crafting Claims

CONNECTION

Share an anecdote from your life to demonstrate what it means to formulate a substantial idea.

"Writers, when you come to the meeting area today, I want you to notice that I have divided the space into four corners. Each corner is for people who are working with a different story. Choose your seat based on the story that you read, because later you'll be talking with others who read the same story."

Once students had settled, I began. "The other day I was out to lunch with a friend, and he asked me what I liked about this other friend of ours, who can be a bit difficult to get along with. And the thing is, I had a hard time figuring out what to say, because my reasons didn't seem big enough. They didn't seem to quite capture why I like our friendship. It was an annoying feeling, like my brain was failing. I kept coming up with little things, with ideas that only showed a tiny part of her, like, 'I like how she is really into video games.' or 'She can be really nice sometimes.' But later on, when I had more time to think, I realized that the real reason I like this friend is that she sees the world in interesting ways, and helps me see it in those ways, too. This felt like a real thing to say about my friend, but it was hard to get to."

Tell students that the next step for them, as literary essayists, is to develop all the thinking they have done into an idea that is big enough to become their essay's central idea—its claim.

"You all have loads of ideas about the stories you've been working on in your notebooks, and even more in your minds. Like the ideas I had initially about my friend, when I thought, 'I like how she is into video games,' your ideas are probably true, and yet they might not yet be some kind of 'big truth' about the text, or the character."

✛ Name the teaching point.

"Today I want to teach you that when literary essayists write about a character, they work hard to come up with an idea, a claim, that captures the whole of that person so the claim (or thesis statement) is big enough to think and write about for a while and can maybe even become the central idea of the entire essay."

I gestured toward the anchor chart, to highlight the new bullet I had added prior to the minilesson.

◆ COACHING

It may be tempting to ramble on about what students have been doing prior to today—because it's an easy way to orient yourself and your students before plunging ahead—but kids will pay closer attention to new information, anecdotes, and stories than to long summaries of what they have already been taught. So if you are accustomed to recapping at the start of a minilesson, try to make that work somewhat interactive ("Let me read over a list of things you've learned, and give me a thumbs up if you feel you have mastered an item on the list, and a thumbs down if you haven't yet practiced it").

> ### How to Write a Literary Essay about Character
>
> - Reread selected bits (best not to start with the whole story).
> - Notice the details, think, talk, write to explore: "Why this detail?"
> - Think, "What does the character really want?" and write long
>   - It can help to use thought prompts (Maybe . . . Perhaps . . .).
>   - Think about the deep down, internal motivations.
> - Once you have an idea about character motivations and some evidence, reread again, reread more of the text, reread more closely, and expect your original idea will change.
> - **Try to generate an idea about the character that encompasses the whole character and the whole text**

TEACHING AND ACTIVE ENGAGEMENT

Point out that to generate a claim, it helps to reread what you've written and review what you've thought, working to generate a collection of possible claims that each encompass the whole character and text.

"To come up with a strong claim about a character, it helps to reread one's entries and notes and to think again about the text, coming up with drafts of 'possible claims.' Let's return to our entries and ideas about 'Raymond's Run,' and as we do so, ask, 'What is the main thing we really want to say about Squeaky?' Let's review the entries we wrote and talked about, including Jamhil's, where he answered that same question by going deeper and deeper with *maybes*.

"As I reread these entries, will you try to come up with a claim that you think is big enough to encompass all of your most important ideas about Squeaky? Your idea might come from these entries or it might come from the story itself. Ready? Pens up?" I read aloud, pausing for kids to stop and jot. Occasionally I said, "After you've jotted one possible idea, try another, and another."

I projected the following pages from my notebook to the class.

> I notice that when people say mean things about Raymond, Squeaky reacts by saying, "I much rather just knock you down . . ." I wonder why Bambara included this detail about Squeaky—that she wants to knock people down. Maybe the author wants to show us that Squeaky is really really angry over how people treat her brother. On the other hand, perhaps Bambara is showing us that Squeaky really loves Raymond—she loves him so much that she's willing to fight for him. Or

This is a writing unit, but of course, it hinges on the reading instruction you and others before you have given to your students. To write a compelling essay, students need to be able to develop and test out ideas about texts, and this work can be infinitely complex. It will be important to teach your students that coming up with an idea requires exploration, time, and thought. Essayists don't grab hold of the first idea that occurs to them. Although you will demonstrate a bit of the process of sorting through notebook entries for ideas, listing and evaluating possible claims, this isn't easily conveyed through a minilesson, and your main goal will be to set students up to do this work and to say those all-important words: "Off you go." They'll learn from doing.

For today's teaching, you'll need to have a way of making the past few days' ideas visible for students. You could follow our model, showcasing the class's thinking by putting a few pages of your notebook on the document camera, with the class's collective thinking prerecorded. Or you could do this just as easily with chart paper and a marker.

could it be that Bambara is trying to show that Squeaky thinks it works better to fight than to talk through stuff?

* * * *

I think Bambara wants to show that Squeaky is a good runner. I think maybe she also wants to show that Squeaky is really egotistical, like she is a rapper saying, "I'm the best!" But it is sad she is running a relay race all by herself. Maybe the author is trying to show that Squeaky doesn't have any friends because she is running all by herself and winning all the spots. I bet maybe she doesn't have friends because she is always attacking kids.

* * * *

Squeaky seems tough and angry, wanting to knock down people, but even though she seems tough, what shines through is how much she loves Raymond. He is disabled in some way, I am not sure how exactly, and having him tag along could make some people crazy. But she wants to stay near him to look out for him. They go everywhere together. If people tease her brother or treat him badly, Squeaky gets mad. She knows he is different and that he can't protect himself.

PROTECT.

That is a good word for what Squeaky does. Squeaky wants to protect her brother from the world. She watches that he walks on the safe side of the sidewalk and knocks anyone down who so much as looks at him. It is like she sees the whole world as enemies to her and to Raymond. Maybe she's gotten tough because people have made fun of her and she uses that toughness to protect Raymond. But while she thinks she is just protecting Raymond, she is also pushing people away and I sort of wonder if deep down, she is lonely.

Use a symphony share as a way to allow multiple students to share the claims that they generated.

"Writers, now let's hear your ideas. Reread the claims about Squeaky that you have jotted, star the one you think best captured her, in all her complexity, and get ready for a symphony share. Remember, I'll be the conductor of the orchestra, and when I tip my baton your way, you read out just one of your claims—your favorite one—as if you are the clarinet or the oboe in the orchestra, coming in on cue."

After giving students a minute to select their best claim (and meanwhile orchestrating it so that a few students captured the claims that were called out on white boards), I tipped my baton to a succession of students, and soon we were sitting among these and other claims:

> Squeaky seems tough and angry, wanting to knock people down, but what shines through is how much she loves Raymond.

As I circled the room, some kids were focused on the fact that Squeaky is a really tough person but that she's that way to protect the things she cares about, like her brother and her status as the fastest runner. Other kids were on about the fact that Squeaky really values the truth and respect. The latter idea didn't come out in the symphony share, but if I had wanted it to, I could have deliberately signaled for that writer to share her ideas. The advantage of listening in first is that you are able to engineer what is shared with the whole group. I just thought for now that I wanted to make the work accessible enough that everyone would generally see the ideas as central to the story.

Deep down, Squeaky just really wants to protect Raymond.

Squeaky acts tough to people and pushes them away.

In spite of her big talk and her toughness, Squeak is lonely. BUT she doesn't want people to know.

Channel students to join you in testing the claims they generated, weighing whether each encompasses the whole character and text. After narrowing the field of contenders, point out that essayists tweak the wording and thinking before settling on a still-tentative claim.

"You'll do this same work on your own later today, generating claims about the short story you have selected. Always remember that after an essayist drafts a few possible claims, he then looks them over, weighing which seems most viable—which encompasses the whole character and which rings truest? Right now, review these claims that we've come up with about Squeaky with the people sitting near you, and decide which you think comes closest to capturing the essence of her. Turn and talk." While the students were talking, I listed the claims that were captured during the symphony share on a sheet of chart paper.

Soon I quelled the conversation and asked, "So let's tackle the really hard question. Which of these seems most encompassing of *all* sides of Squeaky, and why do you say that? Or go for the opposite. Which seems one-sided, like the thought I had that I like my friend because she enjoys video games?"

Hands shot up. Frankie began the conversation. "I think the second claim, the one that Squeaky just really wants to protect Raymond, that one is just about one side because yes, Squeaky *does* want to protect Raymond, but she is more than just that—like she also wants to win the race. That has nothing to do with Raymond. Squeaky has this really huge personality. There is more to her than loving Raymond."

I nodded. "Okay, so we think that 'Deep down, Squeaky just really wants to protect Raymond' might not be broad enough?" When some students nodded, I took that as enthusiastic assent, coming from middle-schoolers!

Sarah added, "Same with the third one—that is true that Squeaky acts tough, but it is just one side. She's not all tough."

I nodded, crossed those two out, and then starred the first and last claims on our list. "So these ideas seem best because they capture different—even conflicting—sides of Squeaky." I reread them, underlining key terms for emphasis as I said, "'She is tough and angry—but also loving.' *Or,* 'She is tough, but also lonely, and intent on protecting herself from anyone knowing that she is lonely.'"

Channel students also to weigh whether the possible claims encompass the whole text, and as they consider that, suggest they tweak and revise and refine and rewrite the claims so they do work.

"You have done some important work that essayists do. But essayists don't stop there." I returned to the anchor chart and emphasized the final few words on the bullet I'd added that day. "Essayists also think about whether a claim can

Notice that today's teaching is longer than usual. You may find that you can condense it, especially if your students have had experience writing essays. One of the hardest things for students to learn in this genre is how to come up with a claim that is big enough that they can then support it in ways that generate a powerful essay. Moreover, you want to teach kids that coming up with a compelling idea takes some time and thought. You don't want to convey that essayists grab hold of the first idea that occurs to them. And so, you model how you can take your students through the process of sorting through their notebook entries for ideas, then looking across these to come up with a possible claim by asking, "Is this the big thing I'm trying to say? Does it convey a full picture of the character and the story?"

be supported by the whole story—the beginning, the middle, and the end—because the best ideas encompass not only the whole character but also the whole text." I gestured toward the final bullet on the anchor chart.

> • Try to generate an idea about the character that encompasses the whole character **and the whole text.**

"Think about that idea and our two remaining claims. Talk about that. Go!" After students talked a bit, I said to them, "I think you are realizing that this process involves not just choosing between a bunch of possible claims, but tweaking the claim that seems closest to what you want to say and rewriting it over and over until it is just right. So get your pens going and try making a claim that is more precise. Those of you sitting near kids with white boards, work on the white board."

As students worked, I looked over their shoulders, giving pointers. "You are aiming to capture something that is not only true about the character but that is important. Try to dig down under what you say first to ask, 'What's *really* important about this?' Is the big thing that she wants to win the race—or what?"

Name a claim that the class seems to agree upon, one that you can imagine as the thesis to an essay on the shared story, and remind students that the next order of business is to read the text with this claim in mind, checking on whether the evidence is there to support the claim.

"Class, so I am hearing new versions of claims, and the new ones seem to encompass several sides of Squeaky as well as a good deal of the story. Here is one that I think is especially strong—it encompasses a good deal of the story, and it is also clear." I drew a line on the chart paper that listed our claims, and below the line wrote the following revised claim:

> Squeaky is fiercely protective of both her brother and herself.

"I like the idea, but if we had time now, we'd still need to check to see if it is really grounded in many parts of the story."

Debrief. Share the realization that students were able to land on a bigger claim by looking across the various initial ones.

"So what you have done is what essayists do. You generated a list of claims and found that some just talk about one side of a person. It is wise to try for one that feels bigger, one that encompasses the whole person. Even after you found a claim that generally worked, you rewrote it, then tested it again. This is a *lot* of work to produce just one or two sentences!"

Listen in to what students are saying so that when you convene the class to put forth a thesis you want to suggest works, you can spin this as if it has come from the class. You may, in fact, have already thought this through yourself.

Good stories prompt readers to have all kinds of ideas, and this is one of those stories. We also found that this claim was a compelling one: Squeaky demands respect for things that matter to her.

LINK

Set students up to start doing similar work with other students who read the same story, leading them toward being ready to do this work on the page of their notebook, settling on a claim for their own character essay.

"You are sitting near others who read the same story as you did. Get with another student or two—not more than two others, not leaving anyone out. Reread your entries about the short story you've read and work together to come up with a list of possible claims. You can come up with one shared list or talk together and jot separately so you each have a list. But as soon as you have a few possible claims, start testing them out to see whether they fit with the whole character, and across the whole story. Get started!"

As students worked, I voiced over. "Remember, you're searching not for facts about the character, but for ideas—for things that are not explicitly said in the story itself, but ideas that you thought up on your own."

A bit later, I piped in with, "Remember that you can look over the writing you've collected about the text and ponder your thoughts about it. It helps to underline or star or list the big ideas you've written about the text."

Then a few minutes later I commented, "Some of you are testing your ideas now, as you come up with them. Let yourself generate a whole slew of ideas—good, bad, whatever—and only afterward, ask questions of one idea, then another, such as 'Can I find evidence that supports this across the story?'"

I watched students work and sent those who weren't working especially industriously with others off to their seats to work alone. Others, however, continued working in pairs or triads for much of the workshop.

This link is extended so that students have a chance to practice with others before they go work on their own. If you feel your class does not need this extra support, you may choose to simply send them off.

Strengthening Claims and Supporting Them with Compelling Evidence

A S YOU CONFER TODAY, expect to encounter challenges. Revising a claim so that it has traction is no easy task, but it is essential to everything else that follows in this unit. Expect to encounter a wide array of needs, from students who struggle to generate a claim instead of a fact (let alone select one that is especially strong), to those who have decided to press forward with a claim that, for one reason or another, you think may not lead to a successful essay, to those with a fairly basic claim that won't lead to rich thinking. And, of course, you'll have students who magically get today's teaching, who are ready to tackle next steps; you won't want these kids to be held up just because others need more support.

So how to get to it all? Begin by familiarizing yourself with the sorts of challenges you're likely to encounter.

Inevitably, some students in your class will struggle to find ideas in their notebooks that they can spin into an *initial* potential claim, let alone one with traction. You may want to pull these kids into a group in which you set them up to revisit some of the earlier work the class did. Remind these students that big ideas come from small details, and that noticing details that will stir big thinking is essential to this work. You might suggest that recurring details are especially worth noting because they are often ones the author uses to reveal something big. Students might notice whether there are particular things a character says over and over or actions he repeats. Are there objects the character has with her often or that she values?

Likewise, you might direct these kids to notice any recurring patterns in the writing they've done in their notebooks. Is there a tendency to focus on a particular aspect of the character—a trait, for example—or on a relationship between the main character and another character? Have they wondered the same types of things again and again or had an ongoing (maybe escalating) reaction to the story?

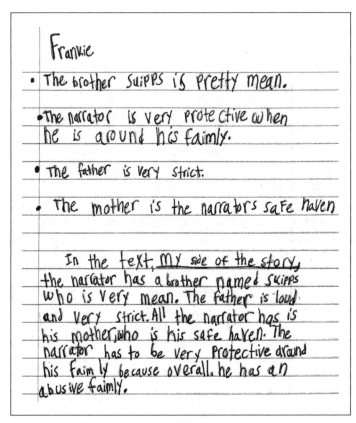

FIG. 4–1   Frankie pushes to find a claim that encompasses the whole text.

You could reiterate some of the previous session's work on motivation. Students might use prompts to move from initial observations to bigger statements that can be supported across the text: "The fact that _____ wants _____ feels important because . . ." "I notice patterns in what _____ seems to want, and these patterns makes me think that . . ."

You'll want to challenge any students whose claims are a bit simplistic to push themselves—and their thinking. Often, this is simply a matter of supporting their first ideas and helping them to say more. Sometimes asking relevant questions will help. "What surprises you especially about this?" "Why do you think this is the case?" Be ready to redirect students to the text itself.

Finally, you'll want to challenge any students who are on target—kids who have successfully generated several possible claims and have landed on one that feels like a strong option and for which they can name supports that cross the story—to begin developing their points. They might do some freewriting in their notebooks, in which they write long about the first support, then the second, then the third, frequently mining the text for precise words, lines, and details that prove each one.

MID-WORKSHOP TEACHING   Planning the Boxes-and-Bullets Structure, Then Finding Evidence

"Writers, many have you have got your claim, your thesis, and are ready to plan your essay, so let me get you started. Remember your essay about the third little pig being an admirable character? To write that essay, you found reasons and evidence to support the claim, 'The third little pig is an admirable character.' To write this next essay, you are also going to need to come up with evidence to support your claims, and your evidence needs to be in *some* categories, *some* buckets. It could be that your evidence, like in the 'Three Little Pigs' essay, can get divided up into *reasons why* the claim is true, in which case your boxes and bullets will go like they did earlier."

(A character) is (a trait) because

- (one reason),
- (another reason)
- and above all, because (a third reason)

"Right now, take a minute and see if you could figure out a plan for your essay that follows that template."

The students worked on this, and I listened in. After a bit I called out, "So Crystal's essay might go like this: 'Jim is not like the men in his family because, one, he doesn't like to hunt, two, he doesn't want to kill a sick kitten, and most of all, three, he has a different idea of what it means to be a man.'

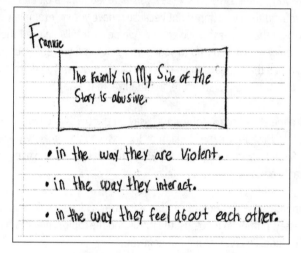

FIG. 4–2   Frankie tries out a structure for his essay.

"That works in the template. On the other hand, to write the class essay, 'Squeaky is fiercely protective of her brother and of herself,' we already have categories. They aren't reasons, but they *are ways* that Squeaky is fiercely protective, one, of her brother and, two, of herself.

"The important thing is that you find the evidence you need to support your claim, and then get it into categories. So will you take the next fifteen minutes to work like the dickens, identifying evidence? Stick Post-its® beside the evidence you spot in the text, and as you work, think about how you can divide your evidence into buckets, into categories, into the bullets in your boxes and bullets."

Drawing on Structure Boot Camp to Organize Evidence

Ask students to return to the essays they crafted during essay boot camp, noticing the techniques that were used to structure their essay.

"Essayists, when you wrote your 'Three Little Pigs' essay, you were laughing a bit and fooling around, but the truth is that what you did then was important because it gave you an example you can follow now. So I'm going to show you the class essay we started (we never totally finished the essay when we were working together, but you can also turn to your own essay). Will you and your partner annotate these essays, marking off all the things in them that can help you when you write this new essay as well? Notice the techniques you used to structure, to organize, that essay."

I showed students a chart-paper-sized copy of the class essay on the third little pig. "Can one or two of you come up and annotate this chart paper version of the essay while others work on your own paper versions?" I asked. Soon two students were marking up the class essay while other students did the same on their private copies.

"Writers, after you have annotated what you notice from this essay, will you make sure you have the start of an outline to your essay, putting in it not just the thesis and the topic sentences but your hunch about the evidence you'll include. I'll come around to help you."

I pulled alongside Chris, who was working on an essay about the character James in "Your Move."

> James is frustrated

- James is frustrated because he always has to take care of his brother.
- James is frustrated because he wants to be in with the cool kids.
- James is frustrated because he is tired of being good.

"Chris, can you pick one of your reasons and start listing some of the evidence you have to support?" Chris sighed. "Yeah. He wants to be cool like he wants to join the K-Bones." I nodded. "Good . . . keep doing that work."

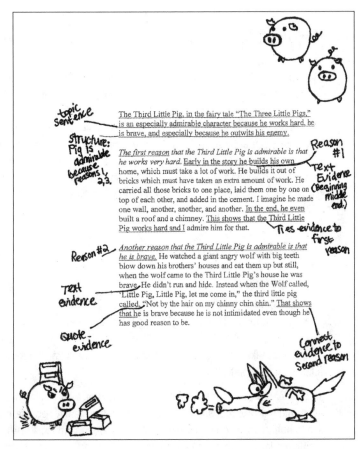

FIG. 4–3   Annotated and illustrated essay on "The Three Little Pigs"

REVEALING THE CHARACTER THROUGH DETAILS

"Tonight for homework, will you go back to the work you were doing earlier, and reread two selected passages in your story, writing about the details you see in those two passages and the ways those details reveal the character? But this time, choose those passages because you are sure you will be writing about them in your essay. So when I do this work, I'll find a passage that is especially strong and relates to Squeaky being protective of her brother and another passage that is especially strong and relates to Squeaky being protective of herself. I am hoping that tomorrow you will have at least one to two pages written in your notebook where you are trying this work.

"Remember some of the things you learned earlier about doing this work."

How to Write a Literary Essay
About Character

- Reread selected bits.

- Notice details, think, talk, write to explore: "Why this detail?"

- Think, "What does the character really want?" and write long.

- It can help to use thought prompts (Maybe... Perhaps...)

- Think about the deep down, internal motivations.

- Once you have an idea and some evidence, reread again, reread more of the text, reread more closely, and expect your original idea will change.

- Try to generate an idea about the character that encompasses the whole character and the whole text.

Conveying Evidence
Summarizing, Storytelling, and Quoting

ᴅear Teachers,

Occasionally throughout these units of study, we'll write a letter to you with some suggestions for the day rather than writing out in detail what we've done. We hope this will give you a welcome opportunity to get your own curriculum-writing feet underneath you. When you do design your own minilesson, with just some scaffolding from us, you'll be able to especially tailor it to your students.

In this session, you continue to support students in the work of going back to the short story they are writing about to collect the evidence that convinced them of their claim in the first place. It is through this close reading of the text and thinking deeply about it that they come to their ideas, as in the one that Jim Howe, in "Everything Will Be Okay," is not like the other men in his family. And now it is time to gather the evidence together in ways that will be equally convincing to other people. To help students do that, you'll be teaching them several ways to harvest evidence.

MINILESSON

The connection in the minilesson will need to return to the content from the previous session, because that was especially important. You will probably remind essayists that yesterday they learned that once they have tested out their claim, it is time to plan how the whole essay will go so that the claim at least *hints* at what the plan for the essay will be. To make this plan for the essay, people who write essays about characters often try to see if this template will work:

A character is (a trait) because (reason A), (reason B), and (reason C).

If that template doesn't fit what the essayist has to say, the essayist sometimes tries out one of these alternate templates:

Common Core State Standards: W.6.1, W.6.9.a, RI.6.1, RL.6.2, RL.6.3, RL.6.4, SL.6.1, L.6.1, L.6.2, L.6.3, L.6.6

> A character is (a trait) because (reason A), (reason B), and (reason C).
>
> A character is (this way) (with person A) and (with person B).
>
> A character is (this way) (in this situation) and (in that situation).
>
> A character is (this way) and (that way) as a (role).
>
> A character is (this way) at the start, the middle, and the end of the story.

The important thing is that once this structure work is underway, writers collect evidence to support their thinking.

Your teaching point, then, might be something like this: "Today I want to teach you that when writing a literary essay, after developing a text-based claim, essayists reread the text through the lens of the claim, searching for the most compelling evidence that can support it. Essayists quote some parts of the text, story-tell other parts, and summarize yet other parts, but one way or the other, they collect evidence."

As you proceed into the teaching and active engagement sections of the minilesson, you'll want to decide whether you will again use "Raymond's Run" as the centerpiece of the minilesson or instead will discuss what a student has been doing and use the story that student has used. Either alternative will work well.

If you use "Raymond's Run," you could say to the class, "What essayists do is they reread the text with their claim in mind, so let's do that now. Let's skim 'Raymond's Run,' looking through the glasses, the lenses, of the claim, 'Squeaky is fiercely protective of both her brother and herself,' so as to recall the evidence that convinced us this claim was a good one."

Before you demonstrate how to do this, be clear in your mind that the goal is not really to find the evidence in this one story. It is to highlight the strategies you hope students use when they look for evidence for their essays. But you'll figure out what the strategies are by doing this work yourself and meanwhile spying on yourself to notice what you actually do. For example, if you start doing this work, you'll probably note that you aren't actually reading the story so much as skimming over it, pen in hand. Teaching students to skim is tricky business but very important. It is tricky because what you or I do when we skim may be entirely different but equally effective. What I do is make a beeline down the first word or two of each line, trying as I do that to cut to the chase of that part of the story. You may do the same (or not). I suggest doing this reading work with teachers at your grade level and talking together about how exactly one goes about doing it. Then decide, as a group or individually, what portions of the strategies you use seem worth teaching to the class and which you will keep in mind as possible tips to give individuals or small groups.

That is, you might decide that although it is the case that you don't skim by running your eyes over every word at triple speed but instead by looking at just a portion of each line and recalling, as you do, what that part of the story says, you may also decide that's a detail compared to the real work that you need to teach.

In any case, as you skim through "Raymond's Run," you'll immediately come upon mention of Squeaky keeping Raymond on the inside part of the sidewalk as they walk down the street. That's being protective, right?

For sure, you need to teach students to mark the evidence and keep going, because in the end, they need evidence from the beginning, the middle, and the end of the story (and if they are not careful they will just get a lot of it from the first five lines of the story or from the all-important scene, usually at the end, of the story). You will also want to point out that the challenge is not just to find evidence, but to find the most compelling and convincing evidence.

As you continue skimming the story, you'll also come upon the part when Squeaky runs into the girls on the street and starts being rude to the girls before any of them actually *say* anything at all to Raymond. You can show to students that you again take note—bingo! More text evidence that Squeaky is protective of Raymond.

At this point, or soon thereafter, you'll have spent as much time skimming and marking evidence as you can afford to spend in a ten-minute minilesson, so point out that you'd normally read more before pausing, but that in any case, at some point you pause to reread the marked evidence, thinking "Which bit of evidence especially makes the point I want to make?"

Suggest that students need to reread closely, pen in hand, annotating the passage, underlining the words that show exactly what they want to show as evidence, and encourage them to do this in a critical mode, expecting that a lot of the passages won't, in the end, be perfect. For example, does the fact that Squeaky keeps Raymond on the inside part of the sidewalk really show that Squeaky is *fiercely* protective? Probably not. But when it comes to Squeaky's interactions with the girls, that's a different thing. Close reading will yield the realization that Squeaky is in attack mode even in her thoughts about the girls. She has mean thoughts about each one—and Mary Louise used to be her friend! And then, just the thought that they are about to say something prompts her to be rude first. That perhaps does qualify as evidence that Squeaky is being fiercely protective.

You might even mine this passage a bit more, suggesting that actually, when Squeaky is so quick to push away the girls, even her old friend Mary Louise, this could also be evidence that Squeaky is protective of herself. These are her peers that she is pushing away. Maybe this scene also shows that she is protecting herself from the pain of seeing her brother teased or from being disappointed in people, like Mary Louise who used to be her friend but who is now instead friends with Rosie, a girl Squeaky actively dislikes, and Gretchen, a girl who is Squeaky's competition. It seems like there's a way in which Squeaky protects herself *so much* that she doesn't have any friends.

In any case, once you have located some evidence to include in your essay, you can demonstrate how you actually bring that part of the story into the essay. Here, you'll want to tell students that there are a few options for how to bring evidence from a story into an essay. They can story-tell the evidence, using their own words and what they know about narrative writing to re-create the portion of the story.

You could show students how you might do this in the first body paragraph of the class's essay about Squeaky being fiercely protective of Raymond.

> Squeaky is fiercely protective of her brother, Raymond, especially when they go for strolls. One day, when Squeaky and Raymond are on a walk down Broadway, Raymond on the inside of course, to keep him safe, they bump into Mary Louise, Gretchen, and Rosie. When Mary Louise tries to talk directly to Raymond, asking him what grade he is in, Squeaky snaps, "You got anything to say to my brother, you say it to me . . ."

Another way to bring evidence into an essay is by summarizing the background of the story and quoting just the key parts of the text. Here, point out how you weave in important phrases or lines of dialogue that work to support your point.

> Squeaky is fiercely protective of her brother, Raymond. We learn right away that Raymond is "not quite right in the head" and that all Squeaky has to do in life is "mind my brother Raymond, which is enough." Another kid might crumble under the weight of looking after a brother with special needs, who is "subject to fits of fantasy" and who might dash into traffic after pigeons. But not Squeaky. She is Raymond's biggest protector. During their strolls, she's careful to keep him on the inside, near the buildings, when they walk down the street. And if "anybody has anything to say about his big head," Squeaky tells us, "they have to come by me."

Here, you'll want to remind students that if they stray from what the actual text says to embellish, they must make this clear to the reader by using phrases such as, "I can imagine this scene . . ." (e.g., "I can imagine this scene. Squeaky leaning in toward Mary Louise, with her fists clenched at her side.") or "One can imagine this began with . . ." or "This must have happened like this . . ."

You may not have time to give other examples, but if you do have a few extra moments, you could also let students know that they could also refer to key details from the text in passing by writing something like this:

> Squeaky is fiercely protective of her brother, Raymond. For example, when she describes how she practices her running exercises while going for strolls with her brother, she says she keeps Raymond on the inside, near the buildings. This is so that he doesn't fall off of the curb into puddles in the gutter, or dash into the street, chasing the pigeons into the island in the center, upsetting the old people sitting there eating their lunches and reading the paper.

Be sure to update the anchor chart with this thinking, so that students can refer to it as they work to convey the evidence they find in their own texts.

In any case, you'll send students off to continue working on their boxes-and-bullets plan and to reread their story through the lens of their claim, collecting evidence. That is, in your link, it is best to send students off to do not only the new work you will have taught that day but also the cumulative work they've been learning to do all along.

CONFERRING AND SMALL-GROUP WORK

Today you may find that some students will need additional support as they think through how best to convey the evidence they've collected in support of their claim. You might gather a group in the meeting area while the rest of the class works independently, and say something like, "Class, this work can be tricky. If you feel a little unsure of how to get started, or if this was hard for you, stay here in the meeting area and we'll work on it more together. If you think you've got a grip on this strategy and now have a way to get writing, off you go to your desks."

Chances are you may need to help some kids with the step you assumed most students could do in a snap: finding evidence that supports their bullets. These kids may have easily come up with supports for their claims, but when asked to show where in the text they see evidence of these, they simply shrug. "I don't know—I just think that," they may say. When pushed, you will see these students pick a scene somewhat at random—and it may or may not really support the idea they are writing about. This isn't surprising. By asking students to proceed from generating a claim to determining bullet points to finding evidence that supports these to finding the *strongest* evidence, you are, in effect, asking students to move from making a large, often sweeping statement to coming up with supports that are increasingly precise and pinpointed. What you—and these kids—may discover along the way is that the challenge lies not in the task itself, but in the claim on which everything rests. Or on the bullet points. That is, this is a chain of work, with each piece relying on the one before and after it. If a student's claim or body paragraph foci are weak, it will be difficult to find evidence anywhere in the text, let alone strong evidence. Be on the lookout, then, for any spots where the process broke down even before today's work—and then help the student redo that work.

If, on the other hand, you find that, in fact, a student who is struggling *does* have a strong claim and strong support, it may simply be a matter of helping that student do the kind of close reading that looking

How to Write a Literary Essay
About Character

- Reread selected bits.

- Notice details, think, talk, write to explore: "Why this detail?"

- Think, "What does the character really want?" and write long.

- It can help to use thought prompts (Maybe... Perhaps...)

- Think about the deep down, internal motivations.

- Once you have an idea and some evidence, reread again, reread more of the text, reread more closely, and expect your original idea will change.

- Try to generate an idea about the character that encompasses the whole character and the whole text.

- Search for the most compelling evidence that can support the claim, then add it to your essay like this:

  - Quote some parts of the text.

  - Story-tell other parts.

  - Summarize yet other parts.

for evidence entails. See if you can get the student to narrow down the text to places where evidence might remotely live, and then help him zoom in closer and closer to the precise line of dialogue or image or action that provides evidence of the point he is hoping to make.

Some of your students may have a clear sense of what evidence to include but may struggle with how to get that evidence down on the page. At the most basic level, they may not know how to retell, or summarize, in a way that doesn't go on endlessly, but rather gets across their main point. Teach these students that essayists know how to "spin" their retells to highlight the parts that best show their point, and that they also try to retell their scenes in a way that is engaging to read, by including some strategies they learned during their narrative writing units, such as slowing down and stretching out the details of a scene to build tension. Then quickly revisit some of those strategies. Make sure you use student essays to demonstrate.

Meanwhile, you will have other kids who aren't sure which parts of the text to quote. You may want to give them highlighters and then read aloud parts of the text, suggesting that they listen with their claim in mind, noting any text that jumps out in defense of it. You could also show them how you might do this yourself, explaining how particular lines of dialogue or phrases or actions work to make your point, and how often it's enough to take a partial quote or to weave one in to one of your own sentences. You might have students try angling their evidence a few different ways in their notebooks, vetting the entries they have written, with the help of a partner, to determine which is strongest.

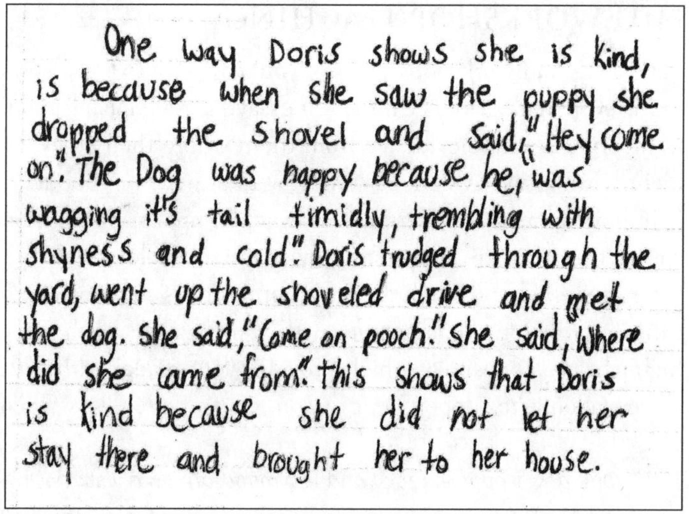

Finally, some students may have chosen evidence with little selectivity; these kids will benefit from learning how to weigh—or rank—their evidence. The cognitive work involved in ranking will have a big payoff for sixth-graders. You will want to emphasize that this strategy is one that students can use far beyond this one day's work, or even in this precise context—to great effect. Try saying something along these lines: "So I have a feeling that once you get the hang of ranking, you are going to be ranking all over the place. You can rank figures from history to see who was the most influential person, or you can rank heroines in books to see which one is the cleverest. And certainly, whenever you are drafting the body paragraphs of an essay, you will always want to rank—in your head or on paper—the evidence you are considering to be sure you include the strongest support for your thinking."

To help students practice this strategy before applying it to their own stories and essays, you might put up a list of scenes that could go with your other reason, "Squeaky is fiercely protective of herself," and then give partnerships a few minutes to rank these in order of "most supportive" to "least supportive." Be sure to coach students to explain *why* they rank the evidence as they do; this is important work for essay writers and will be the focus of the next session. The ability to analyze how a piece of textual evidence supports an idea is a crucial one, and this is a good opportunity for you to quickly assess how easily it comes to your students. In any case, this quick practice will help students get a feel for ranking and for thinking through why a piece of evidence might support an idea strongly or weakly.

One way Doris shows she is kind, is because when she saw the puppy she dropped the shovel and said, "Hey come on." The Dog was happy because he was wagging it's tail timidly, trembling with shyness and cold." Doris trudged through the yard, went up the shoveled drive and met the dog. she said, "Come on pooch." she said, "Where did she came from." This shows that Doris is kind because she did not let her stay there and brought her to her house.

FIG. 5–1   Kevin story-tells his evidence while using quotes.

MID-WORKSHOP TEACHING

For today's mid-workshop teaching, you may want to teach students a strategy for incorporating even more evidence into their essays, through using appositives. As they are working to incorporate more evidence from the text into their essay, they will need to clarify and identify who their evidence is referring to or what it is about. You have continued to highlight how your sixth-graders are more grown-up versions of their elementary school selves, so don't be afraid to use more grown-up terminology with them. Introduce them to the term *appositive*, and teach them how appositives can be a way to provide their reader with extra information. Demonstrate with your own essay, showing how you use commas to highlight the appositive, which provides your reader with further clarification, and even more evidence to support your reason.

> One day, when Squeaky and Raymond are on a walk down Broadway, Raymond on the inside of course, to keep him safe, they bump into Mary Louise, Gretchen, and Rosie. Squeaky thinks about trying to avoid the girls, but they end up having a confrontation on the street. She exchanges words with Mary Louise, <u>who used to be Squeaky's friend when she first moved to her neighborhood from Baltimore</u>, about the May Day race and the conversation turns to Raymond. When Mary Louise tries to talk directly to Raymond, asking him what grade he is in, Squeaky snaps, "You got anything to say to my brother, you say it to me . . ."

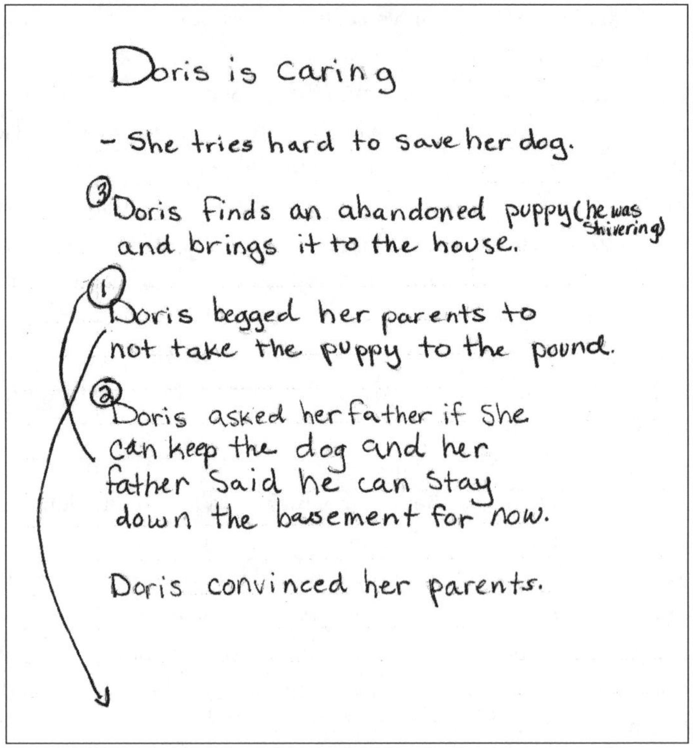

Doris is Caring

- She tries hard to save her dog.

(3) Doris finds an abandoned puppy (he was shivering) and brings it to the house.

(1) Doris begged her parents to not take the puppy to the pound.

(2) Doris asked her father if she can keep the dog and her father said he can stay down the basement for now.

Doris convinced her parents.

FIG. 5–2 Denise weighs the evidence for her essay.

SHARE

You'll probably want to use the share session to do two things. You'll want to teach responsively, and you'll want to rally kids to continue collecting evidence for their essays.

To teach responsively, plan to take all moves that any one student is making and broadcast them. For example, if you noticed that a student that day had been debating whether a moment showed a character's generosity or not, and the student had been thinking, "Was that really generosity or just being nice?" you could celebrate the importance of that effort. When engaged in argument, defining one's terms is a really important enterprise, and yes, it is impossible to debate a claim without clarifying what the terms of the claim mean. Before you can make the case that a character is generous, you need to clarify what the difference is between being generous and just being kind. Paying close attention to the exact meaning of the words used in a claim is a big deal. That means, of course, that to write the class essay, it will be important to examine what the term *protective* means. Is Squeaky being protective? Could her actions be described more accurately as vigilant? As cautionary? As thoughtful? As shielding?

One important thing to stress is that an essayist's claim evolves through this process. The work is not simply deciding which evidence best fits the claim; the work also involves reconsidering the initial claim in light of the evidence.

HOMEWORK: GROWING EVIDENCE THAT FITS YOUR CLAIM

You'll want to set students up to continue growing evidence that fits their claim. You could suggest that before they go home, they need to do what people who cook do all the time. They need to think ahead to what they will be making tomorrow (an essay!) and whip up a quick shopping list of all the ingredients they need to produce that essay tomorrow. Only instead of getting their ingredients from a store, they'll need to produce them through their homework.

   You could help them make a shopping list by telling them that to make a literary essay, they need certain things:

1. They need to be able to introduce the text. Usually this means they will write some background information about it—almost a little tiny report. The background information needs to include the author and the genre, and sometimes it includes a tiny summary of the story.

2. They need a boxes-and-bullets plan so they can write a thesis, a claim, early in their essay and then have a plan for how they will organize the evidence they bring in to support their claim. Will they be talking about the reasons for their claim, the ways it is true, the situations in which it is true, the way it is true in the start, the middle, the end of the story—or what?

3. For each part of their essay, they will need compelling evidence. Some of the evidence will be told in micro-stories, some in lists, some in quotations—and sometimes the evidence is told through a combination of those.

4. The evidence needs to come from all portions of the story: beginning, middle, and ending.

Enjoy designing and teaching the session!
Kate and Kathleen

Studying a Mentor Text to Construct Literary Essays

IN THIS SESSION, you'll teach students that writers can study published literary essays to learn techniques and structures to bring to the work of drafting their own essays.

GETTING READY

✓ A sample literary essay to use as a mentor text, one copy for each student. You could use the example in this session, one written by another student (available on CD-ROM), or one that you have crafted (see Teaching and Active Engagement).

✓ Pens (see Teaching and Active Engagement)

✓ "Things to Look for When Annotating a Mentor Essay" listed on chart paper (see Teaching and Active Engagement)

✓ Planning outline for mentor text, enlarged on chart paper (see Link)

✓ Colored pencils or markers (see Link)

✓ Copies of the Argument Writing Checklists for Grades 5 and 6, one per student, as well as an enlarged copy (see Share)

COMMON CORE STATE STANDARDS: W.6.1, W.6.4, W.6.5, W.6.9.a, W.6.10, RI.6.1, RL.6.2, RL.6.3, RL.6.10, SL.6.1, SL.6.2, SL.6.3, L.6.1, L.6.2, L.6.3

YOU CAN THINK of the work of making an essay as a bit like a barn raising. And if that analogy holds, it's time to build the barn. Your students have many of the materials they need, and they have the framework. Everything isn't done, no, but nothing will rally energy more than letting the work culminate in something that looks not like a lumberyard but like a barn, not like notebook entries but like an essay.

It is time for your students to roll up their sleeves and put this thing together.

Notice that what you are starting with is probably quite a mess. Students will have entries—outlines, lists, jots, blurbs—scattered across the pages of their notebooks. How do they tack all that stuff together when it is locked into the binding of a notebook? How is this thoughtful mess going to clean up into an architectural marvel?

It is tempting to distribute a worksheet that will tell writers that this next step is no big deal: they just pour everything into its proper place, and presto! But instead, we suggest you convey that the work ahead is challenging work. It is not for the faint of heart. The job is to do nothing less than turn notes and jottings into full-fledged drafts, and this requires some of the most intellectually demanding work of all. For example, students will need to read over all their evidence and think, "Which piece of evidence best matches my claim? What stays? What goes?" They also need to think about how evidence is bound together to make cohesive essays. After all, you have not yet taught transitions.

One way to develop the eye to judge is to spend some time reading finished work that is something similar to the essay they'll be writing, written by a mentor author. As they read, they'll ask, "How has she constructed this text? What has she done with her text that I, too, can do with mine?" And they will annotate that text for themselves. Then they will begin constructing their own essays.

As students draft, they will piece their material together. In earlier grades, this work may have been done in a hands-on, manipulative process. Today, however, your grown-up middle-schoolers will engage in a less physical process, doing more of this work in their mind's eye. Eventually, they'll abbreviate this process even more, moving seamlessly from reading and thinking to outlining and writing an essay.

Studying a Mentor Text to Construct Literary Essays

CONNECTION

Celebrate that students are ready to construct their literary essays.

"Writers, today's the day! If you think of the work of making an essay as a bit like a barn raising, then today, it's time to build the barn. You have the materials you need, and the framework. It is time for you to roll up your sleeves and put this thing together.

"Before you begin, though, I want to make sure you imagine how all the pieces will go together. I want to be sure you remember how barns look in the end (only, really, these aren't barns we are making but literary essays about characters).

"Mo Willems, an author of picture books for kids, once said, 'You work like the devil to make something that looks like you just threw it together.' In the end, your essay will look like it was no big deal to write—and months from now, the truth is that writing an essay like this one will be something you can practically do in your sleep—but for now, actually getting the little things right is a very big deal.

"So before you begin constructing your final essay, I want to suggest you take some time to study a completed essay."

❖ **Name the question that will guide the inquiry.**

"Today, then, instead of a regular minilesson, we will do an inquiry. We will be researching this question: What makes for a good literary essay? And what, exactly, does a writer do to go from making a claim and collecting evidence to actually constructing an essay?"

TEACHING AND ACTIVE ENGAGEMENT

Set writers up to study a mentor text, letting them know that they should be thinking about the inquiry question.

"I'm going to suggest that you do a specific kind of reading that writers do before they make a draft. Specifically, I suggest you look over this draft of a literary essay and ask, 'What has this author done that I, too, could do?' This is an

Note how little quotes by authors help add meaning and a little spice to minilessons. So be sure that you have a place where you keep the gems that you run across so you can use them when you develop your own minilessons. Mo's books—Knufflebunny is one and a whole series of Pigeon books—are written for young readers (though adults love them too!). One wouldn't normally think of him as a resource for middle school kids, but in fact his insight is apt. So collect intriguing quotes even when they don't seem to be relevant, and you'll be pleasantly surprised one day when you're in need of inspiration and discover it in your quote collection.

essay about 'Raymond's Run.' It'll be interesting to study an essay that was written off of a text we all know so well. Also, it was written by a student when she was in sixth grade; Yuko is an eighth-grader now. Lots of teachers have said that her essay is quite effective, so it is worth studying." I distributed a copy of Yuko's essay to each student and displayed an enlarged copy on the document camera.

"While I read the first three paragraphs of the essay aloud, notice the different parts of the essay, and label—annotate—what you notice. Listen closely to my intonation as I read aloud." I read the first two paragraphs aloud with intonation that highlighted the claim and its relationship to the supporting ideas, as well as the link between evidence and an idea. (The emphasis, in the essay below, is our own. Students will be annotating clean copies of the text.)

"Now, go ahead and read the rest of the essay on your own. When you finish reading, Partner 1, will you specifically study the bits the author has tacked together to construct her introduction and last body paragraph? And Partner 2, will you do the same for the middle portion of the essay? Think, 'What did the author do that I could try?' and afterward, we'll talk about it."

In the story, "Raymond's Run," by Toni Cade Bambara, Squeaky, the protagonist, is a hard person to love. _She is a hard person to love because she has a negative outlook on life, because she is always looking for a fight, and because she is conceited._

The most obvious reason why Squeaky is hard to love is because she has a negative outlook on life. Whenever she mentions someone, it seems like they are always "stupid," or a "fool." Also, Squeaky thinks that everyone is out to get her and Raymond. For example, when she is walking down the street and runs into some girls she knows, right away she starts thinking awful things about them, like that Mary Louise isn't "grateful" and that Rosie is "too stupid to know that there is not a big deal of difference between her and Raymond." Squeaky doesn't think kind thoughts about people, and she doesn't act kindly towards them either. We have all heard the phrase—"you can't love anyone else until you can love yourself." In this story we see that the opposite might be true too—it is impossible to be loveable if you don't show any love to others.

Furthermore, Squeaky is hard to love because she is combative—she is always looking for a fight. There are many times in the text where Squeaky mentions that she is ready to fight someone, that, in fact, she would "much rather just knock you down and take my chances" rather than talk about anything. At the beginning of the story, Squeaky says that if anyone has something to say about her brother, they have to come through her first. And then later on in the story when she and Raymond see the girls on the street, when Mary Louise asks Raymond what grade he is in, Squeaky says right away, "You got anything to say to my brother, you say it to me, Mary Louise Williams of Raggedy Town, Baltimore."

While as a reader, you kind of understand why Squeaky is so combative, that doesn't make it any easier to love her as a character. Sure, people are probably really mean to Raymond. And she definitely has a lot on her plate as a young kid. However, that doesn't make it right for her to always think about using violence and conflict to get her way. Just because we can understand why she is angry doesn't mean we agree with how she deals with her anger. Squeaky doesn't even give anyone a chance to be nice—it's as if she would rather fight than make friends. This also makes her a very hard character to love.

<u>Finally, Squeaky is a hard character to love because she is pretty conceited.</u> It seems like she is always bragging about her running in this text. Right away she says "There is no track meet that I don't win the first place medal." And even if this is true, the way she says it sounds kind of cocky. Like when she mentions that Gretchen even thinks she has a chance in beating her she calls the idea "ridiculous." And later, when she is talking to Mr. Pearson and he suggests that maybe she could let someone else have a chance this year, she is not gracious about it, she is not kind. Instead she gives him a nasty look and acts like he said something awful. She is so conceited about her running that she doesn't notice that he was just looking out for some of the other girls. Squeaky's ego is so big that it pushes all the love and compassion you might feel for her right out of the way. Her ego is like a force field protecting her, but that force field is also keeping everyone out.

As you can see, Squeaky is tough to love, because she sees the worst in people, she is always ready for a fight, and she is conceited. While at the end of the story she starts to change a little, by smiling at someone for like the first time ever, she is still a hard person to love.

Start annotating the enlarged copy of the essay to help students get started, then once they begin, listen and watch as they do this work and talk in pairs about their observations.

I looked up at the students. "Annotate—mark up—your text." For a moment, I marked my own copy of the essay, then I began looking over to watch as kids worked. To scaffold them, I said, "Here are some of the terms you might use to annotate your essay," and I flipped over a new piece of chart paper to display this list. As I showed this list, I knew full well that it contained terms that the class did not necessarily know, and therefore I expected it would generate a lot of discussion.

```
╭─────────────────────────────────────────────╮
│   Things to Look for When Annotating          │
│          a Mentor Text                        │
╰─────────────────────────────────────────────╯

   * Background information on the text
   * Introduction
   * Claim
   * Topic sentence 1
   * Topic sentence 2
   * Transition between parts
   * Interior transition
   * Story/example
   * List of examples
   * Quote
   * Analysis of evidence
   * Conclusion
```

I channeled students to share their observations with their partner, reminding them they could talk not only about what Yuko did, but also about what she did not yet do. I listened in as the partners talked.

Jamhil announced to his partner, "I noticed quotes." Frankie nodded in agreement.

I gave them a thumbs up, then challenged them to extend their first observation. "If you look closely at a quoted section of the text, you can notice *how* the author quoted that part." I said, then voiced over, "Don't just notice what the author did. Notice *how* she did it. Why is this considered well-done work?"

Soon the students were noticing instances when the cited text was just part of a sentence and other instances when it was several sentences. "What ideas do you have for why Yuko would quote the parts that she did?" I asked. The students launched into a discussion of that. I gestured for them to think how Yuko's work might influence what they did when their evidence involved quoting parts of the story and left to crouch down next to another group.

Of course, Yuko's essay follows just one of many possible structures that literary essayists use—and in fact, hers is a relatively simple one. More experienced essayists entertain points of view other than their own and then provide a counterargument; they compare and contrast one text to other texts, or to life. Then, too, they often raise questions in their conclusions or land new insights. Don't worry about this right now. Soon you will enter a new bend, and with it will come a focus on more complex, theme-based essays—ones that will invite new formats and extended features of essay construction. In Bend III, you will introduce compare-and-contrast essays. For now, it's enough that students see what a finished draft resembles, noticing some of its component parts.

Share some students' observations.

After a bit, I called the writers back together and asked Crystal to get us started saying what she noticed. "I noticed that the essay included what the character didn't do," she began. When I gestured for her to elaborate, she read from the essay, "Squeaky *doesn't* think kind thoughts about people, and she *doesn't* act kindly toward them either. This makes her very hard to love.'" When I asked why she thought Yuko did this, she said she figured that Yuko did this to highlight what the character *did* do.

Interested, I said to the rest of the class, "Hands up if you noticed that, too." I marked the essay with Crystal's observation.

Then, I gave a marker to three other students, asking them to cluster around the document camera, jotting one thing they noticed into the margins of the essay. "Don't forget to use some of the terms that are listed on the 'Things to Look for When Annotating a Mentor Essay' chart. Where do you see 'background information on the text'? Where is the 'analysis of evidence'?" While they worked, I suggested the rest of the class share their annotations with anyone sitting near them in such a way that they, too, could mark new stuff onto their copy of Yuko's text if they agreed with it. Soon each student's copy of Yuko's essay (and the class copy of it as well) bore labels.

I'm aware that giving students opportunities to share their ideas with the whole class can be very time-consuming. My top priority—always—is to keep all students engaged and to protect writing time, so here I make a concerted effort to support both goals.

LINK

Show writers the plan that undergirded the student's exemplar essay that they just studied, and suggest writers prepare to revise their own plans to include elements they may have neglected to include. Tell them that then they will write their essays.

"Before Yuko began writing her essay, she wrote a quick outline to follow as she wrote. She sketched out how her essay would go, jotting key words such as *introduction*, *thesis*, *new paragraph*, *topic sentence*.

"The start of her outline for her essay looked something like this." I revealed the sheet of chart paper where I had jotted down the outline.

Essay Outline
> Introduction
> Thesis
> Body paragraph 1
> Topic Sentence
> List from page 3 from my notebook
> An example with a quote p. 2
> Write more about it (prompts)

"Writers, you have the start to a plan for your essay. Please revise that plan to add elements to it that you may have forgotten, and then spend most of your time today writing your draft. And don't forget, you have so many great ideas already written in your writer's notebooks. Don't let those ideas go to waste. You may want to use colored pencils or markers to go back through your notebook, reading closely, finding entries or portions of entries that can go directly into your draft and color-coding these ideas. Pick a color for your first bullet and then use that same color to mark each supporting entry you find. And keep going with different colors for each bullet and supporting entry. Some of these entries may be in great shape and can go directly into your draft, as is. And some color-coded entries may simply provide you with a starting point and may need further revision as you incorporate them into your draft."

You'll be amazed at how the invitation to use colored pencils to code entries spurs students on to work with great fervor. The notebooks also begin to look more beautiful and personalized, and that leads students to love them more. Writer and educator Peter Elbow once pointed out that it is important for writers to love their writing, because they'll be more game to work at it if they love it. So even if the colored pencils feel a bit over the top—go for it.

Small Groups to Support Students as They Draft

AS STUDENTS CONTINUE DRAFTING in light of the mentor essay, you will find that a few of your young writers just plain freeze up. This is predictable; you have directed your class up until now to write essays with a great deal of direction, and now here you are showing them an exemplar and saying, "Do what you will!" For a sixth-grader, this can be an intimidating task. The fear of making the wrong choice can be paralyzing for the best of us, and our students are no different.

As you pull a small group of students who are having a tough time making their own choices, your main goal is not to make sure they have chosen the "right" or even "best" strategy to make their writing better, but to build their confidence that as writers new (or new-ish) to essays, they have the ability to read a mentor text, identify something that looks like it might help their writing, and implement that strategy right away. This skill—this independence and transference—is far more important than any one particular line or strategy that you might compel them to use in this particular essay.

Start your small group by relaxing the pressure a bit. You might start by saying something like, "We are going to work together today to help each other choose something that Yuko did in her essay that you think will be good in yours. And here is the best part—there is absolutely no way you can make a mistake today, unless you choose not to even try." Then coach your students to repeat what they noticed in Yuko's essay during the lesson, perhaps listing what they say on a piece of paper or white board. Follow up by saying, "Now, turn and talk to the person sitting next to you. Which of these things do you think would help you make your writing better today? And if you can, say a little bit about why."

Then, after the mid-workshop teaching point channels students to note their transitions, you may want to convene another small group and invite them to work together to study more closely the transitions that Yuko used in her essay. You can get them to notice even little details like the commas, which can signal to readers that the text is

(*continues*)

MID-WORKSHOP TEACHING **Using Transitional Phrases**

"Many of you noticed Yuko's transitional phrases at the start of each major part of her essay, which is something most of you learned during fifth grade, to include in your writing. But you are right to remind yourself of the importance of transitional phrases because they help essays flow more smoothly and they set readers up to know what kind of thing will come next in the essay.

"Right now, will you and your partner do a quick study of one of your drafts (it can even be of your essay plan) and notice your transitions, comparing them to Yuko's?

Her transitions are not very fancy, so I am pretty sure some of you will have much more sophisticated ones. Turn and talk!"

I quickly navigated the room, moving from table to table as partners shared their writing with one another. I helped Jacquelyn notice that Yuko used prompts to transition into her supporting reasons, using "Furthermore . . . ," while her partner, Theo, used ". . . this proves that . . ." and "for example . . ." to connect his evidence to his claim. I coached Theo to help Jacquelyn find places where she might include similar transitions.

---

about to say more, to give them more information, to show an example. Bring students together with a copy of the mentor essay and point to the phrase you want them to notice first.

> <u>Furthermore,</u> Squeaky is hard to love because she is combative–she is always looking for a fight. There are many times in the text where Squeaky mentions that she is ready to fight someone, that, in fact, she would "much rather just knock you down and take my chances" rather than talk about anything. At the beginning of the story, Squeaky says that if anyone has something to say about her brother, they have to come through her first. And then later on in the story when she and Raymond see the girls on the street, when Mary Louise asks Raymond what year he will be in, Squeaky says right away, "You got anything to say to my brother, you say it to me, Mary Louise Williams of Raggedy Town, Baltimore."

"See, right there at the start of the paragraph Yuko uses the word *furthermore*, instead of saying something like 'Another reason is . . .' The comma signifies that Yuko is about to say more. And *furthermore* has a cool ring to it. It sounds like you are so confident in your thinking that you are almost saying, 'Not *only* am I right because of this last thing I said, there is even more that shows how right I am!' This is powerful academic language that I bet you could use as well. Let's take a second with Yuko's essay. With your partner, can you underline any other places where she uses a powerful transition word or phrase?"

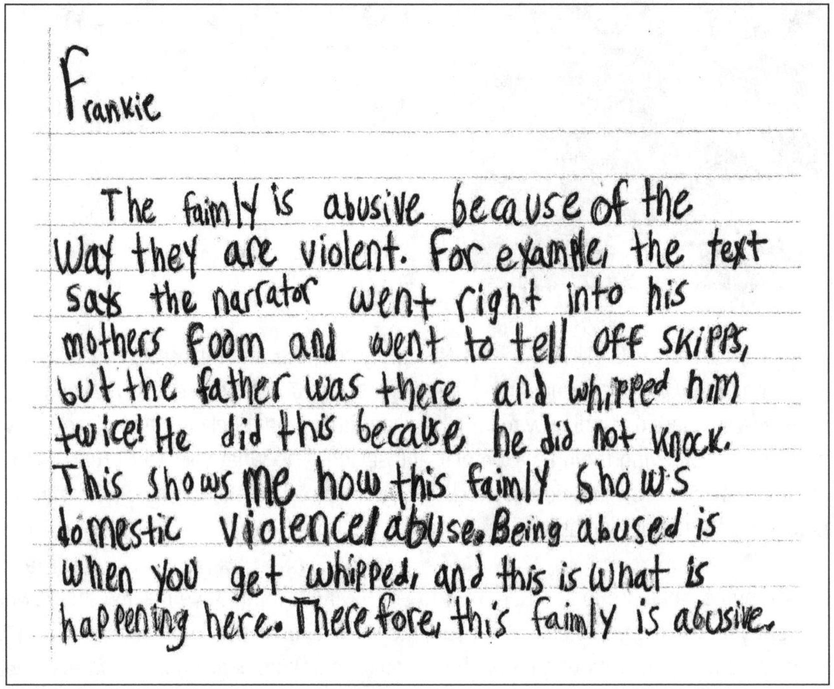

> Frankie
>
> The faimly is abusive because of the way they are violent. For examfle, the text says the narrator went right into his mothers room and went to tell off Skipps, but the father was there and whipped him twice! He did this because he did not knock. This shows me how this faimly shows domestic violence/abuse. Being abused is when you get whipped, and this is what is happening here. Therefore, this faimly is abusive.

FIG. 6–1   Frankie's body paragraph after studying a mentor essay

Using a Checklist for Self-Analysis and Goal-Setting

Emphasize to students that anyone who is looking to improve, no matter what their discipline, takes the time to look back over their past work or performances and analyze what their strengths and weaknesses are.

"Anyone who is looking to improve at something—running, playing the violin, boxing, singing—needs not just to work hard, but also to take pause, reflecting on what they have accomplished so far and making a plan for how to push themselves further.

"As you know, writers also need to pause and think, 'How am I doing?' When you wrote personal narratives, you analyzed your writing against a narrative checklist; there are also checklists you can use for other kinds of writing.

"The interesting thing about writing about reading is that, in a way, it falls into two categories. It can be information writing because the writer is teaching people about a text. Also, literary essays can be thought of as argument writing, because the writer is defending his interpretation. For now, we are going to think about literary essays as argument writing, and so I am hoping you will assess the draft that you have written so far by comparing it to the checklist that writers use at the very end of fifth grade. Once you have aced that checklist and I've taught you a few more strategies, you can compare your writing to the sixth-grade argument checklist—and to parts of the information checklist as well. You'll also see the grade 6 checklist here. Once you make sure you're doing the work you learned last year, then you can move on to using the grade 6 checklist.

"Let's start with the first part of the checklist—structure." I pointed to the first section on the enlarged copy of the Argument Writing Checklist. "Before you look at your own writing, talk to the writers at your table about those points. What do you notice? What will you look for in your own writing?" I gave the students a minute to discuss, then reconvened the group.

"Now that you have a sense of some of the things that are expected of essayists, take a look at the structure of your writing. How does it stack up? If you met the criteria, how did you do it? What are the replicable moves for future essays? And if you didn't yet meet the criteria, what specifically could you do to improve? Don't be afraid to mark up your drafts as well as your copy of the checklist, circling the goals you have for yourself, or making a T-chart in your notebook to keep track of your progress."

As students worked with the checklist, I circulated around the classroom, leaning in and nudging students along, constantly asking them to show me *evidence* of the checkpoints in their drafts or prompting them to formulate ideas for what they might do to improve.

Argument Writing Checklist

	Grade 5	NOT YET	STARTING TO	YES!	Grade 6	NOT YET	STARTING TO	YES!
	Structure				**Structure**			
Overall	I made a claim or thesis on a topic or text, supported it with reasons, and provided a variety of evidence for each reason.	☐	☐	☐	I explained the topic/text and staked out a position that can be supported by a variety of trustworthy sources. Each part of my text helped build my argument, and led to a conclusion.	☐	☐	☐
Lead	I wrote an introduction that led to a claim or thesis and got my readers to care about my opinion. I got my readers to care by not only including a cool fact or jazzy question, but also by telling readers what was significant in or around the topic.	☐	☐	☐	I wrote an introduction to interest readers and help them understand and care about a topic or text. I thought backwards between the piece and the introduction to make sure that the introduction fit with the whole.	☐	☐	☐
	I worked to find the precise words to state my claim; I let readers know the reasons I would develop later.	☐	☐	☐	Not only did I clearly state my claim, I also told my readers how my text would unfold.	☐	☐	☐
Transitions	I used transition words and phrases to connect evidence back to my reasons using phrases such as *this shows that.* . .	☐	☐	☐	I used transitions to help readers understand how the different parts of my piece fit together to explain and support my argument.	☐	☐	☐
	I helped readers follow my thinking with phrases such as *another reason* and *the most important reason.* I used phrases such as *consequently* and *because of* to show what happened.	☐	☐	☐	I used transitions to help connect claim(s), reasons, and evidence, and to imply relationships such as when material exemplifies, adds on to, is similar to, explains, is a result of, or contrasts. I use transitions such as *for instance, in addition, one reason, furthermore, according to, this evidence suggests,* and *thus we can say that.*	☐	☐	☐
	I used words such as *specifically* and *in particular* to be more precise.	☐	☐	☐				

EVALUATING YOUR WRITING USING THE ARGUMENT WRITING CHECKLIST

"Writers, continue this self-analysis at home. Look through the remaining points on the checklist, and determine the work you are already doing well, as well as the work you're going to push yourself to do next. Remember, when you hold your writing up against a checklist, it's not just so you can say, 'Oh yeah, I did that,' and move on. Tomorrow you will have time to revise your essays and work toward the goals you'll set for yourself tonight. We will also have an opportunity to celebrate your hard work tomorrow!"

Session 7

Revising Essays to Be Sure You Analyze as Well as Cite Text Evidence

ONE OF THE CHALLENGES of teaching middle school is that even if students do enter the school having grown up within a strong writing community, something seems to happen between fifth grade and sixth, and the kids need to be reminded of all they know and can do. Prior to now, one focus of this unit was geared toward bringing your students back up to speed. It's not accidental that they didn't assess their essay writing to see if it met end of fifth-grade standards on their Argument Writing Checklists until the session prior to this one!

Today's session, on the other hand, is clearly meant to push forward, and it pushes forward in the one area that will be especially challenging for your students and for middle school students in general. The topic you teach on today is not one of those things where you can show an example of what you hope kids can do and then presto, they do it! This work is challenging; in fact, of all the work of essay writing, analyzing evidence is often the toughest for many teachers and writers. And so, across this session you will offer students other ways of connecting evidence to ideas. This session conveys to students that the true heart of an essay is the degree to which it provides analysis of why or how the evidence chosen supports the claim and reasoning. To that effect, then, today you will teach your class to connect two parts of an essay together through writing—the angled evidence they have gathered and the reasoning that holds that paragraph together.

You'll start the session by communicating to your students that making a claim and supporting it with an example from this story is not, in and of itself, enough. What's needed is for the writer to "unpack" the example, looking closely at the precise words that the author has used, the decisions the author has made, to help essay readers see that evidence as the essayist sees it.

You'll teach students to use some "analytic phrases" that can help them begin to do this work. Some of these aren't new, although they used to be referred to simply as "thought prompts." In prior years, students were taught to "unpack" a bit of evidence by saying "This shows . . ." Now, however, you'll suggest that the essayist actually has to *make* that case. How, exactly, does the evidence support the essayist's ideas?

IN THIS SESSION, you'll teach students that essayists often revise their essays to make sure they explain *why* and *how* the evidence connects with, or supports, their claim.

GETTING READY

✔ Passages from your own literary essay, enlarged for students to see (see Teaching and Active Engagement)

✔ "Ways to Analyze Evidence" chart (see Teaching) 🕸

✔ Students' drafts and short texts that they are writing their essays on and pens (see Active Engagement)

✔ Chart paper with several counterargument thought prompts listed (see Mid-Workshop Teaching)

✔ Student writing sample that shows evidence of a counterargument (see Mid-Workshop Teaching)

✔ Clean copies of the Argument Writing Checklist, Grades 5 and 6, one per student (see Share) 🕸

COMMON CORE STATE STANDARDS: W.6.1.a,b,c; W.6.5, W.7.1.a, RL.6.1, RL.6.2, SL.6.1, SL.6.3, L.6.1, L.6.2, L.6.3, L.6.6

As part of this, you'll suggest that writers need to entertain the notion that others could see that passage as illustrating a different point altogether. In the mid-workshop teaching point, you make the suggestion that by anticipating a counterargument, writers are more apt to be persuasive. You also point out that one of the counterarguments that an essayist can anticipate is the view that the data actually shows something close, but different. Is Squeaky actually protective of her brother, or might there be a more precise term?

"The true heart of an essay is the degree to which it provides analysis of why or how the evidence chosen supports the claim and reasoning."

Today's session focuses on teaching students to "unpack" their evidence and explain the connections between their evidence and their claims, but meanwhile you'll also remind writers that just yesterday, they concluded the workshop by using a checklist to assess their own essay. That self-assessment work will have led most writers to see possible next steps, and they'll be revising to do that work, as well as to do the work your minilesson revolves around.

Revising Essays to Be Sure You Analyze as Well as Cite Text Evidence

CONNECTION

Convey to your students that being able to express themselves clearly lends power to their essays—and also to their own lives.

"When I was your age, there were these times when I said to my mother, 'Why do I have to . . . ?', and her only answer was, 'Because I said so, that's why.' It was as if my mother was saying, 'Why? Because I am the grown-up and you are the kid and you have to do as you are told.'

"Has that ever happened to you? You ask *why* and there is no good reason except, 'Because I said so.' It is really frustrating, right?" The class erupted into stories of guardians and older siblings who had used this phrase often—and apparently unfairly. Above the clamor I gathered their attention.

"Oh my—that certainly struck a chord! Here's my point. When I read over the drafts you're planning to revise today, it seemed to me that sometimes *you* are doing the same thing that makes you so mad. Sometimes you are making claims—'Squeaky is protective of herself,' 'Jim Howe is different than the other men in his family because his ideas about what it means to be a man are different'—and you plop in stuff from the story that you think makes your point, but the reader is left unconvinced. The reader is left thinking, 'So? You still haven't convinced me why your claim is true.'"

Sometimes you begin a connection with a story about your life at your students' age that may at first seem to have nothing to do with the minilesson, but by the end leads directly to your teaching point. Once your students are hooked by your story—and they will be since it's about you, and moreover, you as an adolescent!—they'll be better able to grasp your teaching point.

❖ **Name the teaching point.**

"Today I want to teach you that when an essayist makes a claim and includes evidence to support that claim, that alone doesn't convince readers that the claim is justified. Essayists often revise their essays to make sure they explain *why* (and how) the evidence connects with, or supports, the claim."

TEACHING

Name the work of the day: analyzing the evidence from the text by explaining how it illustrates the support for your claim.

"It can be tricky to learn how to analyze evidence. Let me show you how I get started. The work here is to explain how the scene from the text—my evidence—fits with the thinking in this paragraph and, of course, with my claim. Here is part of the draft that I wrote yesterday—my thinking and my evidence."

> Squeaky's protectiveness of herself also drives her to push people away. For example, in the scene where she is talking to Mr. Pearson before the race, and he asks (jokingly) if she will let someone else win, Squeaky stares him down like he is an idiot. She is so angry that he would even suggest that she not win, that she glares at him until he stops talking!

"So first I want to just name to myself what my work is here. What am I trying to explain? I am trying to explain how the scene with Mr. Pearson shows her pushing people away *and* that this is an example of her being protective." I lifted a finger for each point to highlight that there are two ideas being addressed. "Whoa. That's a lot to explain. No wonder this work is hard!

"I have a feeling we can learn the most from each other today. Can you take a second with your partner right now and try explaining how this scene shows Squeaky pushing people away and that she is protective? Remember, you are trying to really say *how* or *why* this scene shows the idea. Try to avoid saying 'Because I said so!' One way you can start is by using the phrase, 'This shows . . . because . . .'"

The class began to talk, hesitantly at first, so I moved to some partnerships and gave them encouragement and a little push to try out some thinking. I gathered the class together after listening to a few other examples and asked Brian and Janessa to share what they were thinking.

They furrowed their brows. Janessa, looking a little unsure, said, "Um, this shows that . . . Squeaky pushes people away because maybe Mr. Pearson was just trying to be nice to the other girls?" Brian added in, "And she just is so mean to him like no one else matters but her, which definitely pushes him away." I nodded and gathered the class' attention.

"So many of you made a great start to analyzing your evidence. Brian and Janessa used the prompt that said 'This shows . . .' Does anyone have another explanation for this scene?" I nodded toward Sarah and Jaz.

Jaz started. "Being protective means always watching out for danger, so this scene definitely shows Squeaky being protective. Like, if Squeaky lost the race, and lost it on purpose, her reputation as a star runner would be in danger. So this scene shows how Squeaky is protecting herself."

"Wow, guys, did you catch that? Sarah and Jaz actually tried to define what we meant when we said *protective*. "What a great strategy! Here are some others you could try."

It is vital that I name what it is that my evidence is supposed to illustrate—without this clarity any analysis will remain vague.

Of course, I had coached Sarah and Jaz to think about the definitions of words as a way to help explain their evidence, but as I gather the class together I name this strategy as theirs. Having ownership over the work you are doing is an important element of engagement. That being said, as students are talking today, you will want to have the strategies and prompts in your mind so that you can help students to try them on the fly, thereby creating "student-owned" strategies that are also ones you would like the whole class to try.

Ways to Analyze Evidence

This shows... because...

It is important to notice...

_____ means _____, therefore _____

This is significant because...

Even though... (the character)...

"So let's keep going now. Can you try again with your partner, doing the same work? But this time see if you can add onto your explanation by using one of these prompts."

Diamond took charge of her partnership, and so when we came together again I asked her to share her thinking. She said confidently, "I think this scene shows that Squeaky thinks she is protecting herself, but really she is almost building a wall around her. Not that she wants to be friends with Mr. Pearson, but by being so rude, even if you think you are being protective, you are really just making people not like you." I nodded and said, "Which of these prompts might help you close up your thought, Diamond?"

"Oh. Um. I could say, 'This is significant because . . . even though she thinks her rudeness is protecting her . . . um . . . all she winds up being is rude . . . and alone!'"

"Wow!" I said "That was awesome! It's like the prompt just got that brilliant thought right out of your head! Nice work!" Diamond beamed.

ACTIVE ENGAGEMENT

Help students as they work with partners to analyze how a scene supports the rationale for a claim, using thought prompts to push their thinking.

"Right now, will you find the first place in your draft where you supplied evidence? Go to the end of that part of the essay and put a star there. That's the first place where you are going to need to analyze your evidence. So right now, will Partner 1 read aloud your evidence, and then, Partner 2, will you toss your partner one of the thought prompts? One you think might work to get your partner analyzing the evidence. Partner 1, repeat your evidence, then take whatever thought prompt your partner threw your way, repeat it, and keep talking as long as you can. When Partner 1 slows

I urge Diamond to use a prompt here in order to help her focus her big ideas into a powerful line. Often, when students begin to explain their thinking they start to ramble. Making their thinking fit a thought prompt can help with this.

down, Partner 2, throw another thought prompt, one you think will keep the writer analyzing the evidence. Do this for as long as it seems to work. Then if there is time, switch roles."

I walked over to David and Devin. David was looking at his paper, reading the scene he selected. "James wants to do the right thing. For example, even when he is going with the gang he knows it's wrong and is worried."

Devin said, "Um, 'this shows . . .'"

David looked annoyed and thoughtful. "This shows . . . that James knows it is wrong and feels bad."

"Keep going!" I said to Devin.

"Ok. Try 'Even though . . . (the character) . . .'"

David sighed. "Even though. Uh, even though James wants to be bad and join the gang, he can't, because deep down he is a too good a person."

"See that?" I said. "Good work."

LINK

Remind students of the importance of analyzing their evidence to provide their readers with a more compelling argument in support of their claim.

"As you continue to revise your essays, remember that it's not enough to just plop that evidence right into your piece. The analysis of the evidence, the *how* and *why* of it, is what is really going to convince your readers that your thinking is real and true. And this goes not just for writing, but for life. The 'because I said so' reasoning is super frustrating. Supporting your reason with the *why* of it is just as important as the reason itself.

"At the end of the workshop today, you're going to have some time to share your essays with a few others. Be sure to work now to make your essay as powerful and convincing as you can. Think about the goals that you set for yourself last night when you analyzed your writing using the Argument Writing Checklist."

Assuming one partner as "the thinker" and one as "the prompter" helps focus their work, as it allows for fun discoveries. Making your active engagement as active as possible helps keep your class attuned to the work of the session.

Troubleshooting Common Problems with Analysis of Evidence

AS STUDENTS BEGIN TO WORK ON THIS DAY, you will notice two major issues arising. First, there will be your students who have trouble taking the plunge into explaining and analyzing evidence. They will need a bit of cheerleading, a little support.

Try ushering these students to look at the "Ways to Analyze Evidence" chart, putting a bit of pressure on them by saying, "Choose one that looks good now and try it out. Don't worry too much about whether it is the perfect one yet."

(continues)

MID-WORKSHOP TEACHING   Considering the Counterargument

"Writers, I know you are trying to come up with ways to write about how your evidence fits your claim, and you have so far been using thought prompts to help you begin to do the thinking you need to do between what the evidence is and the point you are trying to make. This part that you are working on—explaining your evidence in convincing ways—is the crux of what makes your essay feel like it is the work of a middle school writer. This is the really challenging part of the whole unit, up to this point.

"So I want to give you another tip. You are essentially arguing *for* something, and one of the best ways to argue *for* something is to imagine what the counterargument might be. So it really helps to entertain an opposing idea and to then come up with ways to counter that point of view, to talk back to it.

"There are, again, phrases you might use to put out an opposing view." I flipped to the sheet of chart paper where I had jotted some counterargument thought prompts.

> Some people might interpret this differently. They might argue that this passages shows not that . . . but that . . .

> Some people might suggest that this shows . . . but I disagree because if that was the case, then . . . I think this shows . . .

"You can also pose a counterargument by suggesting some people would differ on the precise term that you use in your claim. Earlier, when I looked over Miguel's shoulder, he was wrestling with whether his character's behavior was *generous* or just generally *kind*. In the same way, you could put forth the notion that some people might suggest your character's behavior can best be characterized a bit differently. Again, posing that argument allows you to defend the choice you have made.

"Listen to the way Jaz uses counterargument in this essay about *Fly Away Home*. When you notice her use of counterargument, give me a signal." I read:

> The Dad in Fly Away Home is not that great a father because he is teaching his son to lie, to hide, to break the law. For example, when they are in the Mall and they notice people looking at them, the son says, "We know how not to get noticed." This shows that the son is almost proud of the fact that they know how to sneak around. I know a lot of people will say that the Dad is doing what he can to keep his kid dry and safe, and that this makes it all worth it, but I disagree. I think there are always choices in life, and that while it is great that the Dad is giving his son a place to sleep, it is not great that he is teaching him how to be deceptive.

"Jaz imagined what someone who disagreed with her might say and then answered that disagreement ahead of time. This is called rebutting the counterargument, and it is an effective way to make your essays even stronger."

Some students will lose the grip of structure in their paragraphs, adding the explanation before the evidence, or in the middle, or in some odd spot that does not make sense. Many times this indicates that the writer does not really understand how a body paragraph works, or even what the different parts are and how they relate to each other. You can help these students by simply coaching them to identify the evidence in their paragraphs, asking them to actually point out those spots, and then gently reminding them that often essayists put their explanations after their evidence. Invitations to study completed essays help as well.

The second very predictable problem—and much tougher issue—is that as they begin to explain their evidence, their thinking goes a little off track. Their body paragraph is about how the character is caring because she helps others, but then in their explanation they begin discussing the character's sadness. When this happens, you can gather your small group together, asking them to take a moment and point out or underline the word or words in the first line of the body paragraph that they are trying to explain, for example, *caring* and *helping others*. Then, ask your students to reflect on their analysis, asking, "Did I explain what I was supposed to explain?" Hopefully your students will recognize that they have gone off the beam a bit, and you can redirect them to try again.

If they do not recognize their misstep, you could check in on how well they are understanding their original ideas. For example, when working with Yeiry, I coached her to tell me a bit about what it means to be caring, and she said, "it means that you, well you care about people and you help them and are nice to them." It was an easy transition for me to ask, "And how is this scene of Doris trying to keep the dog in 'Stray' a good example of that?" She responded by saying, "She is trying to save the dog, which is a way of helping others, so that is caring." I ushered her to write her thoughts in the margins of her essay.

A final thought about these conferences and small groups in which you are going to push your students to analyze and explain: while you will teach and coach and offer support and encouragement, it is true that for some of your students, their analysis will not quite be as airtight as you might have wished. And for sure, when this happens, you will push your students to notice the tangents, to try to get their thinking in line with their essay. But at the same time you will want above all to celebrate the attempts your students make, even allowing for some sloppy thinking here and there in the efforts to get your class more comfortable with having this kind of thinking in their essays in the first place. Remember that this work—analyzing and explaining—is both terribly

FIG. 7–1 Yeiry works to explain her evidence.

difficult for all writers and perhaps the most important part of an essay as students get older. Certainly we strive for perfection here, but if the work is terribly important while also being terribly difficult, we might need to also celebrate the approximations our kids make along the way, so that they have the confidence to try again next time. This is a process in which students gradually build competence and confidence.

Giving Feedback Using the Checklist

Give students the opportunity to share their essays in small groups, using the Argument Writing Checklist as a guideline to offer compliments and feedback to each other.

"Class, right now, will you grab your pens and the essays you've been working so hard to revise and get ready to share? Join me in the meeting area." Once the students had gathered, I began. "Yesterday, you had the chance to use the Argument Writing Checklist to look back at your work and set goals. I am so impressed by each of you and the hard work you've done, not just today, but all week, thinking about ways to make your essays clearer, more organized, and more compelling."

I leaned in, as if to deliver the best news of the hour. "Right now, you'll share your first pieces with one another, to show off all you've already learned to do as an essayist, as well as the work you're still striving toward. In just a moment, you'll meet in small groups, taking turns reading aloud. And, partners, your job as a listener will be to notice the impressive work your friend is doing as a writer so that you can give the kind of compliment that really matters, one that shows you know this kind of writing well. I have a fresh copy of the Argument Writing Checklist for each of you to use as you listen to one another share. You can mark it with stars to help you listen closely and remember the compliments you'll give at the end."

I gestured toward each student, placing them quickly into groups of three or four, as they clustered into spots around the room. I moved from one group to the next, gesturing toward a specific point on the

Create an opportunity for students to share their writing with an audience, celebrating their hard work thus far and reminding themselves of the goals they'll carry on into the next bend. You may have students sit in small groups of three or four writers, asking each to take turns reading their essay aloud, while the others use the Argument Writing Checklist to give feedback in the form of a specific compliment.

Argument Writing Checklist

	Grade 5	NOT YET	STARTING TO	YES!	Grade 6	NOT YET	STARTING TO	YES!
	Structure				**Structure**			
Overall	I made a claim or thesis on a topic or text, supported it with reasons, and provided a variety of evidence for each reason.	☐	☐	☐	I explained the topic/text and staked out a position that can be supported by a variety of trustworthy sources. Each part of my text helped build my argument, and led to a conclusion.	☐	☐	☐
Lead	I wrote an introduction that led to a claim or thesis and got my readers to care about my opinion. I got my readers to care by not only including a cool fact or jazzy question, but also by telling readers what was significant in or around the topic.	☐	☐	☐	I wrote an introduction to interest readers and help them understand and care about a topic or text. I thought backwards between the piece and the introduction to make sure that the introduction fit with the whole.	☐	☐	☐
	I worked to find the precise words to state my claim; I let readers know the reasons I would develop later.	☐	☐	☐	Not only did I clearly state my claim, I also told my readers how my text would unfold.	☐	☐	☐
Transitions	I used transition words and phrases to connect evidence back to my reasons using phrases such as *this shows that. . .*	☐	☐	☐	I used transitions to help readers understand how the different parts of my piece fit together to explain and support my argument.	☐	☐	☐
	I helped readers follow my thinking with phrases such as *another reason* and *the most important reason.* I used phrases such as *consequently* and *because of* to show what happened.	☐	☐	☐	I used transitions to help connect claim(s), reasons, and evidence, and to imply relationships such as when material exemplifies, adds on to, is similar to, explains, is a result of, or contrasts. I use transitions such as *for instance, in addition, one reason, furthermore, according to, this evidence suggests,* and *thus we can say that.*	☐	☐	☐
	I used words such as *specifically* and *in particular* to be more precise.	☐	☐	☐				

checklist as I heard clear indicators, or paused students as they read aloud, asking partners to reflect for a moment or listen once more as students reread key parts.

CELEBRATING PROGRESS AND TRACKING ONGOING GOALS

"Tonight, to celebrate your hard work as an essayist, read your piece once again to someone at home or show it to a friend or relative online. Use the checklist to show off what you've done really well. You might even share the compliments you received today from your friends. Then, using the checklist, track the goals you set and think about how you'll continue to work toward these goals as we move into the next part of this unit. Jot your plan in your notebook or use Post-its on your copy of the checklist."

Looking for Themes in the Trouble of a Text

IN THIS SESSION, you'll teach students that literary essayists look for themes in texts by identifying and analyzing the problems that characters face and then considering the inherent lessons learned.

GETTING READY

✔ Students' copies of the shared text, "Raymond's Run" (see Teaching)

✔ The stories that students worked with in Bend I (see Active Engagement)

✔ "How to Write a Theme-Based Literary Essay" anchor chart (see Teaching and Link)

✔ Chart paper with a table showing motivations, problems, and lessons learned by Squeaky (see Link)

✔ Students' copies of the mentor essay from Bend I (Yuko's essay about "Raymond's Run"), along with their "Three Little Pigs" essays and the essays that they drafted in Bend I (see Share)

✔ Chart paper and marker (see Share)

COMMON CORE STATE STANDARDS: W.6.1, W.6.4, W.6.5, W.6.10, RL.6.1, RL.6.2, RL.6.3, SL.6.1, SL.6.4, SL.6.6, L.6.1, L.6.2, L.6.3

YOUR STUDENTS will be accustomed to the pattern of these units of study. They progress through one cycle of writing—rehearsing, drafting, assessing, studying mentor texts, revising—and then they return to that process again, this time working with greater independence and sophistication. They progressed in this fashion through several cycles of personal narrative, and as they did that, they not only worked with new levels of proficiency, but the nature of the work changed.

In the same way, you're now rallying your students to cycle through the process of writing a second literary essay, writing on the same story and hopefully on a topic that overlaps with the first one, allowing them to reuse some of the material they worked with in the first essay. While their first essay focused on character traits—an especially accessible focus—this new essay will be interpretive. You'll be asking students to think about the larger theme of a story, and by the end of the bend, about how the craft decisions that the author made advanced this theme.

Today's session is just the start, but what a strong start it is. Today, you teach students that literary essayists need not only write character essays, as they have just done. They can spotlight almost any element of fiction. They could, for example, write an essay that puts a spotlight on the setting in a story. One common way to focus a literary essay is to focus on the theme. You'll teach students to read, asking questions such as, "What is this story *really* about?" "What are the life lessons that this story teaches?"

Although the work is intellectually challenging, it is developmentally appropriate for young adolescents. Many young people spend their lunch periods thinking thematically about their lives, considering what the moments in their own life stories and each other's mean to them. This first session aims to help students practice these skills in the texts they are reading so that they can write more sophisticated essays. You will teach your class that often the gateway to thinking about themes in texts and in their lives is to look at the problems people face and to think about what can be learned from the ways people (including characters) handle those problems.

Specifically, the way you will teach students to think thematically about stories is to ask them to return to the character they just thought about, and even to the aspect of that character they just wrote about, and keeping that in mind, to again ask themselves, "What are the deep-down things that character wants, and what gets in the way of the character getting what he or she wants? What are the most important troubles my character encounters?"

"Often, the gateway to thinking about themes in texts is to look at the problems people face and to think about what can be learned from the ways people handle those problems."

It would be rare indeed to find a story that does not revolve around trouble. This trouble serves not only to keep readers invested in the story and to keep turning the pages, but it also is usually our greatest teacher. When you see problems arising in a story, you know that you are about to take on what it means to face those problems, to overcome them. You learn life lessons from the problems in stories, and therein lies one path to discovering theme.

Once your students have found a few possible themes, you will use the momentum of the unit thus far to channel them to draft claims and plan possible essays. If you are in a classroom full of adept, engaged writers, you will find that they have little trouble accomplishing this session's lofty goals. However, we welcome you to spread the teaching of this session across two days if you think your students need more time for any part of the work of this "day."

While we recommend that you take the time your students need, you should, of course, be aware of the demands they will face, especially when taking high-stakes assessment tests. In these timed tests, your sixth-graders will have to do exactly the work of this session—in addition to powerfully drafting their entire essay—usually in the same time we have devoted to the work that follows. So take your time, but be aware that the work here aims to apply just the slightest bit of pressure on your students to get cracking as fast as they can—so that they are ready when there isn't a minute to waste.

Looking for Themes in the Trouble of a Text

CONNECTION

Rally students to be engaged in the new work by talking up the challenges they'll face. Overview the new bend in the unit.

"When I was in school, I played field hockey, first on the junior varsity team—JV—and then on the varsity team. The word *varsity* is just a shortening of the word *university*, and it means the *main* team, the one everyone is invested in and watching.

"I bet you know what I'm about to say. Starting today, we are heading into varsity-level *essay* writing. I wish I could get you all letter jackets to wear from now on! Earlier, you wrote character essays and learned a whole lot about writing essays that you will continue to use now. But I'm not sure you realized that, actually, essayists can write essays on *any* element of a story (people write essays on the setting of a story, on the structure of a story). By far the most common way to write a literary essay is to write on a story's theme, on life lessons, and that's what you'll be doing over the next bend in this unit.

"For the next portion of this unit, then, you are going to think about what the story you selected—the same story—is teaching readers about life. But here is the thing. You needn't leave behind all the thinking you have already done, because the themes in a story relate very closely to things you have been thinking about all along—to the traits and motivations of the characters, and especially of the main character."

❖ **Name the teaching point.**

"Today I want to teach you that often the life lessons that *a character learns* are the life lessons that the author hopes that *readers* will learn. To figure out what those life lessons might be, it helps to look more closely at the troubles a character faces, and how they get in the way of what a character wants, asking, 'What lessons does the character learn from all this?'"

When I describe literary essays this way, I am angling the class toward writing interpretive essays. By channeling them to look for patterns in stories, I'm directing them toward the work that high school educators refer to as literary interpretation.

It's important that students know where they are headed in a unit and where they have been. You also want to start each bend of a unit with a kind of fanfare to keep your students' engagement high.

TEACHING

Tell about troubles you had in life and how you were consoled and empowered when someone pointed out to you that from hard times, one learns lessons. Use that example to accentuate that characters learn life lessons from tackling troubles.

"When I was in seventh grade, I went to my first school dance and had the worst time ever. No one asked me to dance, while my best friend got asked to dance at every slow song, and some girls made fun of my dress. I went home and cried. Then I talked to my dad, who told me that even though he wished all good times for me, most people have to face hard times—and that those hard times were usually when they learned the best lessons—ones that led them to more confidently become themselves. 'No pain, no gain,' he told me, and I have found that to be true."

Point out that the motivations and troubles in a story have universality, and show students how you can think about universal motivations and problems in the shared story, setting the stage for doing the same with the universal lesson (or theme).

"Just as you and I learn the most from the tough times in our lives, characters in stories learn the most through the problems they face. But here is the important thing—readers learn right along with the characters. And readers learn stuff that relates *not just to the character's troubles* but to troubles that readers have as well. That's true because the problems that characters face in stories have what people call *universality*.

"To understand that, it helps to remember that characters in stories have motivations that all human beings share. People want to feel valued, to be understood, to fit in. And people also have universal problems or troubles—things get in the way of what they want.

"Let's try thinking about 'Raymond's Run,' and let's consider the main character's motivations and/or the problems that get in the way of her getting what she wants. But this time, let's try to do this all in words that have universality. Think with me about what Squeaky really wants and about her problems." I left a moment of silence.

"With Squeaky, it takes a while to learn what she really wants (usually you know that at the start of a story), but by the end of the story, what do you think she really wants? Tell someone your idea."

I listened for half a minute as students shared thoughts with each other, and then, nodding, said, "I agree. She wants to have a friend, to feel connected to people. Here is the question: Is that motivation worded in such a way that it applies to lots of people? Is it a universal motivation?" The students nodded yes, so I pressed on.

"What are her problems?"

Again I left a pool of silence, and then said, "Are you thinking like I am? 'Squeaky has to care for her brother who has special needs.' That's true, right, *but* remember, we need to name her problem in a way that is not specific to *this* story, but that instead is a problem many people have. It helps to say to yourself, 'Squeaky, *like lots of people in the world*, has

---

A major focus of this lesson is on helping students to think in more universal, general ways about the stories they read, instead of focusing on the specific details and conditions of this one text. We practice that skill in a number of ways in this session because pushing kids to think more universally is a challenge, and an important skill for an essayist.

Notice the ways that we keep up the pace of this lesson. You will not have time to elicit responses from students, especially because then you will often need to negotiate back and forth to make sure they are ones that you can build on as the lesson continues, but you do want to make sure that students are thinking with you. So you ask for their thoughts but do not necessarily harvest them right now. You are intent on keeping this lesson brief so students have a large chunk of time to transfer this work to their own stories.

. . . what . . . responsibilities or a role that is hard for her?' To stay close to our other ideas about Squeaky, maybe we say it like this: 'Squeaky has a job to do—as part of a relationship—that sets her apart from other kids.'

"She has other universal problems, too. What would you say they are?" While I scrawled onto the chart, the class called out a second bullet for the Problem column of the chart.

Motivations, Problems	Lessons
Squeaky wants a real connection, a real friend	* Squeaky has a job— a relationship- that sets her apart from others kids. * Squeaky has a temper, a defensiveness, that keeps her apart from other kids.

Debrief, naming what you have done in a way that is transferable to other texts.

"Do you see that instead of talking about Squeaky's problems with specificity about *this* story—instead of saying, 'Squeaky has to take care of her disabled brother'—we worded her motivations and problems in a way that we all can relate to? I don't have a brother with special needs, but I sure do want to connect to people. Thinking this way helps readers empathize with Squeaky, thinking, 'This is true for me, too.' This way, readers learn life lessons alongside the character and discover the big themes in the text."

Now channel the class to think of the third and most important universal dimension of stories: the lesson, the theme. Point out that recalling the motivation and the problem (as well as the storyline) is a way for readers to generate ideas about what the life lessons are that a character—and readers—learn.

"Now let's think for a bit about a lesson Squeaky learns about these particular problems. I know that the author is definitely showing me something about life by telling me Squeaky's story. But I am a little lost. I feel like I want to say something like 'Having a temper is bad,' but I think that this is not powerful enough after all of the thinking work we have done about this story. Take a moment with your partner. What is it that Squeaky is learning—about making friends or about her temper and protectiveness? One way you can do this is to focus on the end of the story and what has changed in Squeaky.

As I listened in to the partnerships, I paid close attention to the students who were a little lost, marking them for my first small group of the day. After a few moments of discussion I brought the class together.

"Wow. Writers, you have become true experts in thinking about 'Raymond's Run.' I love some of the ideas you had about the lessons Squeaky learned. I heard Frankie say that he thinks Squeaky learns that when you are defensive you keep the good things out with the bad. Amazing. And Sophie said that she was reminded of what her aunt always says: 'You catch more flies with honey than with vinegar.' As you talked today I wrote down a few of the ways I heard you get started thinking. Here are your ideas on this new chart. As you work today these tips might continue to help you."

How to Write a Theme-Based Literary Essay

- Think about the character's motivations, problems, and lessons learned—and look for patterns.
  - What does the character want, and what gets in the way?
  - How does the character try to resolve his problems?
  - What lessons does the character learn from trying to resolve his problems?
  - Now what patterns can you see?
- Then craft a claim based on one of the themes.

ACTIVE ENGAGEMENT

Challenge students to try this same work in their own stories, thinking about the lessons a character learns by examining the motivations and the problems of the protagonist.

"Writers, let's leave 'Raymond's Run' behind for now. Instead, go ahead and try this work in your own stories. This can be challenging, so right now, rearrange yourselves so that you are sitting with another student who has chosen the same story. You could sit in twos or threes—whatever works best. You'll be brainstorming a bit before you go off to work on your own.

"The important thing is that you talk about your characters' motivations and problems in universal terms. Think bigger than just the particular scenario in your book. Then, see what you and your partners come up with as lessons the character learns. Okay, get to work!"

As students worked, I moved among them, checking in and sometimes saying things like "How is that problem similar to problems we often see in the world? Make it universal." And, "Get out the story. What does your character want deep down—what motivates her—and how might you describe that in more general terms?" As students got going I pushed them to think about the lessons the character is learning, pointing out that the "How to Write a Theme-Based Literary Essay" chart might help them.

Invite students to share their thinking and their process.

Soon I reconvened the group and chose a few partnerships to share their thinking.

Tess said, "In our story, 'Everything Will Be Okay' the narrator wants to have something of his own to love. That's a universal motivation of his. And later, he wants to decide what kind of man he'll be. He wants to choose his own way of living in the world."

Her partner, Shakira, continued, "A problem he faces is that the kitten—I mean, something he cares about—is taken away from him, and, even worse, it's taken away by someone in his family. This not only makes him sad over losing something he loves, it also makes him question his family."

"And what did you decide that the narrator learned?"

Tess scrunched her face up and said, "That was hard. But we said that maybe he learned that you don't always have to agree with your family, and you don't always like what they say or do, but that's okay. It's okay to be different and stand up for yourself."

"Yes!" I beamed. "That's the work. You used your universal thinking about the motivations and problems of the character to help you see more about the lessons learned in the text."

LINK

Remind students that today they'll be aiming for universality as they chart the motivation, problem, and possible theme in the same story about which they wrote their character essay.

"So, writers, by the end of today you will have a claim about what you think a significant theme or lesson in your story might be. I have given you a bunch of ways to get there—by filling out a chart to get yourself thinking, by using a partner to rehearse and troubleshoot, and some prompts to help get you to the lessons the character is learning. These are all tools that can help you if you are having trouble. On the other hand, some of you might already know a significant lesson or theme in the story and may just want to get writing.

"There are many ways to do today's work. What I really care about is that you are trying to name problems and motivations in more universal ways and that you get to a place where you are writing about the lessons a character learns.

When I circulate during the active engagement, I'm assessing and coaching into students' work, but I am also listening for strong examples I can share with the rest of the class to further exemplify the teaching point. Rarely do I call on just anyone who raises a hand in a minilesson, because in the very limited time I have for whole-class instruction, I do not want someone sharing thinking that inadvertently undermines my teaching.

Universal Design for Learning (UDL) pushes teachers to guide students to make their own choices about the methods and strategies that will work best for them in accomplishing a particular learning goal. With UDL, you do not tell the students what to do. Instead you encourage students to think about what will work best for them and to plan accordingly.

"Can you take a second and jot down in your notebook a little To-Do list for yourself? What do you think you need to do to get going today, and which of these steps and strategies might help you? You can use the charts in the room to help you make your To-Do list, including this one.

How to Write a Theme-Based Literary Essay

- Think about the character's motivations, problems, and lessons learned—and look for patterns.
  - What does the character want, and what gets in the way?
  - How does the character try to resolve his problems?
  - What lessons does the character learn from trying to resolve his problems?
  - Now what patterns can you see?
- Then craft a claim based on one of the themes.

"Okay, once you have your plan for the day—I see most of you are going to write a few entries to get yourself going, using the chart to help you and then crafting some claims—you can get started. Remember to use the support you have in the room—your partner, charts, and even your past essay!"

The Power of Compliments

THERE IS LITTLE DOUBT that the work of interpretation is hard, and that some, if not many, of your students will struggle today and in future sessions. I encourage you to see this as a beautiful thing, a moment of true success as a teacher, when you have found a place where your students need you. If the lessons all go without a hitch, then you have to ask yourselves whether or not your students really needed that lesson in the first place.

That being said, because this work is hard for your students, you will need to work extra hard as well, but not in the ways you might think. You should not on this day (or on any other day, for that matter) work to try to fix all of the problems that arise in the room. Instead, work to fill the room with energy and confidence. Work to have every single student in your class feeling like she can rise to the challenge of understanding themes. Work to make your young writers feel capable of solving problems and trying things out.

You can do this through the use of compliments. A well-worded compliment can be the wind in the sails of a writer, but not unless it is a useful one. For instance, it will not help if you simply say to a student, "Good work," or "I like what you did here." And it will not help to compliment what a student is already exceptional at in her writing. Instead, look for the places where a writer is almost doing something, or where she

---

MID-WORKSHOP TEACHING   **Making Claims More Precise and Compelling**

"Writers, many of you have settled on claims that you think are working, and that is great. But I have an awesome way to help you make those claims a bit more compelling. When people write ads or election campaign slogans, they work like crazy to think about each and every word they use. They ask, 'Is this really exactly what I'm trying to say?' and 'Is this the word that will fire up your readers?'

"Alaina decided to do that. Her first draft of her claim about the story 'Everything Will Be Okay' went like this: 'Jim Howe learns that his family is mean.' Alaina underlined the key words and then tried to make them more precise. She underlined *his family* and thought, 'Is it the *whole* family that is mean?' She realized that, in fact, it's the *men* that are this way, so she changed that part of her thesis. Then she underlined the next key part—the words *are mean*."

The men in his family <u>are mean.</u>

"Alaina, tell us what you thought next."

Alaina said, "I thought about the word *mean*. You asked me, 'Is mean precisely what you think the men are? And if so, what kind of mean are they?' So I thought about it a little more and realized that Jim's dad and brothers aren't mean so much as stuck in their ways. Like, they have this really narrow-minded way of thinking about things. And then you asked me what they had narrow-minded views about, and I said, 'About the ways to be a man.' Jim's dad and brothers try to make Jim into a tough guy—someone who wants to hunt and can kill animals without caring."

I said, "So writers, Alaina's thesis went from 'Jim Howe learns that his family is mean' to 'Jim Howe learns that the men in his family have narrow-minded ideas about what men should be like.' Notice that this statement is not only more *precise*, but also more *compelling*. It's more likely to fire readers up. Some of you may want to borrow this technique. If you have figured out what you want to say, work on *how* you want to say it by doing the word-by-word work that Alaina did."

---

tried something once but not again. We recommend using stickers as you move about the room working with students, marking the places in their writing where they had a moment of brilliance, a big step forward.

Notice how in this conference with Devin, I choose my words carefully so that I compliment in a way that names for Devin what, exactly, he has done that works so well. This way, chances are good that he will use the compliment to push his thinking not only today, after we meet, but anytime he finds himself in a similar situation when he writes.

I pulled my chair up alongside Devin's and asked him what he was aiming to do in his essay on "Everything Will Be Okay," by James Howe. Devin flipped through the pages of the story and said, "I'm trying to figure out the theme. There is definitely one here. It seems like the people in this family put a lot of pressure on each other to kind of stick to what the family believes. Like Jim struggles because he doesn't want to hunt like his dad and brothers. So I guess that's a theme—of pressure to fit in. I'm not sure what Jim is saying about it, but um . . ." He looked at me, as if for confirmation.

"Devin, I love that you aren't stopping just because you're not sure. Later, when you get your pen, you can write, 'Maybe . . .' and write your first thought. Then you can follow it with, 'Or maybe he is trying to say . . .' And you can try out this idea about pressure to fit in or about any idea you come up with. When you grapple with ideas in this way, trying to figure out exactly how to say the idea that is starting to form in your head, you are much more likely to land on the words that will get at what you are really trying to convey." Devin looked at me, nodding his head in agreement.

"Remember that whenever you want to deepen your ideas, you can look for the trouble in a text and then write to discover what the story is really saying about that trouble.

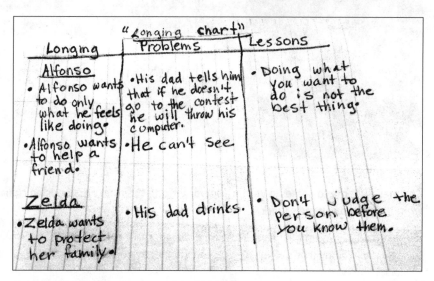

FIG. 8–1   Shakira diagrams possible themes.

Just thinking on the page. You've done this thinking with one theme in this text, but there are often multiple themes that readers can identify and think about."

Then I offered him a tip: "Why don't you try this by writing, because even more insightful ideas often come out when you get your pen moving. You'll probably write to discover what Howe is saying about the ways the narrator is both trying to fit in and fighting against fitting in with his family."

Planning a Thematic Essay

Channel students to come up with a plan for writing their next essay, using charts and ideas from the previous bend's work.

"Writers, by now you should have chosen the claim for this next essay and made a plan for how the essay will go. You'll be gathering evidence for the essay at home and writing it, start to finish, in school tomorrow.

"When you did this for your first essay, it helped to look at both the 'The Three Little Pigs' essay and at Yuko's essay to think about the kinds of evidence you might need to write your own essay. Will you pull those essays out, and also the character-based essay that you just drafted, and talk to your partner about how the essay you plan to write will resemble those three, how it will be different, and what you need to collect to be ready to get started writing?"

Students talked a bit, and then I intervened.

"I heard lots of you talk about how you might structure your essay in similar and different ways to these two essays. That they both will have body paragraphs with evidence from the text and parts where you explain that evidence. You also noticed that you will have to have a plan for how your body paragraphs will go."

Direct the class to talk in pairs about their own possible plans for structuring a theme-based essay, and channel them toward tried-and-true structures.

"It isn't easy to plan a well-structured essay," I said, "so right now will you help each other? Take whatever the life lesson is you think you might be writing about, and write-in-the-air to each other ways that your essay could possibly unfold. In general, if your essay claim goes something like this," and I turned to a fresh sheet of chart paper and quickly jotted a sentence frame.

At first things are difficult, but then something happens for the character and things change for the better, lessons are learned.

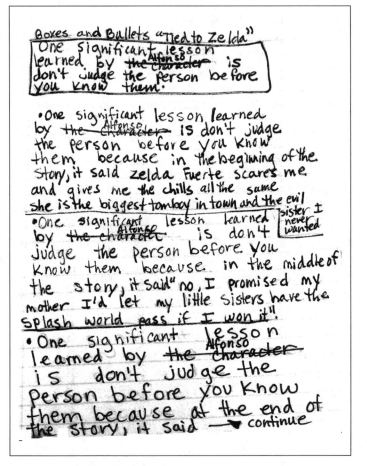

FIG. 8–2   Shakira uses boxes and bullets to find evidence to support her thesis.

"Then it often works best to organize the essay by time frames—by how the theme plays out in the beginning, middle, and end of the story.

"On the other hand, if your claim goes something like . . ." I turned back to the chart paper.

The theme shows up in lots of places in the story . . .

"Then you might organize your essay by ways the theme works in the story. And, of course, you can always work with reasons your theme is true in the story if that works for your claim."

I moved about the room coaching students to try on one structure or another. Some kids came to the realization that the structure they had first selected wouldn't work best given what they wanted to write. Jaz had been planning to use the "reasons why" structure for her essay. Her thesis was: "In 'Thank You, Ma'am,' Roger learns that kindness is more powerful than fear." She was struggling to push her idea forward, and in the end, she decided the most effective supports for her essay followed the "beginning, middle, and end" structure. She came up with this:

> Roger learns that kindness is more powerful than fear

- In the beginning, Roger is afraid.
- In the middle, he starts to realize the woman's kindness.
- At the end, he leaves, but without taking the purse.

Brian settled into reasons for his theme as well but got stuck when he could only think of two. He wrote:

> In "The Gift of The Magi," O'Henry shows us the power of sacrificing for those that you love.

- It's powerful because you find out how much you love that person.
- It's powerful because knowing someone loves you that much is the greatest gift.

Of course, I encouraged Brian to stick with his two great reasons—and reminded him and the class that essays do not need three separate body paragraphs to be good.

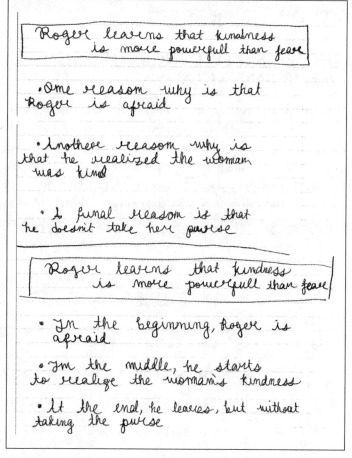

FIG. 8–3 Jaz decides that the most effective supports for her essay follow the "beginning, middle, end" structure.

GATHERING EVIDENCE THROUGH THE LENS OF A THEME-BASED CLAIM

"Tonight, collect evidence for your new, theme-based claim. Just like you did with your character essay, reread the text through the lens of your claim, searching for the most convincing evidence that supports that claim. Remember, you might quote some parts of the text, story-tell other parts, and summarize yet other parts. These are points that you learned as you wrote the character-based essays earlier. I think it's useful to borrow those points from our Bend I anchor chart and add them to our theme-based anchor chart. Tomorrow, you will want to have thoughtfully selected evidence as you sit down to draft a new essay. Be sure you have at least one piece of evidence for each body paragraph of your essay!"

How to Write a Theme-Based Literary Essay

- Think about the character's motivations, problems, and lessons learned and look for patterns.

- What does the character want, and what gets in the way?

- How does the character try to resolve his problems?

- What lessons does the character learn from trying to resolve his problems?

- Now what patterns can you see?

- Think about the patterns you see in universal terms. Ask yourself, "What big life lessons—what themes—can readers draw from the patterns in the story?"

- Then craft a claim based on one of the themes.

- Search for the most compelling evidence that can support the claim, then add it to the essay like this:

  - Quote some parts of the text.
  - Story-tell other parts.
  - Summarize yet other parts.

Drafting Using All that You Know

ear Teachers,

Teaching students to write essays is like directing a play. You have rehearsed each scene so artfully, you've coached your actors, the set designers are working steadily along, but you have no idea how the actual play is going to go when it's finally performed. This is why dress rehearsals were invented, and a dress rehearsal is exactly what your students need for their essay work right now. They need to put together the rich strategy work you have modeled and coached over the first half of this unit, and they also need to show you what exactly they are holding onto, and what is sliding over their backs.

Yesterday, your students laid the groundwork for a theme-based essay, generating claims, mapping out a structure, and for homework, gathering evidence. Today, with all these pieces in hand, you will teach your students to draft an essay in one period without as much help from you as they have received in the past. The goal will be for them to work with more independence and to undertake more steps at once. Certainly you will be there to coach them, and certainly as they write you will confer and pull small groups, but your teaching will be lean. Instead of walking them through each small step of the process of writing literary essays, you'll remind them to draw on what they already know as well as from the resources they have all around them—the charts up in the room, the Argument Writing Checklist, their notebooks, and most of all, their minds.

While the work of the day is challenging, it is also exhilarating. It's the lights coming on for dress rehearsal night; it's the eyes all around asking excitedly, "Do you think we can pull this off?" Enjoy the moment with your class, and celebrate the work they have done so far. No matter where they are on this learning progression or that Common Core State Standard, we guarantee that you will see growth in your students' writing from that first day of essay boot camp when they teased out an essay for "the third little pig is an admirable character."

COMMON CORE STATE STANDARDS: W.6.1, W.6.4, W.6.5, W.6.10, RL.6.1, RL.6.2, RL.6.3, RL.6.10, SL.6.1, L.6.1, L.6.2, L.6.3

MINILESSON

The day comes when the gymnast or pianist no longer practices one part of her routine or composition over and over, then the next in isolation, but instead, she puts it all together and performs the routine or composition in its entirety for an audience. In the same way, writers can spend only so much time positioning themselves, readying themselves. Soon the day comes to write an entire draft, writing fast and furiously, trying to incorporate as many critical notes and parts and as many relevant techniques as possible—while writing on the run, quickly.

Today, then, you'll remind your young writers that essays are often written quickly the first time around. That writers know a draft is just that—a draft, a preliminary sketch or version of something. It is not meant to be the most perfect vision of their idea; it can be a bit rough. That is not to say that their writing should be sloppy and pulled from nowhere. They have done much over the past few days, the past few weeks, actually, to set themselves up to draft successfully.

Your teaching point, then, can be "I want to teach you that when essayists sit down to draft, they draw on everything they know about writing essays, and they often draft quickly, piecing together all the necessary parts—their ideas and their evidence—into a logical structure." As you move on in your teaching, you could explain to the students that it is not as if they are being thrown to the wolves, into the writing wild so to speak, to draft blindly. No, they have a wide variety of resources to draw from as they begin their drafts. Set students up for the day's work by drawing their attention to the charts displayed in the classroom, the Argument Writing Checklist, the mentor text that they used in the first bend, and their character-based essays. Remind them that the work they did in yesterday's workshop (crafting a claim that is precise and compelling, making a plan for how their essay will go and which structure fits it best, collecting convincing evidence to support their claim) can, and should, be utilized as they draft today.

Your goal today is to get your students writing. Keep your teaching brief and precise. For the active engagement portion of the minilesson, you can simply ask your students to gather all they need to draft successfully. Send them from the meeting area to their seats, to prepare their workspace for writing time. Perhaps you will tick off, one finger at a time, all that they could possibly need for drafting. "Writer's notebooks?" "Check!" "Mentor text?" "Check!" "Argument Writing Checklist?" "Check!" "Essay plan?" "Check!" And then by all means, wish them well, and let them have at it!

CONFERRING AND SMALL-GROUP WORK

As students work, keep the class moving by voicing over things like "Remember to use the structure you mapped out yesterday as a guide for your draft—and write each part as long as possible, moving between your universal ideas and your specific examples from the text." Then a little later, you might say, "Most of you are done with your first body paragraph! Remember to go right into your second one when you are done with the first. We are pushing ourselves to write a whole essay today!" You will most likely also highlight the scaffolds and models around the room that will help your class keep moving, pulling a chart of thought prompts to the center of the room and saying "Don't forget to use these charts! They helped you so much before, I want to see them in your essays today!" In this way you are nudging them to remember what they have learned.

You can also nudge students individually, saying to one, "You are stopping too much. Instead of thinking about every word you are going to write, practice just letting the words flow out of your pen. I promise they don't have to be perfect." Or "Remember how we used the author's name when we talked about a text? Try including that in your writing for the rest of the essay."

During your work with students one on one, you will find that many of them need some help in articulating where they are in their essay work. That is, they can point to something they did or did not do, but they are unsure of what to call it. It is important that we have names for things in our writing work, so that kids can say, "I am pretty good at finding evidence, but it is hard for me to analyze it." You can help during your conferences and small groups by giving these things words and names. You will say things like "You know, you used to . . . but now you know . . ." Or "Since you are really good at . . . now you can work on . . ."

Above all else, be sure to encourage and motivate. We often feel like a strange version of an essay cheerleader on this day, making sure to keep the energy high, so our students see us as their biggest fans instead of their assessors. If all goes well, the class will end with everyone slightly out of breath, shaking their hands, and very proud of themselves.

MID-WORKSHOP TEACHING

Once students are done drafting, encourage them to look over their essays with their partners, holding them next to a mentor text, which in this case, could be the teacher's thematic essay. (Feel free to use the one we have provided on the CD-ROM, or craft your own.) Students can discuss what they notice about the mentor text with their partners, maybe even annotating it, in a similar fashion to what they did when they looked at Yuko's essay in Bend I. They can then move on to discussing their own essays, noticing what went well and where they might have some more work to do in revision.

You might say, "So, writers, you are going to spend some time working with your partner, studying a mentor thematic essay. Feel free to annotate this essay, the same way you annotated Yuko's essay last week. Once you have a good handle on the characteristics of a thematic essay, move onto your own essay; study your drafts and mark them up by noticing the different parts of your essays, and label what you think you did well and where you might go for next steps. Then you will discuss and jot on a goal sheet what you will do in your next essay or draft to improve the quality of it. Make a plan for how you will do that work."

SHARE

For today's share, you will once again require students to rely on a tool that they have at their disposal, the Argument Writing Checklist.

At this point, if your students have been using the Grade 5 Argument Writing Checklist, you may want to introduce the grade 6 checklist if you feel your students have mastered the strategies and skills for fifth grade and are now ready to assess their writing against sixth-grade benchmarks. You may also want to share and discuss the Grade 6 Information Writing Checklist, comparing it side by side with the Argument Writing Checklist, working with your students to determine which items on the checklists are appropriate for literary essays. It may be useful for your class to work together to develop a hybrid checklist and then use it to assess where their work falls and decide on writing and revision goals.

Just as you did at the end of Bend I, you will ask your students to hold their writing up against the checklist (grade 5 or 6 argument or the hybrid you create with your class). Ask students to note places where they are approaching or even exceeding grade level standards, as well as to think about *how* they are meeting those standards. Of course, students should also note places where there is room for improvement. What are the standards and checkpoints that they still need to reach toward? And how will they get there? While you were conferring today, you helped students come up with names and words to identify the fantastic work they are doing as essayists. Continue this coaching work across the share. Help students name and describe precisely what it is that they are stellar at, as well as label the weak spots in such a descriptive way that they can easily make the necessary changes. The best part about using the checklist at this point in their drafting is that they don't have to wait long to begin to incorporate those revisions. They can revise on the fly as they finish drafting their essays for homework this evening.

Best,
Kate and Kathleen

Argument Writing Checklist

	Grade 5	NOT YET	STARTING TO	YES!	Grade 6	NOT YET	STARTING TO	YES!
	Structure				**Structure**			
Overall	I made a claim or thesis on a topic or text, supported it with reasons, and provided a variety of evidence for each reason.	☐	☐	☐	I explained the topic/text and staked out a position that can be supported by a variety of trustworthy sources. Each part of my text helped build my argument, and led to a conclusion.	☐	☐	☐
Lead	I wrote an introduction that led to a claim or thesis and got my readers to care about my opinion. I got my readers to care by not only including a cool fact or jazzy question, but also by telling readers what was significant in or around the topic.	☐	☐	☐	I wrote an introduction to interest readers and help them understand and care about a topic or text. I thought backwards between the piece and the introduction to make sure that the introduction fit with the whole.	☐	☐	☐
	I worked to find the precise words to state my claim; I let readers know the reasons I would develop later.	☐	☐	☐	Not only did I clearly state my claim, I also told my readers how my text would unfold.	☐	☐	☐
Transitions	I used transition words and phrases to connect evidence back to my reasons using phrases such as *this shows that. . .*	☐	☐	☐	I used transitions to help readers understand how the different parts of my piece fit together to explain and support my argument.	☐	☐	☐
	I helped readers follow my thinking with phrases such as *another reason* and *the most important reason.* I used phrases such as *consequently* and *because of* to show what happened.	☐	☐	☐	I used transitions to help connect claim(s), reasons, and evidence, and to imply relationships such as when material exemplifies, adds on to, is similar to, explains, is a result of, or contrasts. I use transitions such as *for instance, in addition, one reason, furthermore, according to, this evidence suggests,* and *thus we can say that.*	☐	☐	☐
	I used words such as *specifically* and *in particular* to be more precise.	☐	☐	☐				

First Impressions and Closing Remarks

THIS SESSION IS, first and foremost, a revision lesson. While your students have been revising all along, by using mentor texts and by incorporating the strategies you have taught, much of their revision work thus far has been more in the moment, on-the-fly revision. In this session students stop, look at certain parts of their essays, and work to make them better.

Specifically, in this session you will teach students to craft their introductions and conclusions purposefully and artfully. You will teach them to consider their introductions first. They should think of this first paragraph as the first impression their reader has of them, their writing, and their essays. You will teach your students to write introductions that set up the context for the essay by thinking big about the topics that their essays center around, and you will teach them to try these introductions a few different ways to find the most engaging one.

"You will teach students to craft their introductions and conclusions purposefully and artfully."

Later on in the session, you will move to the conclusions of essays, teaching students to leave their readers with a sense of finality, or something to chew on.

As you work with the class on their body paragraphs, there are times that you and your students will crave the nuance of fiction, the craft and whimsy of poetry. Essays can feel so cerebral at times, and though you have fought to focus on the beauty of the writing in this unit, you might be feeling that for some of your students, the writing is a little dull. This session can help alleviate that—by teaching students to pour themselves into their introductions and conclusions and helping them see that no essay can be truly persuasive without the voice of the author in every word.

IN THIS SESSION, you'll teach students that literary essayists begin their essays with a universal statement about life and then transition to the text-based claim itself, by narrowing their focus to the particular story they are writing about. Then they make sure they end their essays with power and voice, leaving their reader with a strong final impression that concludes their journey of thought.

GETTING READY

✔ "Revision Strategies" chart (see Connection) 📀

✔ An example of one student's writing that shows his process for crafting and revising a lead, enlarged for the class to see (see Teaching)

✔ Student's essay drafts, writer's notebooks, and pens (see Active Engagement)

✔ "Alternative Ways to Conclude an Essay" anchor chart (see Share) 📀

✔ "Conclusions Three Ways," an example of your own writing that shows your process for crafting and revising a conclusion, to show on a document camera (or enlarged for the class to see), as well as copies for each student (see Share)

✔ "How to Write a Theme-Based Literary Essay" anchor chart (see Share) 📀

COMMON CORE STATE STANDARDS: W.6.1.a,e; W.6.4, W.6.5, RL.6.1, RL.6.2, SL.6.1, L.6.1, L.6.2, L.6.3, L.6.6

First Impressions and Closing Remarks

CONNECTION

Celebrate yesterday's hard work, and then help writers anticipate and take ownership of the work that lies before them: revision.

"Writers, yesterday I left class feeling like I had just coached a Super Bowl team. Seeing you take on writing those very sophisticated essays and doing that work with confidence, using everything you've been taught. Wow! For a teacher, this is as good as it gets. Thank you!

"Today you are going to learn a few ways to polish up your work. When writing, people get to do something that you never get to do in life. You get to redo your first impressions. Have you ever met someone for the first time and felt awkward? Well, sometimes when writing on a new topic, a writer can start off in that same awkward way. Today you'll learn ways to go back into a draft and fix up the introduction so that in the end, the first impressions your writing makes on readers will be strong.

"But it is not just the start of an essay that matters—the first impressions. The last impression matters as well. Today I will teach you to start and end an essay with emphasis and insight, so that readers say to themselves, 'Whoa, she nailed it.'"

Explain that this will be one more revision strategy they can add to their list.

"Of course, you will work on other parts of your essay today, too, drawing on the list of revision strategies you've learned this year. I've gathered some revision strategies you have learned during this unit and the one before it, and you can draw on any of those." I gestured toward the chart pad, where I had generated a list of essay revision strategies that the students could call upon.

Hopefully yesterday's teaching will have been a high, and you can give a compliment like this with a straight face. Always remember, however, that the veracity of your words matter. If the preceding day was a disaster and you start today by savoring the good work they did that day, people will begin to lose trust in you.

Revision Strategies

- Think, "What is this essay really about?" and rewrite in ways that better match that meaning.

- Revise through the lens of theme, making sure every detail connects back to that.

- Vary your evidence, and make sure it is compelling and includes important details.

- Incorporate your evidence in a variety of ways (using direct quotes, summarizing, storytelling).

- Unpack your evidence, showing not just how it supports your reasoning, but why.

- Add in new examples to support your theme.

- Use transitional phrases to help readers understand how different parts of the essay fit together.

- Use the Opinion/Argument Writing Checklist to set new goals for revision.

- Use charts to assess writing and revision goals.

- Rewrite whole chunks of text.

- Delete material that no longer fits.

It's important that students don't see units as isolated, genre-specific sets of lessons, but instead, as a reliable source of help when they need it. Reminding students of prior learning will encourage and remind them to use what they already know in the current unit. Of course, it will be even more effective if you have anchor charts hung across the room listing powerful strategies that students might apply across sessions and units. These charts might have titles such as "Revision Strategies that Work" or "Making Scenes Pop." Keep these charts alive and current. Invite students to refer to the charts again and again, and to add to them as they figure out new strategies.

"But the one thing I want to teach you that is a bit new is how to write powerful introductions and conclusions to an essay."

❖ **Name the teaching point.**

"Right now what I want to teach you is this: when literary essayists write introductions, they often lead with a universal statement about life and then transition to the text-based claim itself, by narrowing their focus to the particular story they are writing about."

TEACHING

Use a student's work from the day or year before as your demonstration text. Highlight the steps he took to write a powerful introduction.

"Today Jamhil is going to be our teacher. He did some of this work yesterday, and I'm going to take you on a tour of his introduction and show you things he did that you could do, too."

Using students as mentors in your classroom is powerful for many reasons. First, of course, is the engagement that comes with letting students see a peer's work. But there is also a sense of "I can do that, too." When students see what someone on or near their level of work can do, it makes the work less precious, less formal. Of course, it could very well be that your "Jamhil" did his work in a conference or small group with you the day before. The work does not have to be spontaneous to be a teachable moment.

I placed Jamhil's notebook on the document camera so the class could see his prospective leads and said, "Jamhil first tried out a few different leads and then had to choose from one of these."

- It is tough to find a way to show that you love someone. In his short story, "The Gift of the Magi," O'Henry teaches that the greatest gifts are those that require a character to be willing to make a sacrifice.
- Sometimes, from reading stories, we learn how to be better people. We learn how to sacrifice, how to show our affection, how to be a good person. These are all admirable qualities.
- While we often think of heroes as being extraordinary people who do extraordinary things, I like to find heroes in my everyday life. People who are kind, who sacrifice for others, who show up for the people they love. These are all admirable qualities, as admirable as a superhero's strength or super speed. In O'Henry's surprising story, "The Gift of the Magi," we meet two heroes, Jim and Della, who have many admirable qualities.

I pointed out that Jamhil selected the last of these as his lead. I turned to Jamhil and asked if he would explain a bit about how he wrote his introductions. (We had talked about this earlier in the day, of course.) Jamhil stood and pointed at the first introduction he wrote. "Well, first I just thought about like the big topic of my essay—which I thought was love. And I kind of named a problem in my first line. Then I just kind of introduced the story in the second line with my claim."

I nodded. "Did you try anything different in the others?'

"Well in the last one, especially, I tried to think even bigger into what could, like, connect to the world. And I thought about heroes and stuff, so I started there."

Debrief in a way that leaves students with a step-by-step guide that they can follow when crafting their own introductions.

I continued, "Now, Jamhil wants to make a good first impression with his introduction, so the first thing he wants to do is to sound like he knows what he's talking about. He first thought, 'What's the biggest thing I'm trying to say here?' Jamhil knew that it would be important to introduce the essay as being about something big. So he listed a few of the things that might be good to put up front: like defining what the word *admirable* means by naming things that fit that description, or saying why being admirable is important, or how reading can help us learn how to live life more fully.

"Jamhil then decided what he wanted to highlight—to pop out—and you'll need to make these choices as well. And then, finally, he generated a list of possible leads and chose the one that best represented what he wanted to say in his essay. You ready to try this?"

ACTIVE ENGAGEMENT

Channel students to think about their own essay by first thinking of the essay's larger landscape. Ask them to work with partners to begin to generate lists of possible leads.

"So quickly, jot a few possible general ideas you could say that your essay addresses. In a minute you'll talk to your partner. You did this work a few days ago when you were generating your claims. You reflected on what the larger, more universal ideas in your story and now your essay are. This isn't new work!"

After a moment I said, "Okay, so work with your partner, taking the idea you picked and practicing at least one way your introduction can go. Start by talking about the world or life in general. Don't forget that you know how to spin problems and motivations and life lessons so they are universal, applicable to everyone. Your introduction, too, needs to have universality. 'In life, many people . . .' 'Life is . . .' 'Across the world, many people struggle with . . .' 'The words of the song are true . . .' Try writing-in-the-air an introduction like that now. Partner 2, you go first."

Listening in on the partner talk, I coached in, saying things like "How does that idea affect you? Maybe you could add a line about that, like saying, 'In my life I have always . . . and in the story . . .'" Or "Remember the work we did defining our terms the other day? That is great work to do in your intro. Try saying '(The problem) means . . .'"

LINK

Remind students of the work of the day by summarizing the steps of the lesson. Then, ask them to recall and name what they know about revision.

"So listen up, writers. Today you'll be doing the important work of revising. One way—just one way—to get started is to revise your introductory paragraph.

"If you decide to do that, remember to start by talking about life itself, the world, or many people. You are probably situating your essay by saying many people struggle with whatever your character struggles with or learns about.

"But remember, there are plenty of other ways to revise an essay. Right now, list four other smart types of revision work that people in this room could be doing today. Turn and talk."

The class talked. After a few minutes, I called over the hubbub, asking, "How many of you will be rereading your essay to make sure you have exactly cited the text, unpacking those quotes to show how they go with the idea you are trying to make?" Some students signaled that they planned to do this, and I waved them off to get started, quickly.

Then I suggested other forms of revision, and one by one sent the students who would be doing that work off to their seats to get started. "How many of you will be making sure that you use a variety of elaborations—including stories, examples, quotes, lists, and so forth? "How many of you will be working on an introduction?" Once the meeting area was empty, I headed off to help the writers.

If you find that your students struggle to name an idea in their writing, you could always use the writing you have been doing together, the essay you have been crafting about "Raymond's Run." Or you could go back to the essay that was crafted in essay boot camp, about "The Three Little Pigs." Because that fairy tale is a simplistic one they know well, it may be easier for them to come up with the themes addressed in their writing.

Addressing Struggles

IN THIS SESSION, we are reaching for rigorous, sophisticated work—both in our hopes for our students' introductions as well as in their ability to lean on a repertoire of revision strategies. This being the case, during conferring you will want to be ready to address the struggles that will arise in both areas. For your students who struggle to broaden their discussion of the theme in their essay for the introduction, you can help them to see that there are other ways to introduce a text. They can retell a central moment that highlights their claim, followed by a clear restating of the claim itself, or they can always lean on the tried-and-true introduction that states the claim and the supports for the claim clearly and succinctly from the get-go. The point is that while we want to push our students to write powerful introductions, this is not the end-all, be-all strategy for revision, and many of your students will need manageable ways to write clear, strong introductions relatively quickly so that they can move on to more essential revision work for their writing, such as making sure they have explained their evidence thoughtfully or added quotes powerfully.

With this is mind, I sat next to Frankie. There were multiple drafts of his introduction revision in front of him, and I took the time to compliment his grit. I asked if he thought any of these were working, and his response was a defeated shrug. I followed up by asking him what he thought the most important thing was for him to do today in his revision work, and he pointed to his second and third body paragraph.

"I haven't finished these yet really," Frankie stated. I nodded, complimenting his ability to assess the work in front of him. "Remember, if you feel like things aren't working, like the strategies you've tried out for crafting your introduction don't quite fit, reach for another one. Another option could be to set those introductions aside for a moment and move on to the more important work you felt you needed to get to today. Sometimes taking a break from a portion of your writing that you've been laboring over is just the thing you need to clear your head. So the choice is yours. Work through

MID-WORKSHOP TEACHING Using Academic Language

"Writers, you are learning to use techniques for writing introductions and conclusions that some students don't learn until they're in high school or college. And here's one more trick for your toolbox: your essay will be more powerful if you use the words of your trade.

"This applies to almost any endeavor, even the chicken business. For instance, my eleven-year-old niece and nephew are pretty serious about raising and breeding chickens. They want to be taken seriously by other poultry breeders so they can purchase good birds from them and sell their birds for a good price. As a result, when Melissa and Nick write and speak to adult poultry breeders, they use the words of their trade. They say things like, 'This bird has strong coloring on the undercoat, and its vent is clean and pink.' Or they'll say confidently to a breeder, 'We are looking for a good showmanship bird, one with smooth legs and a good head.'

"Same thing applies in the literary essay business. If you want your literary essays to be taken seriously, use the words of your trade. The main character, as you will recall, is the *protagonist*. The text is written in the voice of the *narrator*. The start of the story is its *lead*. You might describe a story by speaking of its *setting*, *plot*, *theme*, or *point of view*. So one thing you can do as you're revising is to read over your draft and see if you've used the words available to you, and make sure that you have included the vital information of the text you are studying in your essay—the title, genre, and author's name."

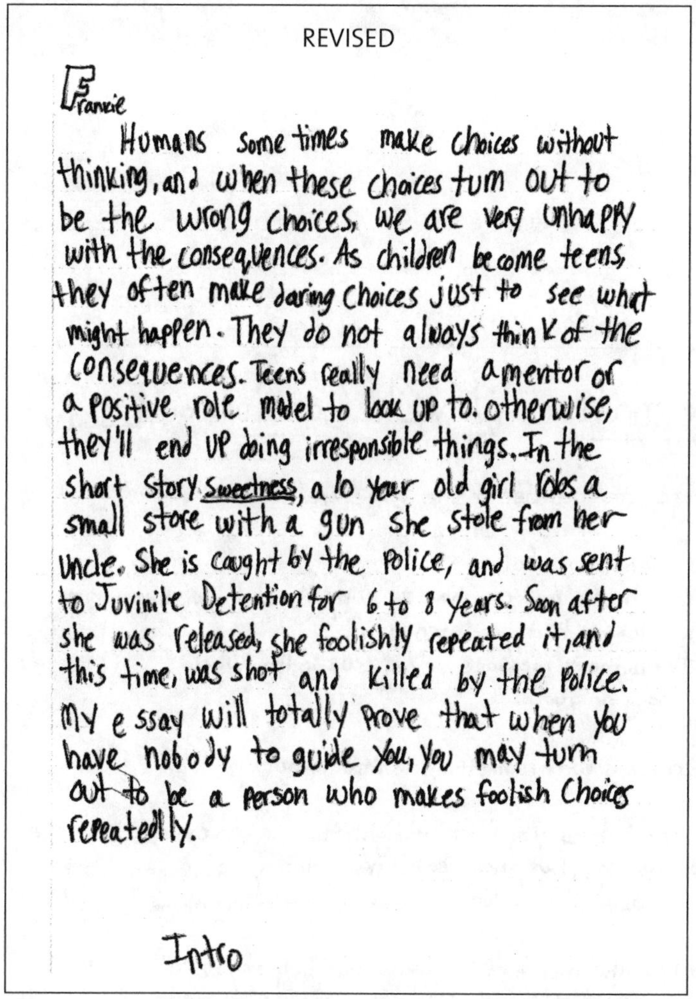

REVISED

⌐5
Frankie

Humans some times make choices without thinking, and when these choices turn out to be the wrong choices, we are very unhappy with the consequences. As children become teens, they often make daring choices just to see what might happen. They do not always think of the consequences. Teens really need a mentor or a positive role model to look up to. otherwise, they'll end up doing irresponsible things. In the short story _Sweetness_, a 10 year old girl robs a small store with a gun she stole from her uncle. She is caught by the police, and was sent to Juvinile Detention for 6 to 8 years. Soon after she was released, she foolishly repeated it, and this time, was shot and killed by the police. My essay will totally prove that when you have nobody to guide you, you may turn out to be a person who makes foolish choices repeatedly.

Intro

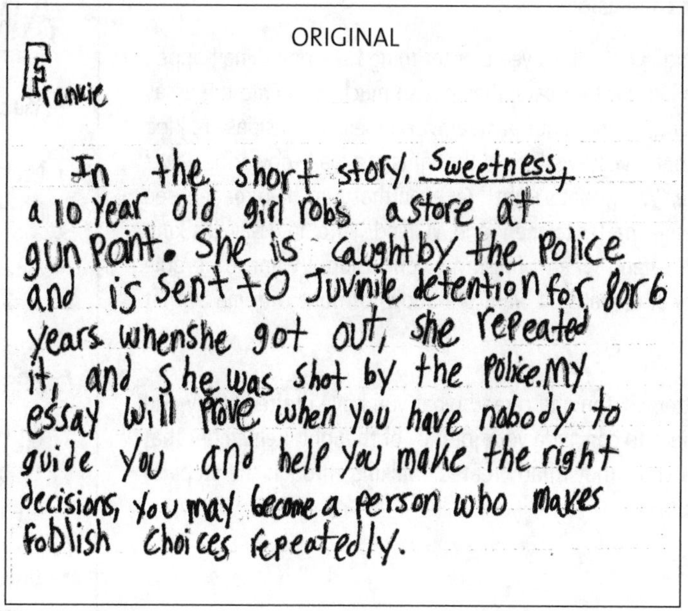

ORIGINAL

⌐5
Frankie

In the short story, _Sweetness,_ a 10 year old girl robs a store at gun point. She is caught by the police and is sent to Juvinile detention for 8 or 6 years when she got out, she repeated it, and she was shot by the police. My essay will prove when you have nobody to guide you and help you make the right decisions, you may become a person who makes foolish choices repeatedly.

FIG. 10–1   Frankie's original and reworked introductions

another introduction? Or move onto your body revision work and then come back to your introduction later."

Frankie looked back down at his papers, then up at me. "I think I'm going to try writing another introduction. If that doesn't work, I'll move onto the body and then come back." Seeming relieved, he got right to work.

An introduction will most likely not take the entire period to write, however, so you will want to be ready to help students be able to lean on their other revision strategies

as they continue working. This is tough for some kids. Their minds go blank and they begin to change a word here and there, to look for spelling issues. Gather a small group of students and ask them to try to name some of the strategies they have learned in the past. Feel free to heavily coach this work, asking, "How many of you have ever reread your piece aloud to be sure it flows the way you want it to?" or "Have any of you tried making sure you are using all of the strategies you learned in writing narrative in your retelling of scenes?" Collect a few ideas and then let kids set goals for the rest of writing workshop time. Some teachers even get the students started writing right in the small group, going from writer to writer, coaching individually as they go.

Writing Conclusions

Tell students that literary essayists craft their conclusions with care. List some choices writers have for their conclusions.

"Can I warn you about something? Over all my years of teaching I see one thing happen over and over. Sometimes when kids write essays, they put so much work into the essay itself that when they get to the end, they run out of steam, and their conclusions are kind of, well, yuck. But it's essential that an essayist's final thoughts are really powerful—that they leave the reader feeling like, 'Wow, that's right!' Or even that they help readers see why this essay or story might really matter to the world. When I write an essay, it's kind of like I think of myself as an MC, and when I finish my conclusion, I want to be able to walk off stage and hear roars of applause. I want the audience right with me at that crowning moment.

"The conclusions you write matter. So, tonight, reread what you have drafted today and then make a strong final statement to conclude your journey of thought. Remember that you have choices." I revealed a chart that I had created, walking through the steps of writing an effective essay conclusion.

Alternative Ways to Conclude an Essay

- Restate the broader theme or generalization.

- Make connections to:
  - ~ Your thesis and emphasize why the claim matters or a life lesson that you learned
  - ~ The author's message or an issue in the world
  - ~ A song or quote

- Leave readers with something to think about.

- Tell about how you first thought this was an essay about the literal meaning, but then read it more closely and came to realize it is actually about a deeper theme. Restate that theme.

- Show how the theme of the essay has helped you rethink your own life. "I used to ... but this story is teaching me to ..."

- Find another way to say the theme, perhaps by bringing in the words of a song, a line from a poem, or another book or movie that makes this same point. This story teaches readers... The words of the song are true: "No man is an island. No man stands alone."

- Suggest a further way of acting (From now on, I will ...) or of thinking, or a new question.

"Let's take a look at a few versions of a conclusion I drafted for my essay. I have printed these out for you to use tonight as you write conclusions. Yes that's right, for homework." I put my copy on the document camera.

Conclusions Three Ways

1. In "Raymond's Run" we learn that being protective can actually have negative consequences; you can end up building a wall around yourself and shutting out others. Like Squeaky, I used to think that if I built barriers I would be able to keep those who I felt could hurt me out. But in reality, I was only pushing away those people who cared about me. This story is teaching me how important it is to open up and let people in.

2. As you can see, one of the themes in "Raymond's Run" is that when you build walls around yourself and others, you don't just end up protecting yourself—you end up closing out the world. There is no guarantee that without walls, you won't get hurt. But what we learn from this story is that sometimes the possibility of getting hurt is worth the risk, because you never know how you can grow, or who you can become or who you can be friends with, without taking a chance.

3. In "Raymond's Run," we watch as Squeaky learns to open up—to stop being so protective that she builds a wall around herself and those she loves. This story teaches us that even a little crack in the wall will do—that a simple smile or a change in thinking could have big results. We can all learn from Squeaky, even if we are not pushing everyone away all of the time. We can all learn to take a risk in our lives and to open up to others a little bit more. Only then will we see the true smiles all around us.

"Take a moment and name with your partner which strategies you see me using in these conclusions and which one you think you will try first tonight. Refer to the 'Alternative Ways to Conclude an Essay' chart if you find yourself having trouble specifically naming the strategies I tried out."

At the end of the share, I reconvened students and asked for their input updating our chart on how to write a literary essay. Soon the chart looked like this:

If you think your students won't be able to hold onto the steps of writing a conclusion, then you might want to create a chart listing the steps and display it during the share so students can refer to it as they try to write their conclusions. Suggest that these students jot these points down in their notebooks so they can refer to them as they do their homework tonight.

How to Write a Theme-Based Literary Essay

- Think about the character's motivations, problems, and lessons learned and look for patterns.

- What does the character want, and what gets in the way?

- How does the character try to resolve his problems?

- What lessons does the character learn from trying to resolve his problems?

- Now what patterns can you see?

- Think about the patterns you see in universal terms. Ask yourself, "What big life lessons—what themes—can readers draw from the patterns in the story?"

- Then craft a claim based on one of the themes.

- Search for the most compelling evidence that can support the claim, then add it to the essay like this:
  - Quote some parts of the text.
  - Story-tell other parts.
  - Summarize yet other parts.

- To write an introduction to your essay, start with a universal statement about life and then transition to the text-based claim itself, focusing on the story you are writing about.

- To write a conclusion to your essay, show connections in at least one of these ways:
  - Your thesis and emphasize why the claim and evidence matter
  - Yourself and the life lesson you learned or realized
  - The author's message
  - Leave readers with something to think about

WRITING A POWERFUL CONCLUSION

"Sometimes you don't know how powerful an idea can be until you see it on the page and it takes your breath away. Tonight, draft a conclusion to your essay. Come up with a few different conclusions that leave readers with a new idea to consider or something to think about. Reread your final paragraph with each of your ending sentence options, and find one that, when you see it on the page, takes your breath away."

Quoting Texts

QUOTES ARE INCREDIBLY POWERFUL. At times, they are indelible.

> I have a dream that one day this nation will rise up and live out the true meaning of its creed: "We hold these truths to be self-evident, that all men are created equal."
>
> —Martin Luther King, Jr.

> Ask not what your country can do for you, ask what you can do for your country.
>
> —John F. Kennedy

What we say matters. We hold on to what we hear people say. Their words inspire us, challenge us to think, spur us to action. And when essayists aim to convey big ideas—to support a claim about a text in ways that will compel and persuade a reader—words matter enormously.

In this session, you will teach your class that a cornerstone of essay writing is the ability to powerfully and succinctly quote from a text. You will convey that while it is a good start, it's not enough to simply say, "Because in the text it says," and then to drop in a direct quote. For starters, the quote needs to be apt, to exactly fit. Your teaching, then, will focus on teaching students to use quotes judiciously and to explore the relationship between the quote and the claim. You will teach students that essayists find parts of the text that will best highlight their evidence or thinking—ones that will prove their claim. Always, they ask, "Does this quote serve to back up a fact or idea I am trying to convey to the reader?" Students will learn, too, that after using just the part of the text that supports their point, they also need to generate an explanation or to reveal their thinking, giving the reader context.

During the day's mid-workshop teaching, they'll learn that it is essential to quote not just in context but also accurately, so that the author's intended meaning is preserved.

IN THIS SESSION, you'll teach students that essayists use quotations from the text to support their ideas, choosing just key parts of a quotation and providing the context for how that bit of text supports their thinking.

GETTING READY

✔ Two quotes from "Raymond's Run" (see Teaching)

✔ The texts students worked with in previous sessions (see Active Engagement)

✔ Student's essay drafts, writer's notebooks, and pens or highlighters (see Active Engagement)

✔ Copies of "Raymond's Run" for students who need support on working with quotations (see Conferring and Small-Group Work)

✔ Examples of student work (before and after excerpts), an enlarged copy written on chart paper or displayed for the class (see Share)

COMMON CORE STATE STANDARDS: W.6.1.b,c; W.6.4, W.6.9.a, RL.6.1, RL.6.2, RL.6.5, SL.6.1, SL.6.3, SL.6.4, L.6.1, L.6.2, L.6.3

Students might ask themselves, "Do I understand this part of the text the way it was intended—and am I quoting it in a way that the meaning is also clear to the reader?"

"What we say matters. We hold on to what we hear people say."

This emphasis on context and accuracy is an effort to both streamline the syntax of quotes students include and to be sure students are not misquoting characters or authors, thus weakening, not bolstering, their claim. The most important message, though, of today's teaching is that essayists rely on the power of the text—its carefully selected words—to craft powerfully worded essays.

Quoting Texts

CONNECTION

Rally kids to see that a quote can capture the essence of a person by channeling them to think of a person in their life who has a frequent refrain, suggesting that the person's life reveals a bit about who they are.

"Today's minilesson will help you use quotes from the stories you are studying in powerful ways—and in ways that support your thinking. Quotes are a big deal. And not just in literary essays. I am willing to bet that right here, right now, you could think of something that someone in your life always says, a quote that that person is kind of famous for. Maybe it is an adult in your life, or your best friend who always says the craziest things.

"For me, I'm thinking of my mom. Whenever I mess up in a way that she used to do as a kid, she always says, 'You come by it honestly.' It's a sweet way of telling me I am not alone in messing up that way, that she'd been there too.

"Can you take a second and talk with your partner? Is there someone in your life who always says something? And here's the important part—what does the quote show about that person?"

I listened in as students talked, some struggling to think of a quote, most sharing either sage advice or wild statements, from "Don't count your chickens before they are hatched" to "YOLO" (you only live once).

I gathered the class together. "What I noticed is that you didn't quote your mom saying 'Clean up your room!' or 'I'll pick you up at six!' Instead, you quoted the memorable lines that capture the person, the speaker. Essayists try to do just that in their essays."

This connection is essentially a little keynote address on the power of well-selected quotes. Notice, however, that you are keeping your students as engaged as possible. You do this by getting them thinking about their own lives, by switching from generalizations to examples, by keeping your pace brisk. One of the interesting things to notice is that the skills involved in writing a minilesson are actually not unlike those involved in writing an essay. Big point, example, unpack the example . . .

❧ **Name the teaching point.**

"Today I want to teach you that essayists know that the words of a text matter, and they make careful decisions, choosing powerful quotes or parts of quotes, to support their thinking."

TEACHING

Walk students through the process of selecting quotes that support their thinking. Demonstrate how you first choose an idea from your essay that you want to support with quotes and then go back into the text to find the appropriate quotes.

"Let's try this with our new essay about 'Raymond's Run.' We could add quotes to any part of the essay, so let's just pick the first body paragraph. Here it is":

> At the start of Raymond's Run, we see just how protective Squeaky is as a protagonist. She is tough. She will fight you if you challenge her. Like when she talks about fighting people all of the time. She is also really conceited. She feels better than everyone else, especially when she runs. These examples show that Squeaky is tough, and they also show her own special breed of toughness. She is tough in a way that is loveable because it is so filled with her funny personality. The examples also show that her toughness comes because she has a hard life and she used toughness to handle her life challenges. Being protective and tough seems at first like the only way she can keep herself and her family together.

"So now that we have picked which part of our essay we are going to be working with, which aspect of our thinking we want to back up with a few quotes, we need to go back to the story, pulling out a quote or two that can back up the idea.

"So I'm looking for quotes to support my idea that at the beginning of the story, we see how tough and conceited Squeaky is. I am going to focus on the conceited part, I think. If we are looking for quotes to show how Squeaky at first wanted to be better than everyone, we can look to the start of the story for those quotes. Reread together, and see what you see." As the students worked, I flipped over a piece of chart paper. "I found many of the same quotes as you just found," I said, pointing to the chart paper.

"Let's take a look at two of the quotes that I pulled from the story." I turned back to the chart pad, where I had copied two quotes, leaving enough space underneath each one so that I could do some writing off of them.

> "So as far as everyone is concerned, I'm the fastest and that goes for Gretchen too, who has put out the tale that she is going to win the first place medal this year. Ridiculous."
>
> "I always win cause I'm the best,' I say straight at Gretchen who is, as far as I am concerned, the only one talking in this ventriloquist dummy routine."

Demonstrate deciding how to select the whole quote or the part of the quote—based on what best supports the claim, compelling language, and fit.

"Let's see, if I take my first quote, 'So as far as everyone is concerned, I'm the fastest and that goes for Gretchen too, who has put out the tale that she is going to win the first place medal this year. Ridiculous.' I need to first stop and ask myself, 'Does this *whole* quotation fit? Or is there just a part of it that really shows the theme that it is better to be yourself than to try and be better than others?

"Hmm . . . What do you think?" I said, and gave students some time to think while I did as well. As their hands started to go up, I asked Crystal to share. "It is really the middle part that is the best."

I underlined that part: "I'm the fastest and that goes for Gretchen too." "Does this part show how, in the beginning of the story, Squeaky is conceited?" The class nodded.

"I could put in the whole quotation, but when a quote is long, it can make things bulky. So it's cool to choose just the best bits of the quote sometimes, kind of like when you are choosing which parts of the turkey to eat at Thanksgiving."

Show students the power of contextualizing their quotes. Falter deliberately to emphasize that brevity is the goal.

"So I've got the part of the quote I want to use, and now I want to really set it up. To set up my quote, I'm both going to name what part of the idea this quote supports, and then in the briefest possible way, I'm going to tell what is going on in the story. Let me see, to name the part of the idea I could say, 'In the beginning of the story, all Squeaky cares about is being better than everyone.' And then to tell what is going on in the story, I could say, 'Squeaky is thinking about what a great runner she is, how she is a much better runner than everyone else. She is even better than Gretchen, who is also supposed to be a good runner. But not as good as Squeaky.'" I quickly jotted my writing on the chart pad, directly under the quote.

"Wait a second, this is getting clunky. I'm going to try now to just use a phrase, a few words, to set up the scene. Hmm . . . what is a phrase that I could use—real short—to set up the scene for this quote? Margaret?"

"You could just say, 'It's not enough for Squeaky to be good at running—she has to be the best—better than you' and then put in the good part of the quote."

Debrief by making the point that the work you have just done with quotes shows what essayists do to make their writing more powerful.

"That feels better to me. See how I framed my quote, both with the part of the idea it supports and the context of the scene it comes from? This is the way essayists work with powerful quotes to support their ideas."

At the start of Raymond's Run, we see just how protective Squeaky is as a protagonist. She is tough. She will fight you if you challenge her. Like when she talks about fighting people all of

Teachers, you'll notice that I try to make this process visible to students. I slow down a process that normally happens very quickly, under the radar. I make a show of thinking aloud, conveying that this is not a simple, one-step process. Then too, I want my students to learn from the questions I ask myself and the ways I try out different possibilities before settling on a juicy quote or the most delicious bit of a quote.

the time. She is also really conceited. She feels better than everyone else, especially when she runs. It's not enough for Squeaky to be good at running—she has to be the best—better than you. She says, "I'm the fastest and that goes for Gretchen too." These examples show that Squeaky is tough, and they also show her own special breed of toughness. She is tough in a way that is loveable because it is so filled with her funny personality. The examples also show that her toughness comes because she has a hard life and she used toughness to handle her life challenges. Being protective and tough seems at first like the only way she can keep herself and her family together.

ACTIVE ENGAGEMENT

Set students up to practice finding and using quotes for their own literary essays, repeating the process you demonstrated.

"Okay, so I am going to leave my example up here on the easel for you to use today. Right now, I want to make sure you feel comfortable with this move. So let's walk through this again, step by step. First step, figure out what idea in your essay you are working on, which part you want to add quotes to. Thumbs up when you have that figured out." I paused, giving students a moment to do this preliminary piece. When thumbs were up, I continued on. "Okay, now take three minutes here in the meeting area and try this out in your notebook. Find a quote that supports your idea, and then write out how you might incorporate it into your essay. Be sure to frame the idea it supports and set up the context of the scene. Try it now."

LINK

Send writers off to work, reminding them of the full array of potential activities they can select from to strengthen their essays.

"So, writers, anytime you are quoting someone—whether it is an author or your mother—you have to be sure that you are focusing on the part of the quote that matches the idea you are trying to highlight, and you also have to pay attention to the context of what was said. Today you are going to be working on writing off of each reason you have for your claim, and as you do, I'd like you to focus in on using quotes to back up your thinking as well. To help you, I am going to leave up my example from today's lesson, as well as the mentor conclusion paragraph from yesterday's share. You should be aiming your writing toward those two marks today as you work."

At times in our active engagements, we will want our students to roll up their sleeves and get started working right in front of us. This way, they are close enough that we can address issues as they come up, and meanwhile they will be working on their pieces, not rehearsing for the work to come.

Finding and Selecting Powerful Quotes

A S YOU CONFER TODAY, you may find that whereas most students are able to quickly locate quotations in the text that support their arguments, other students struggle to do so. This latter group may follow your instruction about placing quotations in context, but without the understanding of how one *first* decides what parts of a text support an argument, they will be at a loss to replicate the work themselves. You might gather these students together for a strategy lesson in which you give them practice locating quotations that go with an idea. You could present them with a simpler idea than the one you used to model—or a fact, even—say, "Squeaky is a

serious runner" or "Squeaky thinks she's a talented runner"—and then give them a few sections of the text that have easy-to-identify lines that support this. In this way, you will be setting these kids up to locate quotes that support a more literal statement first, which will scaffold the work. If they're confused, suggest that they look for any parts in which Squeaky mentions running. From here, you could set them up to find quotations that support a related idea—say, "Toward the end of 'Raymond's Run' Squeaky learns to make way for other runners besides herself." Give students the last page of the story and see if they can identify the lines that support that idea.

(continues)

MID-WORKSHOP TEACHING   Quoting with Attention to Accuracy

"Writers, I have a funny story for you, but it's actually essential to the work you are doing, so listen up. Last night I was instant messaging a few of you while you were doing your homework. This was a part of my conversation with Cindy about whether or not she had to do her math homework."

Me: I'm sure that is not what Ms. Burns (the math teacher) said.

Cindy: OMG yes it was!

Me: What did she say exactly?

Cindy: She said, and I quote, "Don't do it if you don't want to."

"Here is the thing: I know for a fact that Ms. Burns would *never* say that if you don't feel like doing your homework you don't have to." The class laughed.

"But I also know that Cindy is as honest as they get. So as we got to the bottom of this mystery, we realized that what Cindy had missed was what came *right before* this quote. Ms. Burns had said, 'So that is your homework for the night. You could

also do the assignment on the board, but it is extra credit, so *don't do it if you don't want to.*'

"What Cindy had missed was the *context* of the quote. She had just pulled out one phrase without understanding what the bigger picture was, and this caused a bunch of confusion, right, Cindy?" She nodded, saying, "I did my homework, FYI," and the class laughed.

"So here's what you need to know. You've got to quote accurately. Just like when you read a text closely to analyze it, you must read it equally closely to quote it. Remember, each and every word was carefully chosen by the author, and it means something. So when you lift out a section of text to support your thinking, ask yourself, 'Do I understand this part of the text the way it was intended?' And then, if the answer is 'yes,' ask yourself, 'Am I quoting it in a way that the meaning is *also* clear to the reader?' Then make sure you put the quote in context, maybe weaving in bits of explanation to make the quote crystal clear."

And it occurs to me, watching how smoothly he climbs hand over hand and remembering how he looked running with his arms down to his side and with the wind pulling his mouth back and his teeth showing and all, it occurred to me that Raymond would make a very fine runner.

And by the time he comes over I'm jumping up and down so glad to see him—my brother Raymond, a great runner in the family tradition.

And I smile. Cause she's good, no doubt about it. Maybe she'd like to help me coach Raymond; she obviously is serious about running, as any fool can see.

Once they have successfully followed these steps, they should be able to tackle this work in their own stories, looking across a larger swath of text for quotations that "go with" their idea.

Meanwhile, you will surely encounter students who are able to find support-driven quotations but who could use support selecting the most powerful, precise quotes possible. It may be just a matter of encouraging these kids to slow down and look for several quotes that support the argument before selecting one. You might point to several parts of the text they are reading and say, "Read each of these aloud." Then, "If I were to ask you to rank these from most powerful support to least, what rating would you give each one?" Here you will be asking students to do work they did in Session 5, in a slightly different (though related) context.

Minding the Gaps in Essays

Channel students to look back over their essays, noticing areas where there may be gaps. Show an example of this using a student's essay as a model.

"In England, whenever people are getting off a train, the conductor says, 'Mind the gap.' What that means is that there is usually a space between the train and the platform, and this is a warning to be aware of it as you leave the train, or else you could hurt yourself.

"The same is true in essays. Often, after you have drafted there are gaps in portions of your essays, and if you don't fill those gaps, your essays are going to be tough to read and understand. A gap in an essay is usually a place where you haven't highlighted the most applicable part of a scene for your evidence or a place where you haven't explained your thinking well enough, usually when you are analyzing your evidence.

"Let me show you what Hilda did today. She was looking at her essay and came across this paragraph (See Figure 11–1).

"She noticed that when she was analyzing her evidence, she didn't really explain how it shows that without guidance, people can make bad choices. So she went back and added a bit more (See Figure 11–2).

Hilda

Sweetness teaches us a lesson about how without having the proper guidence you can make bad choices even though you are a good person deep down inside. One way Sweetness shows us this is when she saves a baby. In the story it said "Sweetness used to hang out there dause it was quiet, something her house never was. Sweetness figured the baby was glad to see some one, anyone". This makes me relize that you can't jude a book by it's cover because Sweetness made bad choices but that didn't mean that she was a good person in the inside.

FIG. 11–1 Hilda's original body paragraph

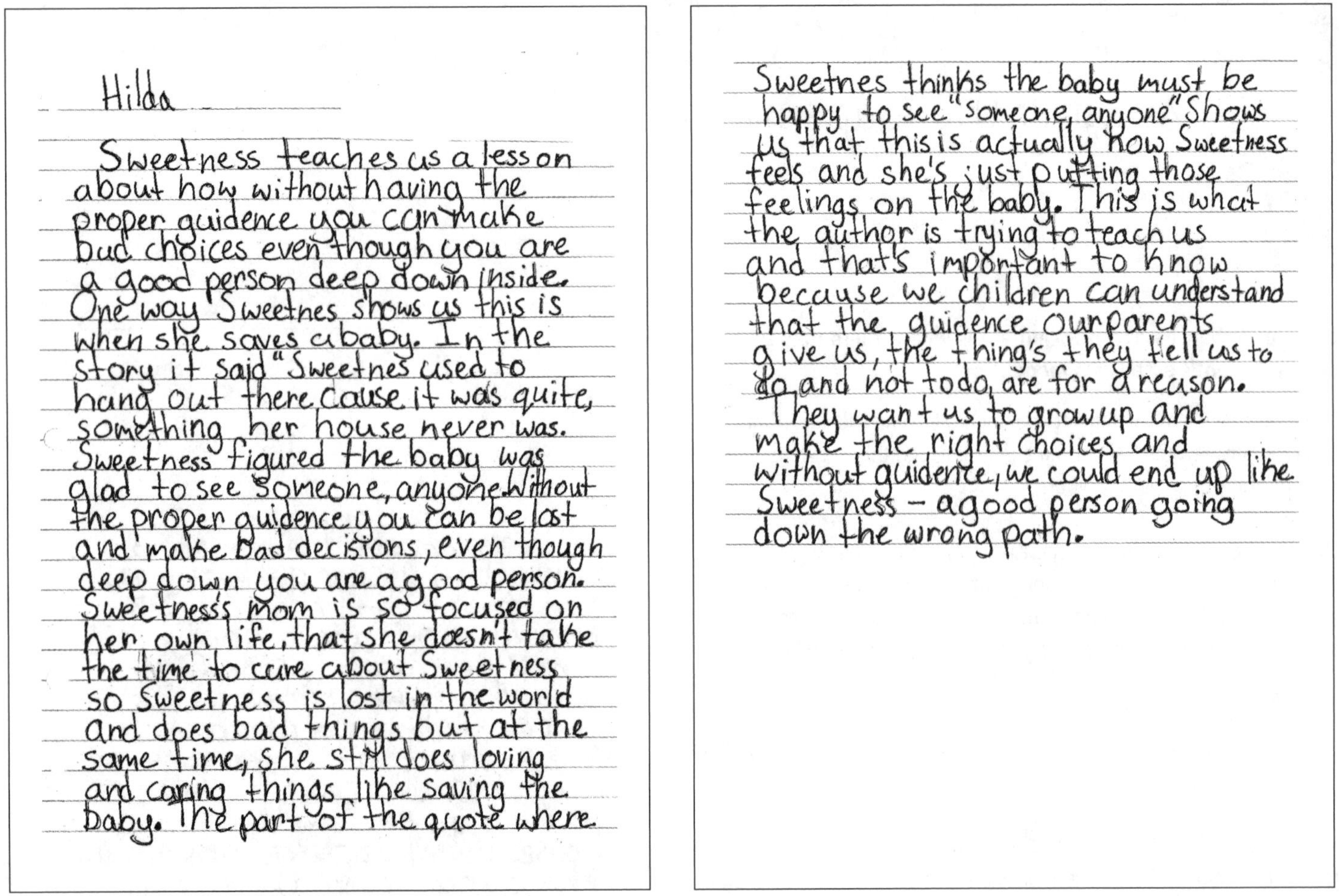

Hilda

Sweetness teaches us a lesson about how without having the proper guidence you can make bad choices even though you are a good person deep down inside. One way Sweetnes shows us this is when she saves a baby. In the story it said "Sweetnes used to hang out there cause it was quite, something her house never was. Sweetness figured the baby was glad to see someone, anyone. Without the proper guidence you can be lost and make bad decisions, even though deep down you are a good person. Sweetness's mom is so focused on her own life, that she doesn't take the time to care about Sweetness so Sweetness is lost in the world and does bad things but at the same time, she still does loving and caring things like saving the baby. The part of the quote where

Sweetnes thinks the baby must be happy to see "someone, anyone" Shows us that this is actually how Sweetness feels and she's just putting those feelings on the baby. This is what the author is trying to teach us and that's important to know because we children can understand that the guidence our parents give us, the things they tell us to do and not todo, are for a reason. They want us to grow up and make the right choices and without guidence, we could end up like Sweetness – a good person going down the wrong path.

FIG. 11–2   Hilda's body paragraph after deeper analysis of the evidence

FINDING AND FILLING IN THE GAPS IN YOUR ESSAYS

"Right now, and then tonight for homework, read over your essay, probably multiple times, stopping every so often and asking, 'Is there a gap here?' And then if you find a gap, for Pete's sake—fill it! This is not a strategy you can choose *not* to do. Every writer pores over their drafts looking for places where they may have not explained themselves well, and you will too. Come in tomorrow with your essay revised, ready to edit your piece. I can't wait to see what you do."

Editing Inquiry Centers

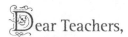 ear Teachers,

Oh, we can well imagine the knot in your stomachs as you get ready to teach your students to edit their writing. Somehow, this work never feels good enough. There is so much to teach, it seems, and then what is taught often doesn't seem to stick. Many believe that students learn conventions best by being immersed in reading and writing, and many educators also think that students need help to notice the conventions in the text they are immersed in, or else it all just washes over them. It can feel like a losing battle, but one that teachers are destined to march toward nevertheless. It is your Waterloo, your Antietam.

But it does not have to be. Here we encourage you to think outside of the box a bit when considering how to teach your students to edit their pieces. We encourage you to consider what may not have worked so far—editing checklists and direct instruction. Instead, you may want to consider some new teaching methods, teaching methods that might be more suited to help students learn better control of conventions.

This session draws from the ideas and lessons discussed in Mary Ehrenworth and Vicki Vinton's *The Power of Grammar* (Heinemann 2005). In that text, the authors argue that students need more than direct instruction to get new convention moves into their natural writing style; they need to be pushed to pay attention to how the conventions work, say in inquiry, and then they need a chance to apprentice themselves to those conventions in their own writing.

This session attempts to address both needs—inquiry and apprenticeship—by setting students up to work in centers, where they look at a snippet of text that exemplifies a certain convention they need to pay close attention to and then try that work in their own writing. This is a high-energy day, with students moving from one center to another, working with partners to name what they see, and then quick as they can editing their own pieces to reflect what they noticed.

COMMON CORE STATE STANDARDS: W.6.1, W.6.5, RL.6.10, SL.6.1, L.6.1, L.6.2, L.6.3, L.6.6

MINILESSON

To help start off the day's learning, you might highlight the importance of having control over our conventions. You could tell a story of a time when you went on a job interview, dressed carelessly, and how you were summarily rejected. You could show photos of people dressed for an important meeting versus dressed for Sunday football on the couch, and then show them two paragraphs—one with flawless conventions and one with many obvious and careless errors. Whatever story you tell, make the point that the care writers put into the conventions of writing shows how seriously they take both the piece and the reader, and that today you are going to give your class a few ways to be sure their conventions are on point. Tell students that they'll learn to use mentor texts to see how rules are applied and will then edit their own essays based on the information they've gathered.

Because today is focused on centers, most of your work will be behind the scenes. You will first need to have assessed which conventions are of the utmost importance for your students to focus on. Most likely you will know this already from your conferences and small groups. If you do not have a firm grasp on what your students need, you might consider collecting a few of their drafts to look over. Remember that you are on the lookout first for the conventions issues that interfere with meaning. While *its* versus *it's* might be your pet peeve, if your students are struggling with verb tense, focus on that much more important issue first. Often in essays, students struggle with the punctuation in direct quotes, with the flexibility of verb tense demanded in essay writing, and as always, with commas in complex sentences.

To set up your centers, you will need examples of each of these conventions in action in an essay. It can be the mentor essay, the essay you have been writing, or really any literary essay, so long as it illustrates the conventions you are focusing on. You will also need a brief description of the "rules" those examples highlight. For instance, to set up your "punctuation in direct quotes" center, you will need copies of the example from your essay that contains this convention:

> In the beginning of the story, all Squeaky cares about is being better than everyone. When she runs into the girls in the street, she brags out loud by saying, "I always win cause I'm the best," and she insults the girls in her head when she calls the conversation, "this ventriloquist dummy routine."

. . . along with a brief description of the convention that you want students to focus on:

Punctuating Quotations

1. Only the portion that comes directly from the text goes inside the quotation marks.
2. If the quote comes in the middle of a sentence, set it up with a comma.
3. If the sentence continues after the quote, set up the rest of the sentence with a comma inside the quote.
4. If the sentence ends after the quote, end it with a period inside the quotation mark.

◆ Punctuating Quotations

1. Only the portion that comes directly from the text goes inside the quotation marks.

2. If the quote comes in the middle of a sentence, set it up with a comma.

3. If the sentence continues after the quote, set up the rest of the sentence with a comma inside the quote.

4. If the sentence ends after a quote, end it with a period inside the quotation mark.

You will need these two supports at every center. Next, divide your class into groups that will travel through the centers together. At each center, students will look at the mentor text and annotate the places where they see the rules happening. Then, they will look to their essays and either mark the places where they correctly use the conventions they are studying or edit their piece to try and get a better grasp on the convention.

Your teaching point can be along the lines of, "Today you are going to focus on doing some editing work in your essays. But we're taking a different approach from what we've done before, your essay in one hand, pen and editing checklist in the other. Just like you learned how to structure and craft your essays by studying the writing of other essayists, you can learn about editing and conventions by studying mentor essays, too.

"Now you'll do some research into the conventions that you are editing for, studying them in context, and then applying what you are learning to your own essay. In your small groups, essay and pen in hand, you'll go from table to table, using the mentor text and the rules list to study and understand the highlighted convention.

"After you have a handle on the rules associated with the convention, turn to your own essay. Are you applying this convention and using it properly and powerfully in your own essays? If you are, fantastic! And if you are not, make that edit. Each group will go to each center today, and you will not leave your center until everyone in your group has edited their essay for that center's theme. You are going to help each other."

You also might, depending on your class, model how to do the central work of this session, which is to learn from a mentor text and use that learning in your own writing. You might take a different convention (or you could take one of the tougher centers, to give your class a leg up on the work), modeling how you notice the convention in the mentor text, and then look at your own writing to see what you can improve based on your inquiry. This might sound something like, "So one thing I saw in the mentor is that when you are retelling from the text, you usually try to use the past tense of the verbs, the action words. So let me see in my piece if I did that. Here is a place where I am retelling—oh wait, I see some present tense verbs here. Let me fix that now."

Then you will want to get the kids right to work. Have the groups begin working in their centers, and coach the groups to get started. Typically students have a tough time getting into this work and may need you to cheerlead them through each step the first time, saying things like, "Look to the mentor to see if you can find any examples of these rules, and circle or underline where you do!" and "Now quick, go to your essays. Where is a place you can look for this editing move in your work?"

CONFERRING AND SMALL-GROUP WORK

Because this session is set up as an inquiry, there will be students who struggle to put all of the pieces together. For instance, you will have writers who have a hard time "seeing" the conventions in the model. Others will be able to identify the rules in another text but may struggle to transfer that knowledge into their own writing. These will be the two camps of your conferring and small-group work today. Similarly to the "boot camp" lesson in Session 1, your conferring work will be on the fly, although you should feel empowered to take a student aside for a longer, more in-depth conference if need be. Mostly, though, you will be moving about the room, coaching students with leans prompts and suggestions, like "Can you point to where you see this rule?" and "Where in your piece do you think you could practice this?" Then, too, you might encourage students to help each other. Once a group has finished with its inquiry and is ready to transfer what they noticed into their own writing, you might have them take a moment to rehearse with a partner, even encouraging your students to help each other practice a few edits that give them trouble.

The stations you set up today will help your students to move through a few possible editing moves relatively quickly. However, your expectation will be that your class uses all that they know about editing to make their pieces as perfect and publishable as possible. Your class may need a bit of a reminder, though, to not only do the editing work of the stations. Use your mid-workshop teaching time to remind students that when writers edit their pieces, they bring to bear everything they have learned about conventions and spelling and grammar, and that their goal is ultimately to make their piece as perfect as they know how to make it.

SHARE

This work will take up much of the period, and so in this session you will want to set up your class for doing the work of editing more independently—both in the time you have left in class as well as for homework that night.

HOMEWORK

You might say, "So, writers, because you are editing right now, your work for the rest of class and tonight is to add these editing moves to the collection of things you look for in your writing when you edit. For homework you will be rewriting your piece, being sure to incorporate all of the work you have done this week, and especially today. I will be really excited to see your clean copies tomorrow, and to hear how this editing work went for you."

Good luck!
Kate and Kathleen

Building the Muscles to Compare and Contrast

IN THIS SESSION, you'll teach students that to compare and contrast, essayists notice the similarities and differences between their subjects, noting their significance, and then categorize their observations into patterns or ideas, in preparation to write a compare-and-contrast essay.

GETTING READY

✓ Concrete objects to model comparing and contrasting, for example, a glass of soda and a glass of juice or two different shirts (see Teaching and Active Engagement)

✓ Chart paper and markers (see Teaching, Active Engagement, and Share)

✓ A collection of concrete objects for students to compare and contrast, set up at individual tables so students can move from one table to the next in centers (see Link)

✓ Julia's comparison of Central Park and Grand Central Station as two important NYC landmarks (see Mid-Workshop Teaching) ◉

✓ Sentence strips and markers, for students to record what they've learned about comparing and contrasting (see Share)

✓ A sheet of chart paper with the heading "Tips for Comparing and Contrasting" (see Share) ◉

COMMON CORE STATE STANDARDS: W.6.2, W.6.4, W.6.9.a, W.6.10, RL.6.1, RL.6.3, SL.6.1, SL.6.2, SL.6.4, L.6.1, L.6.2, L.6.3

M Y FAMILY HAS A TRADITION. We have tasting tests. Each has a different name—the Chocolate Milk Debate, the Peanut Butter Challenge, the Lemonade Litmus Test—but the process is the same. Multiple brands are purchased and laid out before us, blindfolds are donned, and the test begins. We debate which brand is best, comparing one to the other, coming up with categories to compare as we go.

It is fascinating how much you learn about one thing by comparing it to something similar. While at first it seems as though the initial sip of chocolate milk is as delicious as a beverage can get, by the time you taste the third brand, you begin to see that chocolate milk has many layers of flavor—salty, sweet, chocolate-y—that all are in concert at different levels in different brands. By placing these brands next to each other and comparing them, you not only see where your chocolate milk preferences are, but you also learn a great deal about chocolate milk itself.

In some ways, it is also easier to see texts clearly when they are placed next to similar ones. Sometimes the stories you read seem so natural, so real, that it is tough to see them as manufactured by authors. Until you put Dumbledore next to Gandalf, it may seem that the wizard is just, well, Dumbledore. But when placed next to a text that has a similar character, you see something bigger than this character in this text. All of a sudden, next to Gandalf, Dumbledore seems weaker, more fallible, and much more political. And yet you also see that in both texts the wizard character is like this absentee parent—someone the hero desperately needs but rarely has around.

In this last bend of the unit, then, you will teach your students to use what they have learned about writing literary essays and apply those skills to an essay that compares two texts. This is a fast-paced bend—one that leans on what your students already know rather than teaching them loads of new strategies. But it also holds an important lesson—that readers and writers have a history of reading behind them, and that they use that knowledge to make comparisons as they read. Certainly, some of the inspiration for this work will come from the expectation on state assessments that students can do this work of comparing themes, characters, and craft moves in two texts. But more than this, the motivation for this bend comes from the power of the taste test—the clarity of thinking that comes when you lay two things side by side to discern how they are similar and how they are different.

To begin, you will use an everyday example as the focal point for a quick flash essay in which you talk your class through the basics of comparing texts in essay form. Much like the boot camp essay in Session 1, this work will help you to front-load a great deal of picky teaching into one engaging day and will also reveal to you who in your class needs a great

"In some ways, it is easier to see texts clearly when they are placed next to similar ones."

deal more support and who is ready to charge forth. This day, like Session 1, is comprised largely of high-energy whole-class work. Also like Session 1, this day is not meant for poetry; the writing here is quick and messy and is less an assessment of your students' skill as writers and more a sense of how they do with the thinking and structure of comparative lit essays.

Building the Muscles to Compare and Contrast

CONNECTION

Offer students an example of people comparing and contrasting in real life. Connect this example to the work they will be doing in their texts.

"The other day when I was walking to lunch I couldn't help but eavesdrop on a conversation I heard. Crystal and Diamond were debating which game was better—*Mass Effect* or *The Last of Us*, both great video games. What was really inspiring to me was how the two of them were thinking in these great categories when they were comparing the two games. They weren't just saying, '*Mass Effect* is better.' They were saying things like '*Mass Effect's* personalization is way better because you get to choose your character and how they respond, but *The Last of Us* has a better story, with better writing.'

"I bet you do this all of the time. You compare games, movies, singers, dancers, teams. Take a second right now and talk to your partner. What are two things that you might compare, might debate which is better than the other?" The class erupted in talk, loud and engaged. I listened in to a few quick conversations, then brought the class together. "Okay, so let's hear a few. What could you compare?"

Students offered suggestions like "Rihanna and Beyonce," "Giants and Jets," and "McDonalds and Burger King." I nodded. "One thing I notice is that when you compare something, you usually compare two kinds of similar things, right? No one said you debate which is better—Rihanna or the Giants?" The class laughed.

"So today we are going to start a new essay, one that I think you will like. It's a compare-and-contrast essay. Trust me—this is a kind of essay that you want to be able to write, and to write in a flash. It's a kind of essay that you'll be asked to write all through middle school, high school, and college, but more than this, it is a kind of essay that can help you develop really deep ideas about texts. You will learn how to do that over the next few days.

"Before we try this work on texts, though, I want to show you how writing a compare-and-contrast essay can also help you see everyday things a little differently. Things like soda and juice."

◆ COACHING

It is helpful to start with comparing things in real life before doing it with texts as you are teaching students to think in a structured way, which is challenging in and of itself. Kids have much more experience with this kind of comparison than with text comparisons, because kids don't tend to read literary essays, since they are not published.

❖ **Name the teaching point.**

"Today I want to teach you that writers can compare and contrast by putting two subjects side by side and asking, 'How are they similar? How are they different?' Then, they write in an organized way."

TEACHING

Invite students to compare two concrete objects you brought to the meeting area, asking them to notice the similarities and differences between them.

"Let's see how compare-and-contrast works with soda and juice," I said, revealing the two beverages, taste-test style, on a table in the front of the meeting area.

First, I picked up the glass of soda, and then the juice, turning each glass slowly as I inspected them with grave attention. Then I said, "Well, I don't know about you, but the first things that pop up in my mind are kind of random. Like I am thinking, 'They both come in bottles. One is orange and the other is brown. They both taste good—at least I think so! One is bubbly and one is flat. One I was allowed to drink as a kid, and one I wasn't.'

"What I just did—naming a random bunch of comparisons—it's a good start, but I think I can do better. To really do this work of comparing and contrasting well, I have to think more logically than that."

Organize observations by pointing out that a compare-and-contrast essay has a specific structure.

"There is a method to comparing and contrasting. If you want to write an essay that says that soda and juice are mostly the same, one way to do that is to take a trait—name it—and then say how that trait is the same for both items—item A and item B. Then you take a second trait—name it—and say how that trait is also the same for both items—item A and item B.

"Let's try this with soda and juice. Let me start with one trait. Then you do the next. I'll say that soda and juice are mostly alike. They are alike because they both are liquids—and they both are drinkable, and they will both fill whatever container you put them in. They are also alike because . . . Turn and talk."

After a moment or two, the students had shared several other possibilities, and I'd noted a few. "They are alike because they are liquids. They are also alike because of how they taste. Both are sweet, and both are refreshing. Okay, so now our essay could start like this." I turned to an empty sheet of chart paper and scribed our initial ideas.

> Soda and juice are similar in many ways. They are both liquids—you can drink them, and they
> fill whatever container they are put into. Also, both soda and juice taste similar. Both liquids are
> sweet plus they taste refreshing when one is thirsty.

There's a purpose to modeling this mess-up: to show students one of the most common pitfalls to avoid when comparing and contrasting. The main focus of this lesson is to think about structures for comparing and contrasting, but you'll want to give students every chance to understand that observations on similarities and differences are grouped in logical ways—just like any other kind of observation they make in essays.

At some point soon, your students will learn that the point of a compare-and-contrast essay is not only to write about how something is mostly similar or mostly different from something else. Soon you will guide them toward more complex comparative structures. But for now, help your students focus on the need for logical, orderly thinking and writing.

Debrief. Name what you've done in ways that make the work transferable.

"Students, do you see what we just did? We compared two objects, asking ourselves, 'Are these mostly alike or mostly different?' Then we decided to argue that they are mostly alike. We chose one trait—named it—and said how item A and item B are similar with regard to that trait. Then we took a second trait—we named it—and we said how that trait is also the same for both items—item A and item B. Of course, now we could move on to differences, stating, 'But they are also partly different.'"

ACTIVE ENGAGEMENT

Channel the class to try the same work using different objects. Offer two of your shirts for the class to compare and encourage them to think of categories that might guide their thinking.

"Let's try this again. I know that most of you marvel over my fashion sense," I said with a good-humored smirk, "so I brought in two different shirts of mine from home." I produced my shirts and laid them on an upside-down crate covered with a lovely tablecloth.

"Think what you'd write if you were to observe my shirts, and I'll do that too." I was quiet, thinking of what I would say. I paused, and then said, "You've probably brainstormed a bunch of details you think are similar or different. If you haven't already, think now of general traits or categories we could compare, for example, their parts and their purpose. What else?" Students quickly named several other categories in general terms that I helped give words for—appearance, texture, shape, size, purpose.

"To compare and contrast my shirts today, let's focus on how they are different. So now, choose one general trait or category at a time, and be specific about how my shirts differ when it comes to each of those categories. Try writing an essay in the air about the two shirts that is like our essay in the air about the two beverages."

Soon I called on the class to jointly construct a compare-and-contrast essay on my two shirts. This is what they pieced together, calling out lines as I furiously wrote down what they said.

> Our teacher's shirts are different in many ways. They are very different in shape. One is long with long sleeves and a collared neck, while the other is much shorter in length, has short sleeves and a crew neck. The texture of the shirts is also very different. One has stiff material and the other has very soft material. Lastly, the shirts serve a different purpose. One shirt looks more professional, like something she would wear to work. The other is a T-shirt, something she would wear around the house or to the grocery store.

"You also need to write about the similarities between the shirts. How are my two shirts the same? Turn and talk." As the class talked, I wrote the essay they'd constructed thus far onto chart paper, and soon we'd added a second paragraph.

In this lesson, I might have asked students to go beyond superficial comparisons, such as saying that soda and juice both slosh around in similar ways. And I could have taught and then prodded students to consider the reasons or significance for any similarities and differences we identified. But I'm saving that level of discussion for upcoming sessions, when students must delve into what these comparisons mean and what we can learn from thinking and writing about them. Often when planning teaching, it's helpful to save some content to teach as a next step.

Teachers, it is best to elicit only a few ideas or your lesson will be on the long side. You just want to give your students a sense of writing in an organized way.

But our teacher's shirts are also similar in some ways. They are the same color. Both shirts are white. They are also the same size, a size 6. And they both have the same owner–our teacher!

Debrief. Recall the teaching point and put today's work in a bigger context.

"Sometimes it feels like writing a compare-and-contrast essay is like baking a cake—there are measurements and rules and steps to make sure it comes out right. Will you talk with your partner about what the steps might be for writing compare-and-contrast essays?"

The class talked, and after a bit I intervened. "I think you've got the important points. One way to write a compare-and-contrast essay is to discuss both similarities and differences—one at a time. The writer chooses a trait and looks at it across the two items, then chooses another trait and looks at that across the two items."

LINK

Set students up to go off and work in centers.

"Today we are going to do centers again, like we did during our editing lesson yesterday. Normally, I remind you of the strategy I've just taught and then send you off to work on your own important writing projects. Today I'm sending you off to move through a series of centers where you'll have a chance to flex your compare-and-contrast muscles.

"Though you won't be writing about literature just yet, you'll have a chance to use your powers of observation for comparing and contrasting, as well as your writing skills. I've set up different objects around the room for you to compare and contrast in your writer's notebook, just as we practiced here in the meeting area. You'll find photographs of landmarks at one table, vegetables at another, and a table with some musical instruments. I'm going to leave our model paragraph up here for you to use today as well, so you can remember how we write about our observations in organized ways."

To set up today's centers, feel free to use your imagination. As space allows, make up several tables, each with a different theme, and usher students through each center during the writing workshop. So, for example, you might plan a center where students study and then compare and contrast photographs of famous landmarks. Another might have the names and photos of well-known musicians, actors, or athletes. Other tables might display objects like fruits, vegetables, rocks, musical instruments, or tools that students can compare and contrast. Depending on the number of centers you have, plan on giving students approximately seven to ten minutes at each table, ensuring that they have the opportunity to visit each of the stations.

Deepening Students' Initial Observations

IT IS PREDICTABLE that at first your class's observations will be superficial—noticing the way one tiny detail in a picture is different from another or how one vegetable is a different sort of green than another. There is nothing wrong with this. In fact, you modeled doing some of this work yourself a moment ago. You will, however, want to immediately intervene and teach the class to search for larger traits—for categories—under which they can situate their minute observations.

I pulled up next to Jamie, who was at the landmark photograph center and working to compare and contrast the Empire State Building and the Brooklyn Bridge. I immediately noticed that he was creating what amounted to a list of superficial comparisons—the Brooklyn Bridge is long and the Empire State Building is tall, the Bridge and the Empire State Building are both really big and people use them a lot.

"Jamie," I began, "as you look across the similarities and differences you've identified for the Empire State Building and the Brooklyn Bridge, are you noticing any patterns or big categories?" Jamie thought for a minute. "Well, I saw that they both are really big, but how people use them is different," he said.

"Yes, that is exactly what I mean. Here's the thing, Jamie. What you have done beautifully is to dedicate yourself fully to uncovering all the similarities, big and small, between these two landmarks. You have even grouped those similarities together—you are comparing the size especially, and maybe a little of the shape, right?" Jamie nodded.

"Do you mind if I push you to the next level now? Another possibility is that first, I develop a few *ideas* about what I'm comparing—soda and juice, for example—and then I write about the way the idea is true for my first object, soda, and then the way the idea is true for my other object, juice. So, for example, one idea could be that soda and juice are both refreshing beverages. So now let's take a look at your writing and see if we can do something similar. What ideas are you having about the Empire State Building and the Brooklyn Bridge?"

Before long, Jamie developed the following idea: "Both the Empire State Building and the Brooklyn Bridge are important landmarks in New York City."

If your students, like Jamie, are making superficial comparisons, you'll want to move them toward noticing patterns that are more significant. It can also help if you push them to ask, "So what?" and to reflect on the significance of those patterns. "What does this show?" Doing this work in centers will help students eventually observe and analyze along similar lines when they consider characters and themes in literature.

MID-WORKSHOP TEACHING **Grouping Comparisons under the Umbrella of an Idea**

"May I get your attention for a minute? I've met with many of you today, and you've worked hard to notice even the tiniest differences and similarities between the objects at your centers. I wanted to share a bit of work Julia and I just did together, because I think it will be important for us all.

"When we are writing about similarities and differences, we want to be on the lookout for categories we can compare and contrast. In the minilesson, we talked about looking for bigger traits—like appearance, purpose, size. Something else you can do, which Julia is doing, is to come up with *ideas*. An idea can become a kind of category. Then you can compare and contrast your observations under the umbrella of each idea.

"For example, Julia started off by grouping what she noticed into categories—beauty and things to do. She realized she could write a whole paragraph alone on the differences between the beauty of Grand Central Station and Central Park. She also wrote about the things you can do when visiting each landmark—both as tourist attractions, but one as a park and one as a train station with attractions.

"But then, Julia decided to formulate an idea—she thought that both Central Park and Grand Central Station are important New York City landmarks that people visit from all over. Let's take a look at her entry and notice what she did that you might try also." I put Julia's entry on the document camera, and the students turned and talked about what they were noticing.

> Central Park and Grand Central Station are two important NYC landmarks. People come from all over to visit them because of their beauty. Central Park has meadows filled with tall, lush grass and flowers. It has tree lined paths and ponds that make you feel like you are out of the city in the woods enjoying nature. Grand Central Station is filled with beautiful art and architecture. Its ceiling looks like our constellation, with stars twinkling down at you.
>
> Another reason why tourists visit Central Park and Grand Central Station is because there is so much to do. When visiting Central Park a person can visit Belvedere Castle, the merry-go-round as well as the reservoir. Grand Central Station has some of the nicest stores and restaurants as well as a lovely observation area. You can also catch trains that can take you anywhere in New York City.

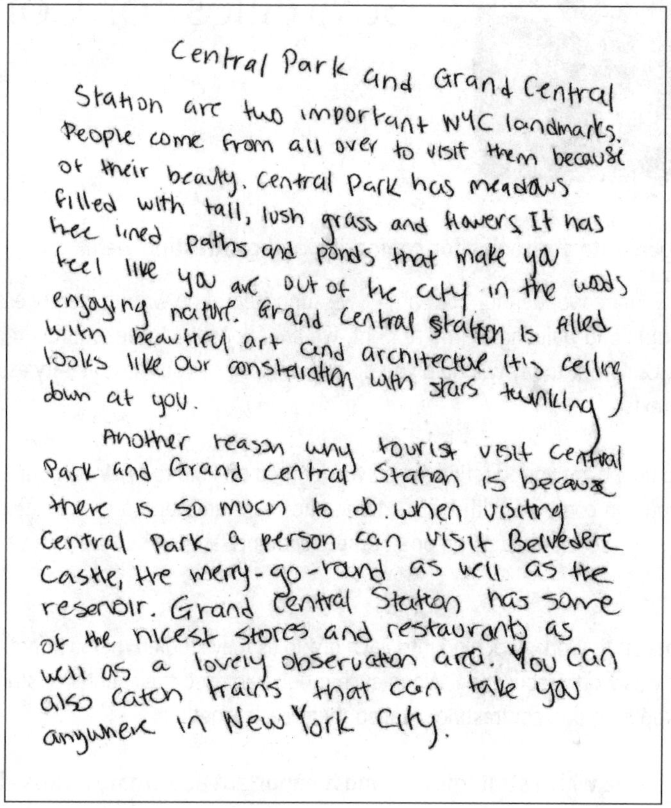
Central Park and Grand Central Station are two important NYC landmarks. People come from all over to visit them because of their beauty. Central Park has meadows filled with tall, lush grass and flowers It has tree lined paths and ponds that make you feel like you are out of the city in the woods enjoying nature. Grand Central Station is filled with beautiful art and architecture. It's ceiling looks like our constellation with stars twinkling down at you.

Another reason why tourist visit Central Park and Grand Central Station is because there is so much to do. When visiting Central Park a person can visit Belvedere Castle, the merry-go-round as well as the reservoir. Grand Central Station has some of the nicest stores and restaurants as well as a lovely observation area. You can also catch trains that can take you anywhere in New York City.

FIG. 13–1 Julia groups comparisons under the larger idea that "Central Park and Grand Central Station are two important NYC landmarks."

Strategies for Comparing and Contrasting

Use inquiry to generate strategies for comparing and contrasting well.

"I'll bet some of you are wondering, 'Hey, aren't we supposed to be writing literary essays in this unit? What's up with the drinks and shirts and buildings?' You're right, we *are* supposed to be writing literary essays, and tomorrow, we'll get back to that. Our work today will help you do that well, since your next literary essay will have you comparing and contrasting two texts.

"Before we wrap up, I want you to reflect on all you learned and did today. With your tables, will you study your writing from today, so you can come up with two or three important answers to the question, 'How do writers compare and contrast?' You'll record each strategy on one of these sentence strips. Then we'll come back together and make a chart of your insights."

I sent the students off to work, coaching into each group as they studied their writing and attempted to name the work they'd done that was worth replicating. When each group had used their sentence strips to record at least two to three strategies for comparing and contrasting, I called them back together.

Help students decide which strategies are most important and create a class chart.

"Writers, you're taking the lead on creating this chart. The decisions about what goes on the final chart will be up to you. Jaz, will you be in charge of collecting the strategies—the sentence strips—the class decides should go on the chart and pasting them up onto this blank piece of chart paper? We'll need a title for the chart, of course. How about 'Tips for Comparing and Contrasting'?"

Jamhil began, sharing on behalf of his group. "We wrote Jorge's strategy on here: 'Group your similarities and differences with ideas, not just traits.'" He looked around the room, and many nodded in agreement or indicated that they, too, had charted something similar. Jaz taped the strategy onto the chart.

Diamond spoke next. "Our group looked at all of our notebook entries, and we saw that we were using tons of transition words we know. We wrote, 'Use transition words to connect your ideas.'"

"That is very important," I said. "Maybe we can leave a little space under your sentence strip so we can fill in some specific transition words kids might use."

At the end of the share we had a chart that looked like this.

Tips for **Comparing** and **Contrasting**

Group comparisons into categories — think about bigger traits or ideas.

Use transition words to connect your ideas.

> They are [similar or different] because...   > By comparsion
> For instance... Also...   > In contrast
> This is..., while that is...   > In addition
> However

Write all about the similarities, and then all about the differences.

You can also compare and contrast your observations under the umbrella of each big idea.

COMPARING AND CONTRASTING

"Tonight, find a few things in your own life that you'd like to compare and contrast and write about them. You might compare your books or clothes or other items in your home; you might even compare people or places in your life. The more time you spend building your compare-and-contrast muscles, the better prepared you will be to use these skills when you compare and contrast two texts. You may want to copy the chart we just made into your notebook so you can use it tonight as you draft your new compare-and-contrast entries."

Comparing and Contrasting Themes across Texts

IN THIS SESSION, you'll teach students that essayists write compare-and-contrast essays by thinking across texts about similarities and differences among themes.

COMMON CORE STATE STANDARDS: W.6.2, W.6.5, W.6.9.a, RL.6.1, RL.6.2, RL.6.10, SL.6.1, L.6.1, L.6.2, L.6.3, L.6.5, L.6.6

I N THIS SESSION, you will build on the momentum you started the day before, channeling your students to begin thinking about—and writing essays on—the comparisons they make between two texts that they know very well. Today feels a bit like a culmination point. There is much from the past few weeks that you will be asking your class to draw upon, to apply, to demonstrate. Be sure that your charts are up in the room and that they are clear. Make sure your students have their mentor texts and their earlier drafts at the ready. Be sure that the checklists and partnerships are ready to go. Most of your students will need some support during this session and in the next few days, and you will not want them to grind to a halt simply because they cannot recall where to go to remember a lesson from the week before.

Your first decision will be how to help your class choose the two texts to compare and contrast. Of course, for the sake of time and efficiency most likely they will choose from texts that they know very well already. We suggest that at least one of these texts should be one of the stories they have already written about. As for the other—here you might open things up a bit. After all, chances are that your class has read a great deal this year. Try offering them the choice of any text they have read and know well—all the while being sure to guide them toward the read-alouds and short stories you know that they have read.

For your own work, you will model off of the short story you have been using all along, as well as the story you used to model in Session 1 for boot camp. This will save you time as you try to quickly show your class how to apply the structure and thinking they adopted yesterday as they now compare texts rather than objects or people.

Often you will see that your students are pretty good at comparing the characters and/or themes in texts—that actually by placing things side by side it is sometimes easier to see each clearly. However you should anticipate that when your class begins to write, things could get messy, so later in this session you will follow up with ways to help students to make their writing more clear and less cluttered.

This session is fast-paced and demanding. We hope that you and your students find it as rewarding as we have to see the culmination of all the work that has been done up to this point. It won't be perfect; it will be messy. But look for the moments where you see that your students have learned something about analyzing texts in writing. These moments will come, and we encourage you to step back and take a moment to appreciate the work you and your students have done.

"There is much from the past few weeks that you will be asking your class to draw upon, to apply, and to demonstrate."

Comparing and Contrasting Themes across Texts

CONNECTION

Point out how the work of this unit is changing the way you see the world and read texts.

"Last night, I watched a romantic comedy. (I'm not proud.) Around the middle of the movie, though, I found myself thinking, 'This isn't as good as that other movie I just saw.' Now, if I hadn't done the work of yesterday's lesson, I might have stopped there.

"But instead, I started comparing the movie I was watching to the other one I liked more, thinking about how the main characters were similar and different, and even about the themes. I saw that in one movie, the lead character was kind of helpless looking for love, and in the other, she was headstrong and brave. And it made me think that the theme of both romantic comedies was about love, of course, but that in one it seemed like the theme was 'Love will make everything okay,' and in the other it was more like 'If you live your life well, love will come to you.'"

Let students know why you think this work is important for them—beyond school.

"So basically I think this unit, this work, has changed my brain. Everywhere I go right now I am comparing things, looking for themes, analyzing people. I could have watched that movie and just been like, 'Whatever, it was, like, okay.' But now I am thinking a little more deeply about things. I want that for you, too—I really do. More so than teaching you to be great essay writers—which I totally care about—I dream that you will all become the most interesting, attentive versions of yourselves that you can be. I think this work can help you to do that."

❖ **Name the teaching point.**

"So today I want to teach you that essayists bring all of their skills to compare-and-contrast essays—by comparing what is similar and contrasting what is different about the themes in different texts."

Comparing and contrasting are habits of mind, and you want your students to be practicing and mastering those mental habits. You want them to be looking at their world thinking, "How are things the same? How are things different? What is the significance of those differences?"

TEACHING

Invite the class to help you make theme-based comparisons of familiar texts.

"Writers, let's practice this work together. The first thing we're going to need to do is choose a text to work with. After we think about the themes in this text, we'll choose another text to compare it with. Let's start with our first text, 'The Three Little Pigs.' First we want to think of a theme from 'The Three Little Pigs.' I was thinking about this a bit, and don't you think that one theme—one lesson we could learn—is that when one way of dealing with a problem isn't working, you should try a new way, a better approach?" The class nodded.

"So now we have to think, 'What other stories carry that same theme?'" I again left some silence. "Remember that the themes in one text will always relate to lots of other texts. That is why they are called *themes*. They are universal. So let's all think for a moment about a few other stories where one of the characters learns to face a problem in a new way. Turn and discuss."

Students talked for several seconds about other characters who resemble the third pig—from Tris Prior in the Divergent series to Ivan in *The One and Only Ivan*. Stephen said "Raymond's Run" about ten times, and when I reconvened the class, I asked him to share his thinking about this second text we all knew well. Stephen explained, "Squeaky is like the third pig. She just keeps doing the same thing. But she finally stops and tries something different, and things start to change. So 'Raymond's Run' has that same thing about when we are repeating the same action and it isn't working, we should try something else." I grinned, "By 'thing' you mean . . ." Stephen groaned. "Theme, or lesson."

"Okay, so Stephen has pointed out what these two texts have in common with each other. Now let's think about the other part of compare-contrast. Right now discuss with a partner what is different about how these texts deal with the theme. To do that you could think about how the different characters react to the trouble of the text, or if there is anything different about their situation."

Within seconds, I gathered the class together. "Well? What do you think?"

Devin raised his hand as I had set him up to do. "'The Three Little Pigs' is messed up. It's really just teaching you that some people are just better than others at dealing with their problems. That's messed up. 'Raymond's Run' teaches you that you can change who you are and how you deal with life. That's a better message I think."

Debrief in ways that pop out the replicable, transferable work you have just done.

"Whoa. Okay. So we did some powerful work here, and I want you to see the steps we took, because you are about to try it on two texts you have read on your own. So first, we chose a text that we know well that we wanted to explore. Then we thought a bit about the themes addressed in the text. Next, we considered some other texts that might carry that same theme. And then we thought about how that theme is similar and different across both texts, first talking about the similarities, and then moving on to the differences. Phew, that is a lot of thinking. I've captured those steps in a chart that can guide us as we do this kind of essay writing."

You may not have a Stephen in your class to chime in at this exact moment. If that is the case, you could demonstrate your thinking about how the two texts are similar, or you could have the class give it a go along with you.

The work you're asking students to do here—to think about themes and how they relate across texts—is work the Common Core Reading Standards for Literature expect your students to be able to do as sixth-graders. The standards expect students to "determine a theme or central idea of a text" (CCSS.RL.6.2) and to "compare and contrast texts in different forms or genres (e.g., stories and poems; historical novels and fantasy stories) in terms of their approaches to similar themes and topics" (CCSS.RL.6.9).

> **How to Write a Compare-and-Contrast Literary Essay**
>
> - Choose one text and think about its theme(s).
> - Consider other texts that address one of these same themes, and select one.
> - Think about how the two texts both address the same theme.
>   - How do the texts address the theme in a similar way?
>   - How do they address the theme differently?
> - Move back and forth between universal themes and specific examples from each text.

ACTIVE ENGAGEMENT

Direct students to compare and contrast a theme across two stories they have read.

"So now take a moment to get yourself ready to do this work on two texts you have read and know well. You will probably start with the same story you used for your character and theme essay. First, think about a theme in your story—which shouldn't be too hard since you just wrote an essay on a theme. Next, work with your partner to think of another story that also has that theme—anything you have read—and use the charts in the room and the work we have done to practice how your compare-contrast essay will go. You might use the chart 'Tips for Comparing and Contrasting,' to help," I said, pointing to yesterday's chart.

As students wrote comparisons in the air with a partner, I moved among them, coaching, saying things like:

"Remember to draw upon all we have read this year when you are looking for a text to compare."

"When looking for a text to compare, you are looking for texts that generally relate to the theme. They don't have to match exactly."

"Instead of jumping from one similarity to the next, try to think through several sentences. Use phrases from the chart, like, 'For instance . . .' and 'Also . . .' to help you keep going."

"Stay close to your theme. Don't write about every little detail that is the same or different. Just those that show how the particular theme you've chosen is the same or different."

A predictable challenge for your students is thinking of another text that deals—generally—with a similar theme as the text they have written about thus far. It will help if for this lesson you have a list of the read-alouds you have read this year, either posted in the room or on a handout, for students to consider.

> **Tips for Comparing and Contrasting**
>
> Group comparisons into categories — think about bigger traits or ideas.
>
> **Use transition words to connect your ideas.**
>
> - They are [similar or different] because...
> - For instance... Also...
> - This is..., while that is...
> - However
> - By comparsion
> - In contrast
> - In addition
>
> Write all about the similarities, and then all about the differences.
>
> You can also compare and contrast your observations under the umbrella of each big idea.

"Remind your partner to use thought prompts to say more. You can even help get her started by interjecting with an appropriate prompt, like 'Because . . . ,' and asking her to finish the sentence."

LINK

Set up students to write their own compare-and-contrast essays, on texts and a theme of their own choosing. Emphasize the importance of this project—that their essays will culminate the unit.

"Writers, you've been building your comparing-and-contrasting muscles for two days, and now you've arrived at an important moment in your essay writing lives. You're ready to do the most challenging work you'll do in this whole unit. Your job over the next three days is to write one last essay. It will be a compare-and-contrast essay."

Gesturing again to the charts in the room I said, "You have already started the thinking behind your essay, and as you get writing you have plenty of resources to draw from. I've added another step to our 'How to Write a Compare-and-Contrast Literary Essay' chart that can help you get started with this." I motioned toward the anchor chart, pointing at the new bullets. "Now, you can delve right into your essay draft; I think you have all the tools you need to get started right away with that. But if you want to take a few minutes to gather more thinking or ideas on your theme or your texts in your writer's notebook, feel free to start there. You don't want to linger in your notebook too long, though; drafts will need to be ready for revision tomorrow. Right now, take a second and make sure that you know where in the room your most helpful charts are. In fact, right now I want you to point to the chart that you think is going to help you the most today."

Teachers, if your students need a chance to gather their ideas on their texts or themes in their notebooks before they jump into writing compare-and-contrast essays, provide several minutes for them to do so. But make sure they move forward quickly to writing their essays.

Throughout this unit, we have suggested ways to help your students use the charts and materials in the room. This is another—having them decide which chart will assist them the most with whatever they struggle with. This also allows you a great entry point in your conferences. Instead of saying, "How's it going?" you can begin with, "What chart are you working with today—and what specific points are you working on in your writing?"

How to Write a Compare-and-Contrast Literary Essay

- Choose one text and think about its theme(s).
- Consider other texts that address one of these same themes, and select one.
- Think about how the two texts both address the same theme.
  - How do the texts address the theme in a similar way?
  - How do they address the theme differently?
- Move back and forth between universal themes and specific examples from each text.
- **Choose a plan for your essay—write all about similarities, then differences, or see-saw back and forth.**
  - **Search for the most compelling evidence that can support your claim.**
  - **Write an introduction and a conclusion that spotlights your claim.**
  - **Use transition words to connect your ideas.**

Taking the Bumps in the Road in Stride

IT IS A GOOD IDEA to anticipate some of the problems your students are apt to encounter today, because this will help you respond more quickly and to the point. Try not to be surprised if your students make simplistic or superficial comparisons between the two texts. For example, you might find a student arguing that in both *Sweetness* and *Tears of a Tiger*, the theme is that seeing someone you care about suffer is difficult, and that in both, there is a girl with a sassy attitude. You'll have a hard time maintaining a straight face over some of their blunders.

When this happens, you might as well get a kick out of your students! Their mess-ups reflect the fact that this is utterly new work—or that it is challenging, or that their sixth-grade hearts and minds are everywhere but here. The good news is that if they are showing themselves to be total novices at this, then it will be easy for them to improve in giant steps.

If a student has said two characters are similar because, say, they have cool hairstyles, two tactics might be especially helpful.

The first thing you'll want to do is to remind students that they are not just looking for anything and everything that is the same, but for similarities that show how the two texts develop the theme, which in this instance is the theme that friendship matters. It usually helps to start with one book and to think about concrete ways that theme is shown. Are there patterns in the actions that support the idea that friendship matters?

Then, second, guide students toward making more substantial comparisons by reminding them of the aspects of books that they already know are important. So, for example, they already know that when writing about a story, it pays off to notice the characters—their traits, motivations, struggles, changes, and relationships. So a student wanting to compare "The Gift of the Magi" and "My Side of the Story" would find it productive to compare any one of those important aspects of the texts and then extend that thinking to themes.

Depending on your students' reading skills, you may also find that some are unsure of their thinking about themes. You might want to pull these students together and teach them a way to develop their ideas. You could begin a small group by explaining why you have gathered them together, saying something like "I've gathered you all together because I noticed that you are having a hard time coming up with a theme that ties two books together." This helps students focus. Then you could name the teaching point of the small group and the work you'll do together. You might say, "I thought it might help you to know that when it is hard to compare themes across books, often it helps to start by comparing the main characters in two books. Again, it helps to start by settling on one aspect of the text. You might decide, for example, that you definitely want to write about Superman. Then you could say to yourself, 'Okay, what character do I know whose life and circumstances are a lot like Superman's?' It could be that Harry Potter pops into your mind, and it is true that there are similarities. Then you could list those similarities. Both Harry and Kal-El are adopted. Both have powers unlike other kids. And both rise to the occasion through a lot of trial and error."

You might then ask students to think about the process they have just gone through with you. What did they notice you doing that they could do, too? You'd want them to realize that if it is hard to think about a theme that relates to two books, usually one can think about characters who are similar, and by thinking about that, one can get to comparisons of theme.

"As you draft a new kind of essay today, I want to share an example of this kind of writing with you so you have a vision of what your essays might start to look like. As I was thinking about this lesson last night, I wrote up a super-fast rough draft of an essay comparing 'Raymond's Run' and 'The Three Little Pigs.' I am going to read part of it to you now. Can you listen for things that you might try as you draft today?" I then read the essay aloud stopping after each paragraph to say, 'What did I do in my essay that you could try?' Jot your ideas down on a Post-it."

One option here is to read part of this essay aloud and then ask students to continue reading their copies on their own. By now, students should be accustomed to reading mentor texts and mining them for useful strategies or ways of using language that they can use in writing their own essays.

It might seem like "The Three Little Pigs" and "Raymond's Run" are very different kinds of stories. One is a fairy tale from a long time ago and one is a short story about kids from the present time. But if you look a little closer, you will see that both stories actually share a common theme. In both stories, the authors teach us that sometimes you have to change how you approach a problem if you want to solve it.

In "The Three Little Pigs," the author shows us that it takes a lot of hard work and clever tricks to solve the problem. In the beginning and in the middle of the story, the first and second little pigs have to run away because their houses were too weak and the big, bad wolf blows their houses down. At the end of the story, all three pigs are together in the third little pig's house. But the third little pig built his house out of bricks so it was strong enough to keep the wolf from blowing it down. The wolf tries to come down the chimney, so then, the pigs try something else to protect themselves. The third pig puts a boiling pot of water in the fireplace—and the wolf falls in. Instead of running away from the wolf, the third little pig comes up with a new idea to outsmart the wolf and solve the problem. The lesson is clear: work hard and try something new and you will succeed.

In "Raymond's Run" the author also shows us that it is sometimes necessary to change your approach to a problem to succeed. In the beginning of the story, Squeaky brags about how tough she is, especially when people try to mess with her brother, Raymond. In the middle of the story, she still acts tough around her classmates and her running coach. She puts people off, just like she wants, but she ends up alone, and unhappy. At the end of the story, Squeaky changes her attitude toward others and smiles at Gretchen and makes a friend. She stops being so overprotective of Raymond so he can shine on his own. The lesson in this story is clear, too: sometimes it takes a new approach to people to life to make you truly happy.

Both of these stories teach us that sometimes you have to change how you deal with a problem, in order to solve it. "The Three Little Pigs" is for little kids, so it teaches you in a simple way. The author shows us how it's possible to approach a problem differently in a physical way because the first and second pig run away from the wolf and the third little pig builds a stronger house and boils the wolf in the pot. "Raymond's Run" teaches us how to change in a harder way—it teaches us how to change our attitude and the way we treat people. Squeaky has to change her outlook on people and how she treats them in order to solve her problem. This is harder to do than building a house out of bricks. Changing how we treat people in the world is the hardest thing to do. This is a lesson we could all learn.

I gave the class a few seconds to share their lists with their partners of the things they might try. "You all noticed that I did a lot of the things from the charts we made yesterday and today. Let's take a look." I pointed to the "Tips for Comparing and Contrasting" chart with the sentence strips that the class made yesterday and to the "How to Write a Compare-and-Contrast Literary Essay" chart I put up today. "Take a moment and think about which of these things you could do in your writing." I paused dramatically. "Okay, tell your partner quickly what your plan is for the rest of the period. Go!"

Being Literary Scholars

Highlight for the class how one student is revising with an eye toward literary language.

"Writers, eyes up here for a minute, I want to share something very cool that Jamie is doing that I hope will inspire similar work from many of you. He's trying out several quick drafts of an introduction, but he's not just thinking about the logistics of introducing the texts and theme he wants to explore. He's putting a lot of thought into the *language* he wants to use. He wants his essay to sound as *literary* as possible. Jamie, can you explain what you're doing and how?"

Jamie said, "I'm brainstorming the kinds of words people use when they are talking about stories. You know, more professional-sounding words. So at first I used the word *character* in my introduction, but then I realized I could use the word *protagonist*, that that would sound even . . . well, even better."

"Jamie," I interjected, "the work you're doing here is very similar to the work professional writers do. Professional nonfiction writers know their discipline and use the language of that the discipline, just like Jamie is doing. In this case, he is using literary language, because he is writing about literature. If he were writing about science, he would use scientific language.

"Jamie, can you read us an earlier draft of your introduction without literary language and then read us what you have now? As the rest of us listen, let's notice what sounds different."

After Jamie read, I turned to the class. "What other literary language did you hear, other than *protagonist*?" As they called out terms, I jotted them on the board and said, "I imagine many of you will want to try what Jamie is doing. As you write and revise, try to incorporate words like these into your essays. I'll add a few more literary words to this list, and I'll also add this learning to our anchor chart."

Literary Language

protagonist   motivation
plot   perspective
theme   mood
tension   conflict
symbol   resolution
tone

In life, people lie a lot every where to everyone. in subw-ys to strangers, in apartments to parents, even in school to teachers. Rather then telling the truth they lie. Some say to get out of trouble. I say to get into trouble. The lesson that Max in "Max Swings for the fences," and Ernest in "Best of Friends," learned is honesty is the best policy.
    Max learned honesty is the best policy from lying to Molly and everyone at school. On the first day of school ant lunch he was talking about himself to his crush, and he was slipping. He

FIG. 14–1 Jamie's student work

CONTINUE DRAFTING COMPARE-AND-CONTRAST ESSAYS

"Your homework tonight is to continue the work you started today. Try coming in tomorrow with a draft written of your first compare-and-contrast essay. Tomorrow we will dive into revising your writing using all you have learned, so it will really help if you have a solid first draft written. I have made copies of my essay for you take as a model, if you think it would be helpful. You can also copy the steps on the "How to Write a Compare-and-Contrast Literary Essay" into your writers' notebooks.

How to Write a Theme-Based Literary Essay

- Think about the character's motivations, problems, and lessons learned and look for patterns.

- What does the character want, and what gets in the way?

- How does the character try to resolve his problems?

- What lessons does the character learn from trying to resolve his problems?

- Now what patterns can you see?

- Think about the patterns you see in universal terms. Ask yourself, "What big life lessons—what themes—can readers draw from the patterns in the story?"

- Then craft a claim based on one of the themes.

- Search for the most compelling evidence that can support the claim, then add it to the essay like this:
  - Quote some parts of the text.
  - Story-tell other parts.
  - Summarize yet other parts.

- To write an introduction to your essay, start with a universal statement about life and then transition to the text-based claim itself, focusing on the story you are writing about.

- To write a conclusion to your essay, show connections in at least one of these ways:
  - Your thesis and emphasize why the claim and evidence matter
  - Yourself and the life lesson you learned or realized
  - The author's message
  - Leave readers with something to think about

Applying What You Have Learned in the Past to Today's Revision Work

IN THIS SESSION, you will teach students that essayists use what they already know about essay writing as well as a variety of resources to revise their compare-and-contrast essays.

GETTING READY

✔ Charts from across the unit, hanging around the classroom for students to see (e.g., "How to Write a Literary Essay about Character" from Session 5, "How to Write a Theme-Based Literary Essay" from Session 8, "Revision Strategies" from Session 10, "Tips for Comparing and Contrasting" from Session 13, and any others your students use often) (See Connection, Teaching, Active Engagement, and Link)

✔ "How to Write a Compare-and-Contrast Literary Essay" chart (see Teaching)

✔ A student's compare-and-contrast essay, to use as a model for making a revision plan based on all she knows to do but hasn't yet done in her writing (see Teaching)

✔ Students' notebooks and drafts to be brought to the meeting area (see Active Engagement, Link, and Share)

✔ Conferring tools, such as copies of student drafts and essays, class essays, conferring sheets, the Argument Writing Checklist, and mentor text (see Conferring and Small-Group Work)

COMMON CORE STATE STANDARDS: W.6.2, W.6.5, W.6.9.a, RL.6.2, SL.6.1, L.6.1, L.6.2, L.6.3

THIS SESSION ASKS STUDENTS to apply everything they have learned about writing literary essays to their compare-and-contrast essays. This is important culminating work—perhaps in some ways the most important, as it asks students to synthesize the work they have done over the last few weeks in ways that allow them to carry it forward. All too often, students are obedient. They do what you teach them, in the moment, and then wait for the next lesson. They sit in their chairs waiting for you to tell them how they are doing and how to move to the next step.

Of course, if your students are to be successful in school (and one might argue, in life), you will want to find ways for them to understand—on their own—what they are doing, how they are doing, and what next steps they can take. All along in this unit we have encouraged you to push your students to self-assess, to use checklists and mentor texts to evaluate themselves and set goals. Now you will teach them to do this on a much grander scale.

Today you will teach your class to figure it out. You have set them up to write compare-and-contrast essays—a form unfamiliar to some students—and now you leave it to them to make those essays as strong and significant as possible as they revise their way toward publication. You have placed them on the edge of the pool, as it were, and now you will ask them to jump in. While you will not be teaching them every nuance of compare-and-contrast essay planning and drafting this time around, you will show them that the work of the unit so far has given them the foundation of literary essay writing to stand on. The rest, you will say, is up to them.

Point out the charts you have made. Guide them to their checklists, their mentors, their partners. Then, step back and allow them some space to explore. This session channels the energy of the toddler with a bucket of Legos: she knows the basics but is always creating new structures based on how the Legos worked the day, week, and month before. Encourage your sixth-graders to summon the same level of energy and enthusiasm for writing essays that they once had for creating fantastic Legos structures.

Applying What You Have Learned in the Past to Today's Revision Work

CONNECTION

As students gear up to revise a compare-and-contrast essay, remind them to draw on everything they already know about writing powerful essays.

"Writers, some of you might be wondering why our classroom resembles a huge walk-in closet, with our strategy charts hanging from clothes hangers and pieces of string. It may look haphazard, but there's a purpose to what looks like madness. I want to make sure that everything you've worked so hard to learn across this unit is front and center today. You've recently begun a new endeavor (compare-and-contrast essays), and it is critically important that you use all that you've learned about writing all kinds of literary essays as you tackle today's revision work.

"I recently bought a new video game, booted it up, and sat down to play for an hour after my work was done. Because it was a new game, I had a lot to learn. How does this character move? What are the rules of the game? What are the cool things I can do in this game world? What are all the ways I can fail, and how do I get around those obstacles?

"But what I didn't have to do was ask, 'How do I use this controller? What is a video game? How do you use the controller and stare at the screen at the same time?' Why didn't I have to ask these things, Jeff?"

Jeff, startled, said abruptly, "Oh, um, you already knew all that, because you played a bunch of games before."

"Right. Exactly. You all are revising a new kind of essay—the compare-and-contrast essay. And while there will be differences in the details in how you revise your essays today, mostly you will be using what you already know about revision to help you make this particular kind of essay as powerful as you can make it. Today, you are going to be like me playing a new video game. You are going to use what you *already* know to figure it out.

"None of you are new to revision. But we can probably agree that really revising our writing is, well, it's super hard, right?" Heads nodded. "Talk with the person next to you for a moment about what you have learned or done in the past that has been particularly helpful when you revise a piece of writing. You can refer to our 'Revision Strategies' chart for some ideas, too."

All through these units of study, you and your students have created anchor charts that are valuable resources. Encourage your students to use these charts again and again until they internalize the steps and strategies. There are also charts less central to the learning of each unit, but helpful nevertheless. You will have to find the right balance between a bounty of helpful charts and an overwhelming overload of charts. Keep present only the additional charts you know your class can use, above and beyond the anchor charts for each unit. You may want to make smaller versions of these less central charts and provide them at the writing center for students to access as needed.

After about thirty seconds, I reconvened the group and said, "I've heard all good tips for anyone who is about to revise. I'm going to add them to our 'Revision Strategies' chart so you can all refer to them as you revise today."

"Even though you've only learned about compare-and-contrast essays for two days, you know enough about writing essays in general to do this newer work well. And you know enough about revising to really lift the level of your current drafts."

❖ **Name the teaching point.**

"Today I want to teach you that essayists ask, 'What do I already know—and what resources can I use—that will help me do this revision work well?' Then they hold themselves accountable for drawing on all they've learned before as they revise their drafts."

TEACHING

Highlight how one student used the resources at her disposal to plan for thoughtful revision work.

"Yesterday, Diamond and I were talking. She showed me the compare-and-contrast essay she has been working on, comparing 'Your Move' to 'Thank You, Ma'am.' She is trying to show that both of these stories are about how we always have a choice whether or not to do bad things.

"I want to show you what we saw when Diamond and I looked at her body paragraphs. Look with us, thinking about whether Diamond has used everything we have learned this unit.

> In both texts, there is a young man who faces the choice of whether or not to commit a crime. In "Your Move," James decides whether or not to do graffiti to join a gang and in "Thank You, Ma'am" Roger has to decide if he is going to steal the lady's purse. They are the same because in both the boys don't do the crime because of love. Like in "Your Move," James loves his brother Isaac so he doesn't join the gang because it would be dangerous for his family and in "Thank You, Ma'am" Roger doesn't steal because the lady shows him love and care.

"Diamond and I took a look at her essay, and right away, we noticed a lot of things she is doing well. For instance, she pairs generalizations with the concrete specifics from the text to back them up," I said, pointing to examples in her essay. "Also, she not only tells about a part of the text that matches her claim, she actually quotes what the text says. Furthermore, to prove a point, she doesn't just support it with one sentence. She writes several sentences to support that point.

Revision Strategies

- Think, "What is this essay really about?" and rewrite in ways that better match that meaning.

- Revise through the lens of theme, making sure every detail connects back to that.

- Vary your evidence, and make sure it is compelling and includes important details.

- Incorporate your evidence in a variety of ways (using direct quotes, summarizing, storytelling).

- Unpack your evidence, showing not just how it supports your reasoning, but why.

- Add in new examples to support your theme.

- Use transitional phrases to help readers understand how different parts of the essay fit together.

- Use the Opinion/Argument Writing Checklist to set new goals for revision.

- Use charts to assess writing and revision goals.

- Rewrite whole chunks of text.

- Delete material that no longer fits.

"Even though Diamond does a lot of great things in her essay, she pushed herself even further. She thought about everything she's learned about revising, and about essays. Diamond, would you briefly tell the class what you did to get ready to revise?"

"Well, one thing I did was study the Argument Writing Checklist again. And I realized that even though I write several sentences in some parts, there are other places where I could say more. I also reread our charts. I figured I'd be able to find at least a couple of things to work on. Like here," Diamond said, pointing to a bullet on the "How to Write a Compare-and-Contrast Literary Essay" chart. "I didn't use a lot of transitions words, and I figured there were places I could write more," she said, this time pointing to the "Tips for Comparing and Contrasting" chart. "Which is why I put a star here and here," Diamond said, pointing to the margins of her draft, "because those are places where I want to go back and do that work."

To prepare for this discussion, I met with Diamond the day before to help her name all of the moves she made to push herself further in her revision work. While I have hopes that every student will soon have the language to discuss his or her writing powerfully, I want to support students along the way.

How to write a Compare-and-contrast Literary Essay.

- Choose one text and think about its theme(s).
- Consider other texts that address one of these same themes, and select one.
- Think about how the two texts both address the same theme.
- How do the texts address the theme in a similar way?
- How do they address the theme differently?
- Move back and forth between universal themes and specific examples from each text.
- Choose a plan for your essay-write all about similarities, then differences, or see-saw back and forth.
- Search for the most compelling evidence that can support your claim.
- Write an introduction and a conclusion that spotlights your claim.
- Use transition words to connect your ideas.
- Use literary language.

ACTIVE ENGAGEMENT

Direct students to review their own drafts and all the resources available to them, so they can plan meaningful ways to revise their essays.

"Writers, right now, will you start—or if you've started, continue—the same kind of work that Diamond is doing? Will you study your draft, study the charts, study the Argument Writing Checklist—study your memory, even, for any past learning!—and ask yourselves, 'What have I forgotten to incorporate into my writing that I could work on?' Take a minute to do some reading, and then go ahead and talk with your partner about what you're noticing."

As students talked, I moved among them, coaching into their work. To one partnership, I said, "Don't just breeze through the charts. Read them *expecting* to find something to work on." To another, "Start talking now. What learning are you remembering as you revisit these resources?" And to another, "When you get an idea for something to work on, make a note in the margins, like Diamond did with those stars, so you know where you need to go back and revise."

LINK

Encourage writers to call forth and use everything they know about writing strong essays, and send them off to work.

"Right now, take a moment to start a list—either at the top or in the margins of your draft—of the things you want to work on as you get your essay ready for publication. When you get back to your seats, you might spend a couple more minutes studying your draft and the resources at your disposal and then adding to your list of goals. But don't let too much time pass before you roll up those sleeves and get to revising!"

Teachers, to ensure that students don't spend too much time making a plan you'll want to signal the students after about five to eight minutes to put their plans into action.

Thinking about *How* to Write an Essay, Not Just *What*

I N YOUR CONFERRING TODAY, it will be important to look closely not only at *what* your students are writing, but *how* they are writing it. Often when students write essays, their writing is bereft of tone or voice and instead defaults into a generic, even wishy-washy voice that uses language like "it could be" or "maybe."

To shed light on this for your students, you might explain that writers think a lot about *how* to convey their ideas. After all, they want others to agree with them, or at least get them to think about new ideas. To decide on the tone of their essay, writers ask themselves, "What will my essay sound like? Will it be more assertive, or will it be more tentative? Will I declare my views in some places, while I allow my thoughts to be more exploratory or questioning in other places?" To help your students understand this, you might liken this to talking to adults versus to kids their own age. You might ask, "Do you find yourself speaking differently to different people? If you're talking to your grandparents, you probably sound different than when you talk to your friends." If your students need this explained further, you might say, "Do you remember when I called you together for our writing boot camp? That day I was pretty strict with you. You'll probably remember I said things like 'Do this now' and 'No, not like that. Like this.' You

(continues)

MID-WORKSHOP TEACHING   **Problem Solving as Students Revise**

"Writers, let me stop you for a moment. I just had the best conference with Jonah, and I want to tell you about it. Jonah was having a tough time with his essay. Things were not working as he started writing. When I sat down with him, he looked at me and—I hope you don't mind me quoting you here, Jonah—he said despondently, 'This stinks.' Now, I knew his essay claim was great, and when we looked over his structure it looked good too, so we had to sit back and ask ourselves, 'What's wrong here? How can we fix it?'

"What was so nice about the conference I had with Jonah is that he was really trying to solve his own problems. We were two writers trying to make a piece better, not a teacher telling the student what to do. And between the two of us, we figured out that his structure looked great, but when he actually started writing, he realized he didn't really have enough evidence in the text to keep himself going. So today he decided to change things up and go at it a different way.

"This is a huge deal, not just for essay writing, but for your lives. There will be lots of times—in school, in work, and in your life—when problems arise. Like all of us, you may want someone to come and fix it. But often, it will be up to you to figure out how to solve a problem. Jonah did that today, and we talked a bit about his process—how he knew things were 'stinking' in his essay and how he went about trying to solve the problem. I'm going to have him explain how he did it. Jonah?"

Jonah stood up and said, "Well, we talked through what I did, and I guess first I just thought, 'This isn't making any sense.' Then I stopped and thought about what might be wrong, and then I guess I went over everything we have learned, all the charts and stuff in the room, to try and figure out what might help. I really needed some stronger evidence, so I started looking for good quotes or small bits of the stories that tied into what I was trying to say in my essay."

I beamed. "I cannot tell you how important it is that you all learn to do this—to recognize when things aren't working in your writing and to figure out for yourself what it takes to fix it. Today and anytime you are writing, try to be aware of when your writing isn't working, and do what it takes to fix it."

---

might even say I was being a bit bossy. But from my language it was clear that I knew what I wanted you to do. We call this being authoritative."

You will ask the group to listen in on the work you will do with one student so that they can then try the same work. "Evmorfia, what tone do you want your essay to have?"

"I want to show a tone of hope."

"Why hope?"

"Well, because Miriam was so lonely without her parents but then isn't as lonely because the family gave her a rabbit. This makes Miriam feel better. So it gives hope to everyone that during bad times there are people in the world who step up and do something."

"What will you do to your writing to make the tone sound hopeful?"

When Evmorfia appeared stumped, I asked her and the rest of the group to think together about how she could bring out a hopeful tone. I suggested that perhaps they might look more closely at the introduction or conclusion to see if they could reveal tone there. The group decided to look first at Evmorfia's conclusion. They decided that Evmorfia couldn't write that the girls were hopeful or that they never gave up hoping. Evmorfia took their suggestion and began revising.

Next, I encouraged the other students to practice this skill themselves on the drafts they had in front of them. I coached them to adopt a tone, and then to choose a part of their essay to apply this strategy to, holding that tone in their minds. By rewriting the same part of a draft a few different ways or with a few different tones, students will discover that with some simple shifts, their writing can have dramatically different impacts.

Another issue that you will see arise—if you haven't already—is that under the influence of these very supportive thought prompts, your students' writing might be starting to sound boilerplate. If every writer in your class is mechanically, unsparingly using the same few phrases, like "Furthermore …" and "This reveals … ," they will be robbed of their own voice, even as they are finding ways to add to their content. It's important that you help your students craft alternative ways of introducing new information or adding an explanation, inviting them to experiment with words and phrases that best match their particular style. Then send them off to try this out in their writing.

Teach that by conveying emotions and feelings through specific word choice, the author creates tone. Direct students to look at places in their writing where they described a character, his or her relationships, or something that happened and to consider what words they might add to those descriptions to bring out the tone they are hoping to convey.

FIG. 15–1   Evmorfia revises her conclusion to bring out a tone of hope.

Offering Constructive Feedback

Rally students to offer a critical eye, this time drawing on past learning to suggest ways their partner might revise.

"Writers, you all know from past work that partners are another invaluable resource. Sometimes writing partners act as cheerleaders, giving the encouragement we need to keep going. Sometimes they act as a sounding board, helping us think through something challenging. But there are also times when writing partners must assume the role of critic, offering suggestions in a helpful, constructive way, saying things like, 'Hey, I'm noticing you have a problem here,' or 'This part is hard to understand. Can I help you make it clearer?'

"One of the beauties of working with a writing partner is that they bring fresh eyes to your writing, often seeing things that you missed. So right now, would you meet with your partner and work to hold one another accountable to past learning? This will work best if together, you take one person's piece and study it carefully. Remember to use all the resources available to you—charts and checklists and any other past learning that dwells in your memory—and use them to add to the list of goals you both think the writer still needs to work on."

REVISING AND WORKING TOWARD GOALS

"Writers, between the work you did on your own and with your partner, you should all have a list of goals to work toward as you revise your essays. And that list could continue to grow, meaning that as you check things off, you might look for new things to work on. Make sure you bring all your available resources home with you tonight, so you can keep working through and even adding to your list of things to do before you publish your essay in just a few days."

Identifying Run-Ons and Sentence Fragments

ear Teachers,

In the last editing lesson, you moved your students through several centers where they did an inquiry into a variety of conventions by studying passages that contained these conventions. For this editing lesson, we suggest focusing in a little more. Of course, what you choose to teach will have to depend on what your students most need to learn. You will want to pause before teaching any editing lesson so you can collect a swath of student work and get a bird's-eye view of the convention issues in your classes. In general, you will first want to focus on any issues that interrupt the meaning of a piece—the errors that make it tough to read and understand. This is not the time to unfurl your hatred of *your* vs. *you're* errors; this is not the time to use your particular pet peeves as a soap box. This is instead a time to help students have better control over the conventions that will make their writing easier to understand and smoother to read.

In this session, we suggest teaching students to consider their sentences. In particular, we suggest you help them be more aware of run-ons and fragments in their writing. To do this, you will give students a lens to read their work through—something that will help them stop and ask whether or not they need to make some corrections.

In some ways, however, the power of this session lies in the conferring and small-group work you do. As students go off to work independently, you will put all of that preassessment to good use as you confer and work with small groups. Forming groups based on need, you will help your students to become powerful wielders of language. You will help them to say clearly what it is they really mean, in a way that their audiences can understand.

MINILESSON

Begin this lesson on a positive and motivating note. Try not to begin with an exasperated sigh over all of the convention work that still needs to be done. With middle school writers, half of the battle over editing is just getting them to pay attention to what they are doing in their writing. And there is no surer way to make sure a sixth-grader *doesn't* pay attention to something than by saying, implicitly or explicitly, "You are bad at this." Instead, begin your lesson by rallying kids to do the work ahead. Make a connection to the work of editing as being like producing a hit single—perhaps even showing a quick video of music producers at work. What a producer does is to minutely tweak the detailed sounds of a song. When you watch them work, it is all subtle twisting of dials here and there until the exact right sound is found. Editing is very much the same work for a writer. The rough material is there, but it needs a tweak here, a twist there, to make it "sound" right to the reader.

Teach your students that one of the ways they can fine-tune their writing is to make sure that their sentences have the right rhythm. For your teaching point, you might say something along the lines of "There is nothing worse than a sentence that goes on too long or stops short. It's like a song with an irregular beat. It is the job of the editor to fix that. One thing you can do is look for words that are used instead of periods." Then, on a document camera or on chart paper, reveal a few examples of paragraphs from your own essay where you have purposefully placed run-ons. You should have at least two paragraphs, so that on one you can demonstrate how you locate sentences that need work, and then on the other the class can practice, before going into their own work.

As you demonstrate, give the kids some tips on what to look for. When looking for run-ons, for example, you might look for words that often are used instead of a much needed period—words like:

and

and then

so

when

because

These words can serve as "red alarm words"—words that make you as an editor stop short and ask, "Does it sound right to go on, or do I need a period there?" Of course, your students may discover other red alarm words in their writing, but starting them off with a few will help. While you will not be able to teach your students, in this one lesson, everything there is to know about subjects and predicates and the like, you can help them to be more careful with their sentence construction. You can help them make the best choices in their convention usage.

At the end of the lesson, you will want to be sure that your students know that when they edit, they are not just looking for one thing; instead they are using all that they know about editing to make their piece as tight as possible. Using an editing checklist might help with this work, but be sure that the checklist you develop is one that only includes conventions that you are confident your students have been taught before.

CONFERRING AND SMALL-GROUP WORK

When conferring during an editing lesson, it makes little sense to always work one-on-one. Conventions invite group work—not only because your students will so often clump together in the work they need to focus on, but also because having a partner or group to work with will ease the way so much. Here are some groupings we have found to be productive:

1. Kids in this group have so many issues with the conventions in their writing that it is difficult to know where to start. They have problems with punctuation, spelling, syntax, handwriting, coherence, length—the whole nine yards. For these students, you may want to prioritize the areas that should be addressed first, rather than overwhelming students with a barrage of "things to fix." Allow them to practice one or two important conventions and master them, and then move on to another convention a bit later.

2. Students in the next group write quickly and confidently and generally do not have many glaring issues—although the ones they do make stand out. These writers make all the common mistakes mixing up *there*, *their*, and *they're*, and so forth.

3. You will want a group for your English language learners who are literate in another language and are using that language to help them in their writing of English. While this is a great support in many ways, it brings about its own issues. For example, these students sometimes put an adjective after the noun it modifies, mix up their gender-related pronouns, struggle with tenses, or spell phonetically. Also, they may not be able to respond to red alarm words or be able to tell when something "sounds right" or not, as native English speakers do. Something else to keep in mind is that students who speak different first languages will have different issues with English conventions, depending on first-language structures, syntax, and origins.

4. Then there are your kids who seem close to perfect. There are few errors in their writing, but this may bring about another concern. Often when students write correctly, this also means they write simply, forgoing any attempt at incorporating complex sentences or vocabulary. For these students, trying new sentence structures or using new vocabulary words has become too risky, for fear of making mistakes. Carl Anderson, author of *Assessing Writers* (2005), has called this the "syntactic shackles" teachers put on kids when they emphasize correctness over experimentation.

Before you teach these small groups, look closely at a few of their pieces. What, realistically, do you expect them to be able to learn, and perhaps master, by the end of this unit? This year? Looking to the Common Core Language Standards might help you to focus in on what the best next step for each group might be. For example, for the group with more issues in their writing than you can count, the emphasis will have to be to first help them with their paragraphing and basic sentence construction—that is, having ending punctuation in their writing. Meanwhile, your group with perfect but overly simple writing could benefit from using a mentor text to try on different "apprentice sentences," as Mary Ehrenworth and Vicki Vinton describe in the book, *The Power of Grammar* (2005).

You will, of course, want a host of strategies to teach students for the issues you expect to see with their conventions. We suggest Chantal Francois and Elisa Zonona's *Catching Up on Conventions* (2009) as a great resource for these lessons.

MID-WORKSHOP TEACHING

For your mid-workshop teaching, urge your class to use partners as editors. Let them know that every writer needs an outside editor to look for mistakes they have made; rare is the writer who can do it all himself. You then could have partners read each other's work, with a clear focus in mind. A writer might say to her partner, "Today I want you to look for run-on sentences," for example. You might also tap a few students who have an eye for certain conventions to become "deputy editors," moving about the room helping students with their verb tenses or their spelling.

SHARE

Today for your share, you will want to end as you began—on a positive, celebratory, motivating note. Have your students share with the class a few before-and-after sections of their writing from today, highlighting which convention move they are working on. The motivation to make our writing clear is always other people; it is the desire to make meaning in our communities. Capitalize on this today, and make your students' editing work public to show how they are polishing their work with the goal of making meaning.

HOMEWORK

For homework, you will be sending your class off to finish editing their essays, and then to write their final draft, being careful to incorporate all of the great revision and editing work they have done so far. Part of the motivation to push through their final draft (besides the deadline set by you) will be to take part in tomorrow's celebration! Be sure to highlight what your celebration will entail so that your class knows what to look forward to.

Best wishes,
Kate and Kathleen

Celebrating Literary Essays

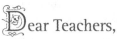ear Teachers,

Congratulations! It is time to close this unit and celebrate the work of literary essays with your hard working writers. Admittedly, finding an authentic, engaging way to celebrate literary essays is a bit tough. Poetry invites the poetry slam, fiction begs for an anthology, but the literary essay leaves room for far fewer opportunities. It may be tempting to just have kids hand in their essays or to sit one last time with their checklists and name how they have grown. They will, in fact, do both of these things, but we encourage you to take the time to find a way to truly celebrate—that is, to have some *fun*. The fact is that the better your celebration is for one unit, the better your next unit will go. When you celebrate with gusto, finding new and original ways for your students to step back and marvel at their work, you make connections from your writing workshop to the rest of your life.

Essays are meant to be shared. They are written with the intention of articulating, logically and persuasively, our thinking about a text, and this implies that there is someone reading them—someone besides you. However, we feel the need to be honest: not many people would choose to listen to a series of lit essays read aloud, nor do we particularly want to read someone else's essay—especially about a book we have never read. Here are three ideas for literary essay celebrations that have energized the work students have done as well as the work to come:

1. **Have a party.** Once your students have gotten to know the characters and themes of a text like the back of their hand, have them come to a party dressed up as a character from a story they wrote about. Make sure they bring a snack they think their character would want to eat, and of course you'll remind students to behave like that character for the duration of the party. You and your class can develop conversation starters that might help students reveal aspects of their characters. Ask questions like, "So, what do you like most about yourself and why?" "What's the biggest problem you've faced?"

"How have you changed?" "What lesson did you learn, or what realization did you have?" Students might use their published essay and the text itself to reference specific examples, recall precise behaviors or lines of dialogue, and support their conversations about the character.

2. **Publish essays on a wiki or blog.** If your class or school uses a wiki or blog—or if you can set one up—your students could publish their completed essays online. This would provide an exciting opportunity to invite a broader audience to read and perhaps comment on the essays. You may want your class to do some quick research to see how literary essays are published online in literary journals and zines.

3. **Translate essays into another genre.** We may not want to hear a litany of literary essays read aloud, but what about a song written off of that literary essay? Or a YouTube video of a kid talking about his story and what it means to him? Or a book trailer to encourage more people to read the text? Have your students take a day to translate their essay into another form, and then have students celebrate in groups, performing or reading or playing their "reconstituted essays." You might choose to audio record or videotape these performances and post these clips on a school or class blog. You might similarly post book reviews online for the public. This interaction with a larger audience helps connect young writers to the world, helping kids realize the purpose and power of their writing, their ideas, and their voice.

4. **Hold book panels.** If your students choose from a smaller selection of texts, then most likely there are many students who have read the same story. Get students together to compare claims and argue whose claim holds the most truth. Urge students to find opportunities for some debate. We highly suggest filming these panels. You might even encourage your class to dress like college professors. Again, students would have their published work on hand to present their argument and support their claims.

Above all, you will want to show your students how proud you are of their work. You will want to give them a literal or figurative high-five. Help them articulate what they have learned about essay writing in this unit, in ways that carry the skills learned and strengthened across this unit forward. After all, this is the first of many essays they will write in middle school and beyond.

Congratulations, literary essayists!
Kate and Kathleen

Even in the darkest times, people still show compassion. This theme is reflected in both stories, The Lily Cupboard by Shulamith Levey Oppenheim, and Katie's Trunk, by Ann Warren Turner. In The Lily Cupboard, and Katie's Trunk, both stories are about young girls who must survive a time of darkness, when both characters are left alone in another's hands, or alone, but still, there is always someone who turns up making a sacrifice of compassion.

In The Lily Cupboard, even in dark times, people still show compassion. During the period of World War II, a young Jew named Miriam faces a dark time when Nazi's are after the Jews. She must stay with a family she doesn't know, to keep her safe. Trusting someone you don't know can be a challenge. Young Miriam feels lonely, until the nice, non-Jew family gives little Miriam a rabbit to keep, in which she names after her father. Very soon after, Miriam becomes close friends with the young non-Jew boy. After the rabbit event, and Miriam becoming close friends with the young boy, Miriam isn't as lonely as she was before. This family is showing compassion to her, but they are also putting their lives in danger for hers.

In Katie's Trunk, even in the darkest times, people still show compassion. During the period of the Revolutionary war, Katie is a Tory who was betrayed by her best friend, and unaware of why. Katie goes through a dark time, when rebels break into her house. Katie and her family are led by their father out into the forest to escape. Katie decides to turn back, and try and save her home. She hides in a trunk, hoping for the best. Katie is about to be revealed, unit a rebel who Katie has known from their past, decides to show compassion. He knows Katie is in the trunk, and lie's saying that people are coming. Katie is very appreciative of this man for risking his life for hers by showing compassion, and not revealing her.

Being in a dark time is frightening; you never know what's going to happen next. You don't know if you will ever get to see a speck of light again. Everyone agrees that going through a dark time is tough to get through. In both The Lily Cupboard and Katie's Trunk, the characters go through a time of darkness, but in both books, there are people who show compassion. They were both stuck in a time of desperation, but there have always been someone there who shows compassion by risking their life for others.

By Evmorfia

Even in the darkest times, people still show compassion. This theme reflected in both stories, The Lily Cupboard by Shulamith Levey Oppenheim, and Katie's Trunk, by Ann Warren Turner. In The Lily Cupboard, and Katie's Trunk, both stories are about young girls who must survive a time of darkness, when both characters are left alone in another's hands, or alone, but still, there is always someone who turns up making a scarifies of compassion.

In The Lily Cupboard, even in dark times, people still show compassion. During the period of World War II, a young Jew named Miriam faces a dark time when Nazi's are after the Jews. She must stay with a family she doesn't know, to keep her safe. Trusting someone you don't know can be a challenge. Young Miriam feels lonely, until the nice, non-Jew family gives little Miriam a rabbit to keep, in which she names after her father. Very soon after, Miriam becomes close friends with the young non-Jew boy. After the rabbit event, and Miriam becoming close friends with the young boy, Miriam isn't as lonely as she was before. This family is showing compassion to her, but they are also putting their lives in danger for hers.

In Katie's Trunk, even in the darkest times, people still show compassion. During the period of the Revolutionary war, Katie is a Tory who was betrayed by her best friend, and unaware of why. Katie goes through a dark time, when rebels break into her house. Katie and her family are led by their father out into the forest to escape. Katie decides to turn back, and try and save her home. She hides in a trunk, hoping for the best. Katie is about to be revealed, until a rebel who Katie has known from their past, decides to show compassion. He knows Katie is in the trunk, and lie's saying that people are coming. Katie is very appreciative of this man for risking his life for hers by showing compassion, and not revealing her.

Being in a dark time is frightening; you never know what's going to happen next. You don't know if you will ever get to see a speck of light again. Everyone agrees that going through a dark time is tough to get through. In both The Lily Cupboard, and Katie's Trunk, the characters go through a time of darkness, but in both books, there are people who show compassion. They were both stuck in a time of desperation, but there have always been someone there who shows compassion by risking their life for others.

FIG. 17–1   Evmorfia's final essay 🌀

Sweetness

The realistic fiction story Sweetness by Angela Johnson teaches a lot of lessons. One lesson it teaches is it is important to notice if someone is in trouble or not doing as well as they should be doing, so one can go and give attention to him or her. The author tells us this through the story by showing how she shows she wants attention from different people. These people include her mother, her best friend Reyetta, and strangers or people in the neighborhood.

One way Sweetness shows she wants attention is she attempts numerous times to get it from her mother. I know this because in the beginning of the story Sweetness finds an abandoned baby, so she reaches out to her mother with the problem, but her mother ignores her and hangs up. This leads to trouble because Sweetness is extraverted and needs attention. After she does a good deed and drops the baby off at the nearby police station, she does a bad deed by robbing a convenience store. (Remember, this is only for attention) This eventually lets her get some recognition, but not the good kind. She ends up in Juvenile Detention because of her actions. The example is on page 1, "An hour after she dropped the baby off, she robbed a convenience store with a gun she stole from one of her uncles." This supports my claim because due to her not getting enough attention, she gets herself into a lot of trouble and mischief.

Another way Sweetness shows that she wants attention is by hanging out with her best friend Reyetta a lot. This shows that Sweetness wants attention from Reyetta because she is at her house or somewhere else with her countless times, meaning that she knows the more time she hangs out with Reyetta, the more attention she will get. She goes to her house without her mother's permission, she can go at in appropriate times, and she can annoy Reyetta's mother because she is always anxious to be with Reyetta. I know that Sweetness loves to hang out with her friend more than ordinary people because the first thing Sweetness does is go to her house is she went away and came back home. "Five years ago, when the welfare gave Sweetness back to her mom, the first thing Sweetness did was ride her bike over to my house. I remember how hard we pedaled as hard as we could to the Dairy Queen, celebrating that the only things Sweetness cared about were me and ice cream." This supports my claim because it clearly shows that she really relies on Reyetta for attention.

Sahm   Sweetness

The realistic fiction story Sweetness by Angela Johnson teaches a lot of lessons. One lesson it teaches is it is important to notice if someone is in trouble or not doing as well as they should be doing, so one can go and give attention to him or her. The author tells us this through the story by showing how she shows she wants attention from different people. These people include her mother, her best friend Reyetta, and strangers or people in the neighborhood.

One way Sweetness shows she wants attention is she attempts numerous times to get it from her mother. I know this because in the beginning of the story Sweetness finds an abandoned baby, so she reaches out to her mother with the problem, but her mother ignores her and hangs up. This leads to trouble because Sweetness is extraverted and needs attention. After she does a good deed and drops the baby off at the nearby police station, she does a bad deed by robbing a convenience store. (Remember, this is only for attention) This eventually lets her get some recognition, but not the good kind. She ends up in Juvenile Detention because of her actions. The example is on page 1, "An hour after she dropped the baby off, she robbed a convenience store with a gun she stole from one of her uncles." This supports my claim because due to her not getting enough attention, she gets herself into a lot of trouble and mischief.

Another way Sweetness shows that she wants attention is by hanging out with her best friend Reyetta a lot. This shows that Sweetness wants attention from Reyetta because she is at her house or somewhere else with her countless times, meaning that she knows the more time she hangs out with Reyetta, the more attention she will get. She goes to her house without her mother's permission, she can go at

FIG. 17–2   Sahm's final essay

The final way that shows that Sweetness needs attention to thrive because she does nice and responsible things for strangers and people around the neighborhood. This shows that Sweetness wants attention because she does it a lot more than average, (According to Reyetta.) Examples of this kind of thing are odd jobs, compliments, praise, Etc. I know this because on page two it reads, "I don't hink that I've ever seen Sweetness frown. Sweetness lives up to her name honestly. She says 'thank you' and 'yes ma'am' to my mama. She helps carry groceries to old people's cars and gives up her seat on the bus a lot." This shows that Sweetness wants attention from strangers because she acts really nice to them, in high hopes of getting more than enough attention from them.

As you can see, Sweetness tells a very important lesson to notice if somebody extraverted because it can lead to trouble if you don't . This applies universally because very bad things can happen one does not get enough attention. For example, people have killed themselves because of bullying and not getting any help with it.

154

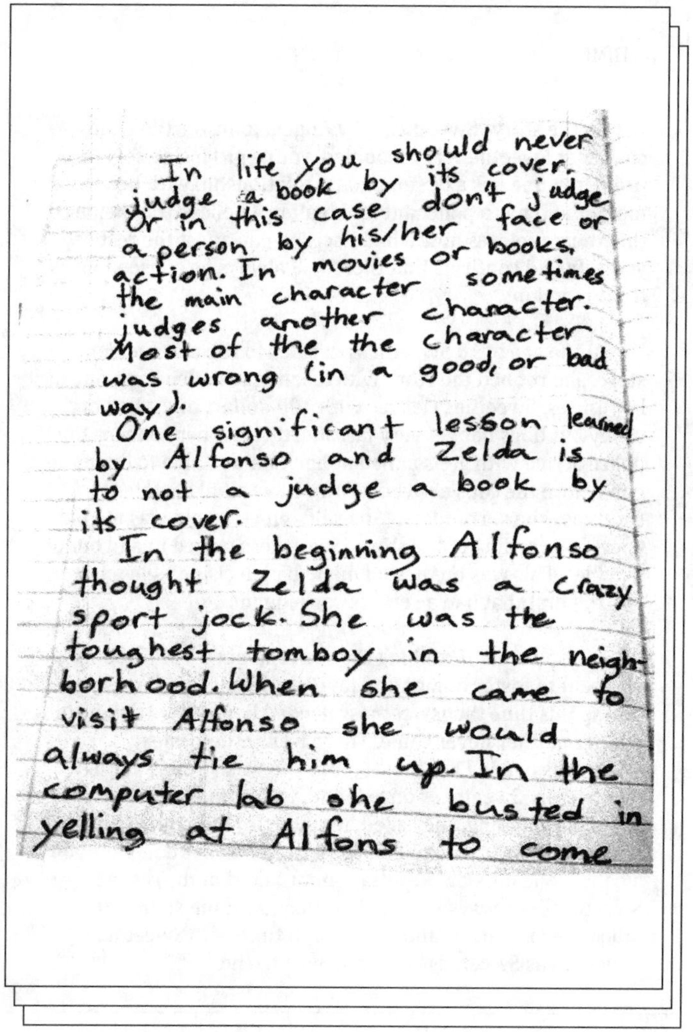

In life you should never judge a book by its cover. Or in this case don't judge a person by his/her face or action. In movies or books, the main characters sometimes judges another character. Most of the character was wrong (in a good, or bad way).

One significant lesson learned by Alfonso and Zelda is to not judge a book by its cover.

In the beginning Alfonso thought Zelda was a crazy sport jock. She was the toughest tomboy in the neighborhood. When she came to visit Alfonso she would always tie him up. In the computer lab she busted in yelling at Alfons to come practice with her. "Umm, can't you find someone else to be your partner for field day?" Alfonso squeaked. "I can't you know the rules. Monday we'll practice. We're going to win!" She said and left while slamming the door. This shows she's tough and crazy, but deep down she had a soft spot.

In the middle of the story, Zelda thought Alfonso was horrible at sports. In practice he would always trip or miss catching the egg. They started doing the 3legged race, but Alfonso tripped and made them fall. "You okay?" Zelda asked, (told you she had a soft side). Alfonso nodded and they started again and again. Zelda sometimes got annoyed when Alfonso tripped but didn't show it. Alfonso is a great athlete deep down in him.

In the end, they both thought they could never be great friends. They both won the 3legged race, without tripping (told you Alfonso was a great athlete deep in him). Alfonso knew he wouldn't catch the egg when they separated further and further. So he told his best friend Jorge that if he miss the egg he's going to give him the Sphlash World ticket for the Sport Camp ticket. And that's what exactly happened! Alfonso missed the egg (actually it hit him in the face and he fell). When that happened Jorge jumped up and down and told Zelda the deal. Then she began jumping up and down and ran to Alfonso. She gave him a high five a punch in the arm. She put her arm on his shoulder, and he did the same, together they walked without being tied together. So they were friends in end and they all lived happily ever after!

That proves why you shouldn't judge a book by it's cover. That's it pretty much. Bye. You can close the book now. BYE! No, seriously you can go.

FIG. 17–3 Shakira's final essay

In the story "Sweetness" by Angela Johnson, the main character Sweetness is a troubled, young girl facing several problems. She has a dysfunctional relationship with her mother and has a penchant for stealing. I believe the theme of this story explores how a bad decision can affect the rest of your life and confirms that there will always be consequences to your actions.

At the age of 10 Sweetness decides to rob a convenience store. She robbed the store with a handgun stolen from one of her uncles. Sweetness leaves with 100 dollars and a box of candy but does not get very far. Shortly after her robbery the police arrive with guns aimed at her. She was able to ditch the gun before the cops arrived. With a mouth full of stolen chocolate she surrenders. "She said ten years old was too old to cry". According to the story "Sweetness stayed in and out of trouble". This was the first of many bad decisions she made and the first that had a serious consequence.

As a result of robbing the convenience store Sweetness was sent to foster homes and juvenile detentions. It was during this time that sweetness needed her mother the most, but her mother never came. There were other times Sweetness needed her mother, but she wasn't there for her then either. Sweetness once found a baby on the side of a burnt out building, she called her mom for help but instead her mom hung up the phone on her, leaving her daughter and a baby alone outside. Reyetta's mom said that the reason Sweetness is always in trouble is that her mom spends too much time in church and not enough time with Sweetness. Reyetta was Sweetness only and best friend.

There is usually an event that happens in our lives that changes us. For Sweetness this was during Easter when her mom yelled at her. When Sweetness was a little girl she used to pray with her mom. Sweetness prayed to see god and her mom would say if you don't see him he's not with you. So little Sweetness went looking for him everywhere. She looked behind cars, at churches even at her friend's house. And because Sweetness couldn't find him she refused to give her Easter speech. Her mom yelled at Sweetness real bad, she stopped going to church and looking for god after that. Sweetness was eventually sent back to her mother but leaves immediately for Reyetta's house where she stays. Sweetness is older now. She tells her friend she will be right back but never returns. Sweetness goes back to the convenience store and robs it again. Sweetness got caught again, but got shot and died.

As you can see, the author gives us a clear picture of how bad decisions can affect our lives. Sweetness was a young girl ignored by her mother and as a result made poor decisions that landed her in trouble. The end of this story is really sad but effective. We have to realize that there are consequences to our actions and I hope that reading my essay will help you think twice before you act.

FIG. 17–4   Autumn's final essay ⊙

Sweetness

In the story "Sweetness" by Angela Johnson, the main character Sweetness is a troubled, young girl facing several problems. She has a dysfunctional relationship with her mother and has a penchant for stealing. I believe the theme of this story explores how a bad decision can affect the rest of your life and confirms that there will always be consequences to your actions.

At the age of 10, Sweetness decides to rob a convenience store. She robs the store with a handgun stolen from one of her uncles. Sweetness leaves with 100 dollars and a box of candy but does not get very far. Shortly after her robbery, the police arrive with guns aimed at her. She ditches the gun before the cops arrive. With a mouth full of stolen chocolate, she surrenders. She said "Ten years old was too old to cry". According to the story "Sweetness stayed in and out of trouble". This was the first of many bad decisions she makes and the first that has a serious consequence.

As a result of robbing the convenience store, Sweetness is sent to foster homes and juvenile detentions. It is during this time that Sweetness needs her mother the most, but her mother never comes. There are other times Sweetness needs her mother, but she isn't there for her then either. Sweetness once finds a baby on the side of the burned out building, she calls her mom for help but instead her mom hangs up the phone on her, leaving her daughter and a baby alone outside. Reyetta's mom says that the reason Sweetness is always in trouble is that her mom spends too much time in church and not enough time with Sweetness. Reyetta is Sweetness only and best friend.

There is usually an event that happens in our lives that changes us. For Sweetness this is during Easter when her mom yells at her. When Sweetness was a little girl, she used to pray with her mom. Sweetness prayed to see God and her mom would say if you don't see him he's not with you. So little Sweetness went looking for him everywhere. She looked behind cars, at churches, even at her friend's house. And because Sweetness couldn't find him she refused to give her Easter speech. Her mom yelled at Sweetness real bad; she stopped going to church and looking for God after that. Sweetness was eventually sent back to her mother but leaves immediately for Reyetta's house where she stays. Sweetness is older now. She tells her friend she will be right back but never returns. Sweetness goes back to the convenience store and robs it again. Sweetness got caught again, but got shot and died.

As you can see, the author gives us a clear picture of how bad decisions can affect our lives. Sweetness is a young girl ignored by her mother and as a result makes poor decisions that land her in trouble. The end of this story is really sad, but effective. We have to realize that there are consequences to our actions and I hope that reading my essay will help you think twice before you act.

When reading stories we encounter characters that have different personalities. We determine their personalities by their actions and dialogue. Both Max in Max Swings for the Fences and Ernest in Best of Friends by Mac Barnett are deceiving. Both Max and Ernest are deceiving because they tell lies to make friends. They are also deceiving because the way they act is different than the way people see them. People see them as nerds and they try to keep away from them. When the other kids actually understand who Max and Ernest are they realize their true personalities.

Both Max and Ernest are deceiving because they tell lies to make friends. Max says that his father is a superstar baseball player Beau Fletcher. He does this so that Molly can like him. He knows Molly would like him if he said this because Molly expresses that Beau Fletcher is her "hero." This shows that Max is deceiving because he liked to get people to like him. Max knew the town he moved to was baseball crazy and if he said his father was Beau Fletcher then they would love him. It seems as if Beau Fletcher is their Derek Jeter or David Wright. During the story, Max had a chance to set things right and tell the truth, however he just made his lie worse. In a like manner, Ernest told a lie to make "friends." Ernest tells everyone he won a "Nesquick Sweepstakes" and he can bring one best friend. He says the "Nesquick Sweepstakes" entails a plane trip, a stay at a hotel, a ticket to the factory, and an hour in the waterslide park. This was so exciting because a Nesquick commercial showed a Nesquick factory and deep inside was a chocolate milk water slide that leads to a chocolate milk pool. After Ernest told everyone in his class they all wanted to be "Best of Friends" with him. They greeted him everytime they saw him, the played with him, they wanted to go out to eat dinner with him, and even go over to his house for a sleepover. This shows that Ernest is deceiving because he took something that everyone wanted to do and he told them that he was going to be able to do it with one other person. Slide down a chocolate milk waterslide into a chocolate milk pool. Instead of becoming jealous everyone wanted to be his friend. They all wanted to be the one person that got to go with Ernest. Max and Ernest are misleading because they make stories so other kids can be their "friend."

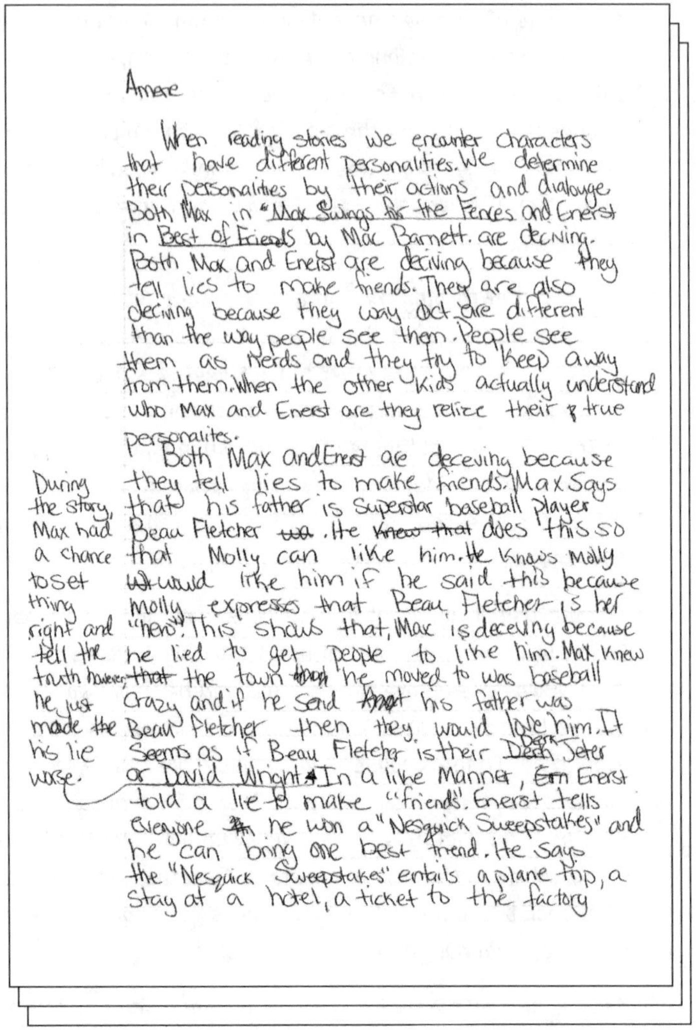
Amere

When reading stories we encunter characters that have different personalities. We determine their personalities by their actions and dialouge. Both Max in "Max Swings for the Fences and Enerst in Best of Friends by Mac Barnett. are deciving. Both Max and Enerst are deciving because they tell lies to make friends. They are also deciving because they way act are different than the way people see them. People see them as nerds and they try to keep away from them. When the other kids actually understand who Max and Enerst are they relice their true personalites.

Both Max and Enerst are deceving because they tell lies to make friends. Max Says that his father is superstar baseball player Beau Fletcher. He does this so that Molly can like him. He knows Molly would like him if he said this because Molly expresses that Beau Fletcher is her "hero". This shows that Max is deceving because he lied to get people to like him. Max knew the town he moved to was baseball crazy and if he said his father was Beau Fletcher then they would love him. It Seems as if Beau Fletcher is their Derk Jeter or David Wright. In a like manner, Enerst told a lie to make "friends". Enerst tells everyone he won a "Nesquick Sweepstakes" and he can bring one best friend. He says the "Nesquick Sweepstakes" entails a plane trip, a stay at a hotel, a ticket to the factory

During the story, Max had a chance to set thing right and tell the truth however, he just made his lie worse.

FIG. 17–5 Amerie's compare/contrast essay

Both Max and Ernest are deceiving because the way they act is different from the way people see them. For example, both Max and Ernest tell corny jokes. Max says "Ready Freddie" whenever someone is waiting on him and he is ready. One example of this is on the first day of school. Molly was his "official new student buddy." Max felt mesmerized by Molly's beauty and he just stood there. Molly asked, "Are you ready?" Max replied by saying, "I'm ready. Thanks. Thank you. Ready Freddie." This shows that Max is deceiving because he uses phrases that most people don't say. Almost no one says "Ready Freddie" unless a guy named Freddie is waiting on you. Max did not say this because Molly made him nervous because later in the story he says it again as encouragement to himself. Most people would look at Max and not at all expect him to say things like "Ready

Freddie." Ernest says at least two corny jokes in the story. His first one is about horses. "When is a horse not a horse . . . when he turns into a pasture!" This joke makes sense, but is not funny at all. This shows Ernest is deceiving because even though people look at him as a nerd they would never expect him to be so corny but to talk intelligently. On top of that, Ernest tells jokes that are not funny at all. In fact his first "joke" is nasty. No one in their right mind would think a joke about horse manure is funny. Only people with crazy imaginations. Another example of Max being deceiving by saying corny things is when Logan says bye to Molly, Jenny, and Max. Instead of saying "bye Max" he says "You too Venus." Max replies by saying "More like Serena." This shows Max is deceiving because he doesn't get Logan's way of making fun of him and makes it worse. Max should have been able to realize that Logan was not complimenting Max on playing tennis but teasing him about it. By calling Max Venus he was implying that tennis is a women's sport, even though Max plays tennis. Another example of Ernest being deceiving by saying something corny is when Dean came over to his house and he tries to entertain the both of them by telling a "scary story." Dean already knew the "scary" part and was not surprised, shocked, or spooked at all. Ernest didn't even know the chronological order of the story. This shows that Ernest is deceiving because he told a scary story in which everyone probably knows. Dean seems to be in the know about many things so if he knows the "scary" part then Ernest's story must be very unoriginal and corny. On top of that if you are trying to tell a story then you should at least memorize it. Ernest and Max fool other people by their looks when their corny sayings say something totally different about them.

All in all, both Max and Ernest are deceiving. To begin with Max and Ernest lie to make friends. Finally, Max and Ernest act in a way that is surprising to the way people see them. Anne Ursu and Mac Barnett are trying to say something about friendship. It seems that Anne Ursu and Mac Barnett are saying that being deceiving and lying to get a friend is not going to get you a true friendship even if you do end up to have "friends."

Learning to Respect Others in "Thank You, Ma'am"

by Julia

Respecting other people, even people you don't know, means trusting that there is more to them than you think. In the story "Thank You, Ma'am," by Langston Hughes, the character Mrs. Luella Bates Washington Jones treats the boy Roger with respect in many different ways. She doesn't let his violence scare her, she talks to him honestly, and she is generous to him without expecting a payback.

In the beginning of the story, Roger mugs Mrs. Jones—or tries to mug her. But this violent act is not enough to scare this woman away from helping the boy and showing him respect. It is late at night and Roger "ran up behind her and tried to snatch her purse". Most people run away if someone would did that to them. Mrs. Jones "turned around and kicked him right square in his blue-jeaned sitter." This doesn't seem like respect, but actually it kind of is. Instead of treating Roger like a criminal (when he actually is here), she holds him so she can talk to him and teach him a lesson. She treats him like he's her son even though she doesn't know him and he just tried to rob her.

Later in the story, Mrs. Jones takes Roger to her home and makes sure he gets cleaned up. The she continues to talk to him honestly and with respect. She lets Roger know that she understands what it's like to want things that you can't have. Just like Roger wants blue suede shoes and that's why he tried to rob her, she says "I have done things, too, which I would not tell you, son—neither tell God, if he didn't already know." Even though she doesn't say exactly what she did, she is telling Roger that she is not perfect too. This kind of honesty is not what you would expect from a stranger, especially someone you just tried to rob. Roger must feel very respected and trusted at this point. In fact it says "he did not want to be mistrusted now."

Another way that Mrs. Jones shows Roger respect is by being generous to him but not so she gets something back. She lets him know that he could have just asked her for the money for a pair of shoes instead of mugging her. That seems unbelievable, but then she is also cooking him a meal and talking to him without expecting anything back. When Langston Hughes writes "The woman did not ask the boy anything about where he lived, or his folks, or anything else that would embarrass him" it shows that Mrs. Jones doesn't even make the boy talk. It's like she is ok with just giving Roger ten dollars, which is probably a lot of money for her since she is eating cake that only costs ten cents. And Roger doesn't even manage to say thank you by the end of the story.

Throughout this story, Mrs. Luella Bates Washington Jones treats Roger with respect, even though it seems like he doesn't deserve it. I think that Langston Hughes wants the reader to understand that everyone deserves respect, even people who make bad choices. I think that Mrs. Jones teaches Roger that even when you are desperate, you should not give up on people. These are important lessons, because it's much easier to assume people are bad, and then either act badly to them or not try to help them. Everyone should remember Mrs. Luella Bates Washington Jones.

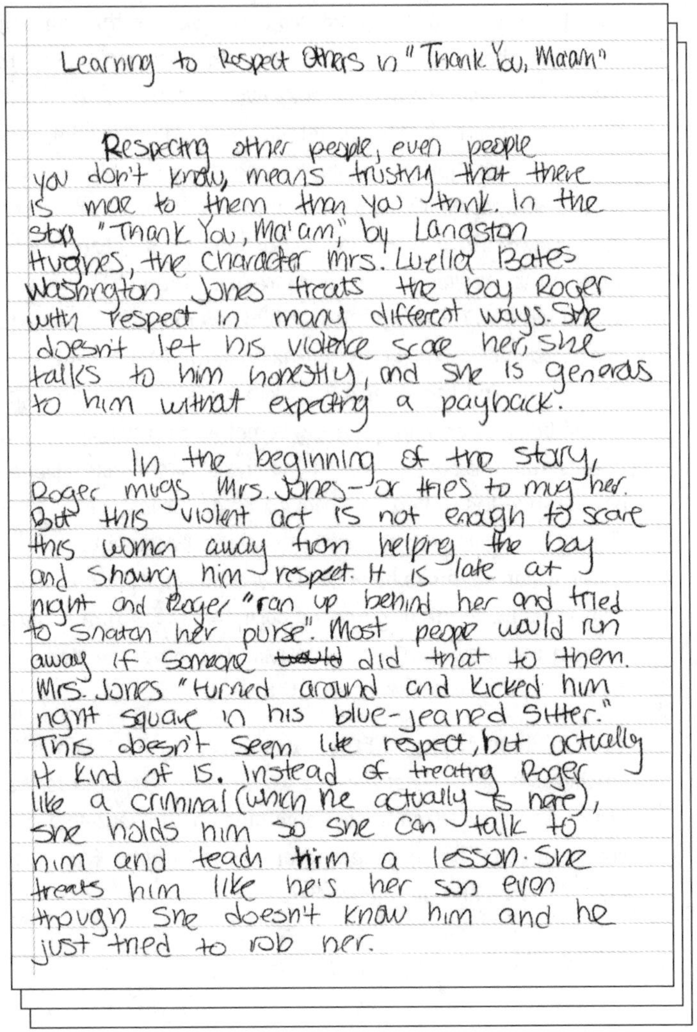

Learning to Respect Others in "Thank You, Ma'am"

Respecting other people, even people you don't know, means trusting that there is more to them than you think. In the story "Thank You, Ma'am," by Langston Hughes, the character Mrs. Luella Bates Washington Jones treats the boy Roger with respect in many different ways. She doesn't let his violence scare her, she talks to him honestly, and she is generous to him without expecting a payback.

In the beginning of the story, Roger mugs Mrs. Jones—or tries to mug her. But this violent act is not enough to scare this woman away from helping the boy and showing him respect. It is late at night and Roger "ran up behind her and tried to snatch her purse". Most people would run away if someone ~~would~~ did that to them. Mrs. Jones "turned around and kicked him right square in his blue-jeaned sitter." This doesn't seem like respect, but actually it kind of is. Instead of treating Roger like a criminal (which he actually is here), she holds him so she can talk to him and teach him a lesson. She treats him like he's her son even though she doesn't know him and he just tried to rob her.

FIG. 17–6 Julia's final essay